MASTERING
—THE—
MOMENT

MASTERING

—THE—

MOMENT

PERFECTING THE SKILLS AND PROCESSES OF EXCEPTIONAL PRESENTATION DELIVERY

TIM POLLARD

Founder and CEO of Oratium

CONDER
HOUSE
PRESS

WASHINGTON, DC

ISBN: 978-0-9982373-4-3 pbk
ISBN: 978-0-9982373-6-7 ebk

Published by
Conder House Press
Washington, DC

Edited by Floyd Largent and Stacey Aaronson
Book design by Stacey Aaronson

Photo credits: Vasa photo used with license through alamy.com.
All other photos are the author's, used with express permission, or in the
public domain.

Printed in the USA

Dedication:
To a dying breed of book lovers

It's hard to overstate the importance of books when it comes to the development of the human brain. In the world that predated the written word, humans were severely limited in their ability to deal with complex or abstract ideas. But when the printed word came on the scene, that all changed. Writers could now lay out substantially more complex and multilayered arguments, taking as many pages of printed text as they needed in order to do so. But this created a problem: the "aural brains" of the time were ill-equipped to handle this new mental challenge. Instead of this killing the new medium, however, something rather wonderful happened. Neuroscientists have only recently discovered that brain wiring isn't nearly as fixed as was once thought, and that our brains are capable of some pretty radical internal rewiring when needed (for example, after a stroke). And that's exactly what happened here: as books presented society with more complex and multifaceted arguments, major areas of the brain started to be given over to higher-level cognitive functions, allowing people to engage in deeper conceptual reasoning, to break down complex arguments into their essential elements and, crucially, to increase their capacity to focus for extended periods. When Gutenberg's printing press ushered in the era of the mass availability of books, the brain wiring of essentially all humanity changed. Books not only gave us new things to think about; they profoundly changed the very way we think.

You can probably guess where I'm going here. The explosive rise of digital media is, once again, changing the way we consume our information, and in a truly profound way. Studies show that we're being reprogrammed to consume information in smaller, more immediately gratifying "bite-sized" chunks, rapidly toggling between text, audio, and video nuggets of ever-decreasing size. Physical newspapers are being replaced by online equivalents, and more importantly, the content within them has changed. Long articles have been replaced by brief and pithy summaries, peppered with hyperlinks that encourage the reader to flit superficially between multiple information sources, rather than engaging deeply with any single one. And here's the problem: as satisfying as such "browsing" may feel, this change is not without its neurological consequences. Evidence suggests that the human brain is once again rewiring itself—only this time, it's in a more troubling direction. While the brains of centuries of book readers got deeper, the brains of the web generation seem to be getting shallower. Attention spans are shortening, and more worrying, people may be losing their ability to undertake complex and abstract reasoning. The Internet isn't evil, but it's pretty hard to argue that its neurological byproduct is going to be helpful to our society.

Which brings me to the point of this dedication. I'm not a crazy person. I don't live in a cabin in the woods of Montana (I do live in Montana, but not in the crazy part), and I don't want to smash the machines. I love technology, and like my Millennial children, I will happily graze over vast fields of electronic information, pausing here and there to nibble at just a few plants. **But everything I've learned tells me that books do still matter for the sake of the brain.** Traditional books (whether paper or electronic) can help protect both our ability to focus and our ability to wrestle with deeper and more challenging intellectual questions. So, as you read this book and ponder its ideas, you're helping to keep alive, at least within your own head, the five-hundred-year-old legacy of reason that helped humanity climb out of the Dark Ages; hence, I'm dedicating it to you. I don't want mankind to destroy the machines . . . but I also don't want the machines to destroy mankind.

In Memoriam
Eva Kor

Eva Kor was the greatest natural communicator I've ever encountered. As a young Jewish girl, along with her twin sister Miriam, she was taken from her home and forced to endure the medical experiments of the Nazi doctors in Auschwitz. By pure determination, and only by the narrowest of margins, she found a way to survive and walked out free on January 27, 1945. Based on what she experienced there, Eva devoted the rest of her life to traveling the world, speaking to groups (especially high school kids) on the vital topics of tolerance, prejudice, and forgiveness. Her lectures were an impossibly perfect combination of riveting poignance, and wit, but above all, they were deeply provocative.

You will encounter different aspects of her story in the pages that follow, but sadly, on July 4, 2019—on the very day this book went to the editor—Eva passed away, and my unhappy final writing task has been to change the references to her from present tense to past. She died peacefully in a hotel close to Auschwitz as she led yet another group on an educational tour of that hellish place. While she lived most of her adult life in Indiana, it seems that everyone who knew her story agrees that it was thoroughly fitting and comforting that she passed away so close to the spot where the lives of most of her family were taken all those years ago.

A wonderful light has finally flickered out. We've lost an exceptional communicator, but an even better human being. I was deeply honored to know her, but as sad as her passing is, I can't help but rejoice that her life came to an end only after many full and rewarding years, and not prematurely in the camp that tried to take it. In every way that matters, she beat them.

Rest in Peace: Eva Mozes Kor,
1/31/1934 – 7/4/2019

Eva doing what she did best:
teaching a group of high school students in the prison of Auschwitz

TABLE OF CONTENTS

SECTION THREE: WHO YOU ARE ON THE DAY

MASTERING

—THE—

MOMENT

INTRODUCTION

Setting the Context for Presentation Delivery: The Story So Far . . .

⁓⧼⧽⁓

This is a book about exceptional communication, specifically what happens on the big day of your presentation. At some point, most people are called to speak to some kind of assembled gathering, and whether it's large or small, ballroom or break room, wedding or workplace, it's a moment you want and need to get right. Of course, before this big day comes, there's a wider context to consider. The paradox of presentations is that success actually has much less to do with what happens on that day, and much more to do with what happened on previous days in the room where the presentation was put together.

Communication is like many other fields: whether it's sports, warfare, or dating, how things go on the day is largely determined by how well you've prepared beforehand. As obvious as this is, I'm often shocked by how many presenters I see who underinvest in the design phase, implicitly hoping they can rescue sloppy material with their sparkling onstage performance. But it never works. When you "firehose" your audience with an excess of poorly structured, confusing content, embedded in a hated deck of dense slides, no amount of delivery polish can redeem the inevitable disaster. When it comes down to it, message design is far more important to get right than message delivery.

So, shouldn't we be talking about presentation design? Yes, which is why my first book focused exclusively on that topic. *The Compelling Communicator: Mastering the Art and Science of Exceptional Presentation Design* took 275 pages to explain the importance of message architecture, and to provide a detailed process for crafting exceptional communication. And because that book creates the context for this book, it's worth reviewing its more "load-bearing" ideas, particularly as they relate to design. So, Book One in six conclusions.

Communication Matters

Communication is a critical skill in life and business. Many times, when you stand up to put your ideas in front of others, a great deal is at stake. Perhaps it's a sale you particularly need, a project you desperately want to get funded, or a dangerous teenage behavior that seriously needs to be modified. When you communicate well, you're judged favorably and are more likely to get the outcomes you want. But when you communicate poorly, you're judged unfavorably and are less likely to get those outcomes. Communication affects careers.

We Typically Aren't That Good at Communication

Despite its importance, most people don't communicate nearly as effectively as they'd like. With depressing regularity, surveys show that the typical presentation is dull, lifeless, and forgettable, with the experience often made even more miserable by a speaker's cocaine-like dependence on slides as the vehicle and crutch that holds everything together.

If You Want to Be Excellent,
You Must Get Message Design Right

At its core, great communication is always great because it's been designed well. Despite what you've been told by traditional presentation skills training, audiences don't judge communication based on the presenter's eye contact or body language; indeed, these are things they rarely even notice. They engage and judge based on the quality and structure of the argument. When Abraham Lincoln stood over the blood-soaked fields of Gettysburg and ended his brief speech with: ". . . that government of the people, by the people, for the people, shall not perish from the earth," the words became immortal entirely because they contain a brilliant and carefully crafted idea, not because they were delivered in some particularly special way. Sparkly delivery might entertain, but it will not enlighten.

The Key to Communication Design Is
Understanding the Brain

The human brain wants and needs to consume information in a certain way, and this creates a set of "natural laws" of communication. For example, the brain stores images better than it stores numbers. The brain remembers information well when it's presented in a logical narrative, but forgets random ideas easily. When you align the design of your communication with these natural laws, you begin to see the breakthrough that we're all looking for. The best news of all is that anybody can understand these laws, which puts communication excellence within the reach of anyone willing to invest in a little learning; it's no longer mystically confined to the "naturally gifted."

Brain-Aligned Communication Will Have Certain Hallmarks

Communication that connects with the collective brain of an audience will possess a distinct set of fingerprints.

➤ GROUNDED IN IDEAS. At the very core of **brain-aligned design**, and arguably its highest precept, is the principle that ideas must sit at the center of your message. Ideas are the currency of the mind. Good ideas stick, and most importantly, they get retold. Imagine you've attended a presentation, and someone later asks you what it was all about. How would you answer? You wouldn't play a tape of the entire meeting; you would naturally and automatically boil it down to the two or three big things that stuck in your mind. You can never truly understand communication if you don't understand the central role played by ideas. For this reason, the most important principle of message design is: **"Powerfully land a small number of big ideas."** In other words, make sure you know what your big ideas are, and make sure they come across clearly and powerfully. As Victor Hugo famously said, "A stand can be made against invasion by an army; against an invasion by an idea, no stand can be made."

➤ ANCHORED IN AN AUDIENCE/CUSTOMER PRIORITY, hopefully causing ever-more distracted people to set aside their phones, lean in, and listen.

➤ CRISP AND SIMPLE, not "dumbed down" by any means, but built to be elegantly simple. Complete and compelling, yet staying within the bandwidth of the hearer's brain.

➤ WELL-SEQUENCED, unfolding as a logical "story" or argument, making it easy to track with and understand.

➤ **ENGAGING FOR BOTH THE LEFT AND RIGHT BRAIN,** bringing left-brain facts to life with right-brain story, imagery, and metaphor. Visual aids finally fulfill their true purpose of illuminating ideas visually, rather than simply being memory-jogging bullets for the ill-prepared speaker.

➤ **CAPTURED IN A CRISP, CLEAN DOCUMENT.** Even the best presentation is subject to the biological limits of human memory. While it's not strictly a principle of brain-aligned message design, a great document containing your essential argument is the key to getting your audience beyond their limits of unaided recall. Which leads to . . .

➤ **RE-PRESENTABLE.** The highest goal for communication is not simply that it is understood in the moment; you want your messaging to stick in such a profound way that your audience can both remember and re-present the story at a later time (which is made vastly more likely if they have a great document to help them). This is how messaging becomes truly viral, and this is how messaging leads to action. When the budget committee discusses your proposal a week after the presentation and you aren't in that room, the **re-presentability** of your story is everything. Put another way, the goal isn't effective communication, but effective re-communication.

The "Carbon Atom" Is the Model That Gets You There

How do you build communication that has these fingerprints? By applying a set of tools embedded in the model we call the "Carbon Atom," which is shown on the next page. This model provides a practical process that is applicable in almost any communication setting, from a TED talk to a training course.

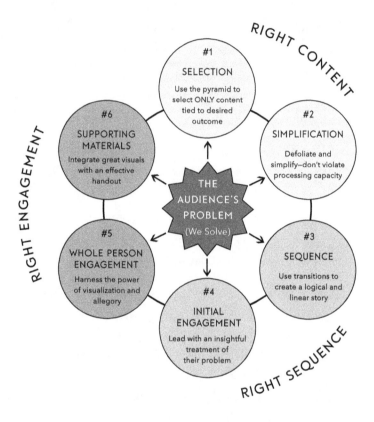

The "Carbon Atom"
A process model for the architecture of outstanding communication

The readers who took the full journey of *The Compelling Communicator* seem to have been well rewarded, and I continue to be humbled by the stories people send us. Salespeople and surveyors, accountants and architects, pastors and parents all report wonderful breakthroughs in the effectiveness of their communications. But by resurrecting this argument that it's all about message design, I'm raising a potentially embarrassing question. Why do we need a book on message delivery at all? Which leads to, "Isn't it hypocritical of me to write it?"

WHY DELIVERY MATTERS

A few months ago, I was sitting with my daughter, Rosie, shortly before she left for college. When I mentioned I was writing a second book, she jokingly replied, "Why, Dad? Did you leave the first one on a cliffhanger?" A pretty funny comment, given it was a business book. But after a little contemplation, I answered, "You know what? Actually, I did."

I'd never thought about it that way, but it's true, and here's why.

> **Even if you've got your presentation beautifully designed, you need to make absolutely sure that this presentation—and nothing else—is what actually shows up on "game day," and that it lands with all the impact you hope for. As it turns out, this isn't quite as simple as it appears to be.**

The problem is that however good your message design, there is still such a thing as the "delivery dilemma," by which I mean the various traps, landmines, snares, pitfalls, and ambushes that, on game day, can seriously derail an otherwise outstanding piece of communication. I'll describe a few below. You've seen them all, and you probably bear some of the scars yourself.

The Delivery Dilemma

Have you ever stood up to present and had your brain momentarily seize up on you, resulting in some less-than-impressive mumbling coming out of your mouth? Or perhaps a technical difficulty left you frantically trying to get your laptop to talk to the projector while your audience looked on in mute disapproval, waiting for you to begin. These opening nightmares, once experienced, are often the source of people's residual fear of presenting: the terrifying seconds where, in front of a large audience, your brain seems to freeze over, while all you can hear is the strange rushing sound of the blood in your own ears.

Or perhaps you navigated the opening just fine, but across the presentation itself, the precise language you were hoping for seemed to elude you, and you didn't land your points with exactly the punch you expected. There is almost no greater frustration for a presenter than when the articulate phrasing you *thought* you had locked in was replaced onstage by language that was clumsy, repetitive, and dull. Much like the golfer who makes one hundred out of one hundred four-foot putts in practice but misses one in the final round of the Masters, it's the well-known ability of the big moment to turn your otherwise reliable brain to mush when it matters most.

Or perhaps the argument was coming out perfectly when one seemingly innocent question became a discussion you couldn't rein in, quickly becoming an extended and agonizing trip to the briar patch . . . and by the time you wrestled the train back onto the tracks, you were two-thirds of the way through your time, but only one-third of the way through your material, leaving you to choose between the three lethally bad options of speed-talking, banning questions, or cutting content.

These aren't fabricated scenarios. Indeed, I'm certain you've seen and experienced some or all of them, just as I have. And of course, this is just a tiny sampling from a much longer list. It's alarming how many different ways a presentation can be blown up when the lights go down, however strong its content may be. It can happen in so many ways, in fact, that if we truly understood them all, we might never get up there in the first place.

Each of these challenges—from nerves, to misbehaving technology, to brush-fire discussions—has its specific remedy, and we'll discuss them all. The larger point here is simply that there are many ways in which the live event can under-deliver against the plan we had going in, with the added agony that presentations are like live TV: there are no do-overs. Whatever happens, happens. It goes in the books.

So here's our foundational premise:

> **Delivery matters, because everything that happens on game day has the potential to either significantly enhance or significantly undermine the quality of the message you've designed.**

Of course, there are some situations where getting delivery exactly right isn't actually that important. If you're making a toast at a friend's birthday party or offering a warm reminiscence at a colleague's retirement, while you do want it to be a sweet and memorable moment for the guests, there's no great penalty if it doesn't go quite as planned (although truthfully, a misfired wedding speech can have lifelong implications!). However, those aren't the settings I'm concerned with. This book is about those moments when there's something truly important at stake, where you're aiming to persuade others to take an action that has genuine meaning, and where getting it right or wrong has real consequences.

THE INTRIGUING RELATIONSHIP BETWEEN
DESIGN AND DELIVERY

The idea that presentation design and delivery are both important probably isn't that surprising. But how exactly are they related? At first blush, the answer to this question seems simple: surely, "Design is what you say, delivery is how you say it." While that's correct, it's also a gross oversimplification. Their real relationship is far more nuanced, but you need to understand it if you're to communicate effectively. The key to understanding exactly how design and delivery intersect can be found inside a little-known proverb in the Old Testament of the Bible, which, even though written thousands of years ago, is perfectly relevant today. Proverbs 25: 11 reads:

**"A word aptly spoken is like apples of gold
in settings of silver." (NIV)**

When I stumbled on this proverb many years ago, it captured my heart, because embodied in that ancient text is a perfect description of how communication truly works. The first part of the proverb, "A word aptly spoken," describes the two core aspects of communication. There is the "word" itself, representing the "idea," and there is "aptly spoken," the *way* that word is spoken. But the second part of the proverb explains *how* they are related, with the relationship being likened to fine jewelry. They are "like apples of gold in settings of silver," and it's the jewelry image that unlocks the nature of the relationship. This proverb is saying that your words or underlying ideas are like the gold at the center of a piece of jewelry. But the *way* those words are delivered is like a "setting of silver," whose entire purpose is *to draw attention to the gold*. This idea is clearly seen in a different translation, where the same proverb reads: "An idea well-expressed is like a design of gold, set in silver" (Good News Translation). Clearer, though a little less elegant.

Ancient as it is, this proverb is profoundly insightful in the way it clarifies a relationship that we tend to misunderstand. The ideas within your message that you've striven so hard to create are the things that matter most—just like the pristine diamond that sits at the heart of a beautiful engagement ring. But the delivery of those ideas is so much more than just "how you say it." Delivery is the setting that puts those ideas on full display, making sure they come across in the best possible light. This book is about how to get that right: how to make sure your ideas sparkle like diamonds.

A FRESH TAKE ON DELIVERY

Having determined the role that delivery plays in communication effectiveness, the next natural question is: where should you focus? The answer is that you need to dig into what truly matters while steering away from the tired, outdated thinking of the past. Traditional presentation skills training continues to cling to an exaggerated focus on physical delivery, exalting eye contact and body language to the highest level of importance. Many of you reading this have been put under the spotlight of a video camera to be purged of the sin of having your hands in your pockets and to be set on the righteous path to confident body language. It's absurd, and most people who take that training *know* it's absurd. No one ever leaves a meeting saying, "That was awful. She didn't make enough eye contact," or "What a wonderful presentation. Such effervescent body language!" And if that's not what people are judging, then how much difference can working on those "skills" actually make? And yet this outdated focus lingers on, solidly hitting the bullseye on the wrong target.

Of course, that's an unfair generalization. Today there are some excellent books on presentation skills that reflect far more modern and scientific thinking, content that can have a highly positive effect on most communicators. However, these make up a distinct minority, and if you're in the market for live training . . . well, buyer beware.

The best proof that what matters in delivery *isn't* what we traditionally think is epitomized by my hero, Holocaust survivor Eva Kor, who, as I mentioned at the beginning of the book, recently passed away at age eighty-five. As described in my earlier book, Eva's lectures pierced the heart because they were so brilliantly designed. Her three big ideas were clear, powerful, and life-altering. But what about her delivery? Well, she clearly didn't spike in traditional delivery skills. Later in life she delivered her lectures seated, so her body language was best described as nonexistent. Her strong Hungarian accent was charming but not the easiest to understand. And she typically looked down while presenting, which helped her keep her focus but isn't quite textbook eye contact. But here's the big question: does this mean her delivery was poor? Not at all. It was exceptional because she got the right things right. One example: I heard Eva speak many times, and I noticed that **her important points always came out exactly the same way.** In fact, it's inspiring to realize just how precise her delivery was. Eva had ideas that were truly diamonds, and she instinctively knew that only the right language would do when it came to putting those ideas on display.

I hope you see my point because this one is easy to miss. I'm not saying that Eva's delivery wasn't good, and that she made up for it with other things. Far from it. Eva's delivery was always world-class, because she inevitably nailed the things that matter—the things that are the subject of the rest of this book, with powerful and precise language being one of the most important. They just don't happen to be the things that traditional training would tell her to do.

WHAT ARE THE THINGS THAT MATTER?
A VISION OF A DIFFERENT FUTURE

As I close out this introduction, I want to paint a fuller picture of what we're going to be talking about, because precise language is only one of numerous skills we're going to explore—and I'm going to do this by means of a simple vision of the future. My goal in presenting the bigger picture this way is pure motivation: I want to show you what reading this book and applying its principles will actually do for you.

Alex Goes to Phoenix

It's an ordinary Tuesday in Chicago when your CEO calls and hands you, Alex, a senior finance manager, the assignment of making an important presentation at the company's leadership meeting three weeks hence in sunny Phoenix. It's an ultra-high-profile moment and an unmistakable opportunity; the senior leadership group doesn't know you well, so a home run here could open up numerous future career options. But if you lay an egg, the consequences are too frightening to contemplate. **The exposure door swings both ways.**

— ❈ —

You put great thought into designing the material to present, but as the big day finally drew near, you transitioned into delivery execution mode. As efficient as it would have been to take the last flight in, you didn't, because that's a rookie mistake. One bad delay and you get no sleep, or heaven forbid a cancellation—and there's no presentation at all. But in your case, you got to Phoenix fully protected from airline malfunctions. When you arrived at the venue you were fresh and rested. You also got there early—earlier than you needed to be there, and much earlier than the typical speaker, because you knew that a) the hotel wouldn't have the room layout, lighting, and temperature exactly the way you wanted it and that, more importantly, b) those things need time to fix. As a result, the room that would have been soporifically warm wasn't, and the tables that initially had poor sightlines didn't. You played with the lights to get them just right: bright enough for the handout, but without washing out the screen. Your tech run-through occurred in plenty of time to iron out an odd laptop connection glitch, and you talked to the hotel to make sure they wouldn't set up lunch until you were done, as well as about the leaf-blowing going on outside. They happily agreed to move their folks to a different part of the property, and with that, your room was set up for success. Of course, when your audience came in, they were completely oblivious to the field of landmines you had defused, but that's precisely the point: you only see landmines when they go off.

Yet, you're a finance manager. Is all this stuff like moving furniture really your job?

**Of course it is. One hundred percent.
No one else is going to do it.**

When the big moment finally arrived, there were some opening nerves, but you knew the techniques to mitigate them and no one noticed. Thanks to several rounds of careful, out-loud rehearsal, the great argument you had designed was fully "grooved" in your mind and was exactly what came out of your mouth. More than simply being precise, your language was imaginative and muscular, making quiet use of several tools of rhetoric that you knew would help heighten a particular point. Flowing from your understanding of how style correlates with effectiveness, you particularly dialed up the authenticity of your delivery. Finally, you handled questions deftly, answering those that needed to be answered, while graciously deflecting a couple of dangerous invitations to the briar patch. Despite the discussion, and the fact that the previous speaker's overrun caused you to start a few minutes late, you still wrapped up calmly at 12:28, against a promise of 12:30, because you knew how to trim some secondary material, invisibly, on the fly. Hitting that planned finish time was a surprising achievement that your audience both noticed and thoroughly appreciated.

Most importantly, they absolutely loved the presentation! **Of course, if pressed, they couldn't necessarily articulate precisely why it had gone so well.** Yes, they noticed that you finished on time, and they especially noticed (and loved) that you shut down "Grandstand Graham" before he could derail the whole session. But most of what you were doing evaded their conscious perception; they saw none of what you'd done behind the scenes to get the room and technology right, and while they did hear everything you said, it's unlikely they would have discerned what you were doing linguistically and stylistically at a conscious level. No one came up and said, "Alex, I love that you presented your main idea as an antithesis," but they were nonetheless impacted by that idea at a deep, unconscious level. **Most importantly, your content was the focus and star of the show, put on full display by a largely invisible cocktail of highly advanced delivery skills.**

And that is expressly what you had worked to achieve, knowing that **when great design meets great delivery, that's when magic truly happens.** Apples of gold in settings of silver.

ADVANCED . . . BUT NOT COMPLICATED

This is a book about the advanced skills and practices that will transform an average presenter into an exceptional presenter, from the standpoint of their message delivery. But within it is a fascinating paradox, which we see in Alex's triumph in Phoenix. In that story, she certainly displayed a range of advanced skills, but was anything she did especially complicated? No, and that's important. **Advanced doesn't mean complicated.**

Gary Player is a golf legend, and one of the greatest putters who has ever lived. Recently, I was watching one of his videos on putting, and in it, he taught that when you get onto a green, you should walk up to the hole and look to see which side is more worn. Why? Because the worn side has been hit by a lot more balls, which means that it's the downhill side, so even though your eyes may tell you differently, this is the way the ball is going to try to go. That insight is utter genius. It's highly advanced, and yet it's childishly simple to understand and apply. (How come I never thought of that?)

The same is true of presentation delivery skills.

In general, the practices we're going to discuss aren't advanced because they're complicated or especially hard. They're advanced because average speakers don't employ them, which is why they routinely get blown up by landmines that in most cases could have easily been defused.

That's very good news.

In some fields, like fly-fishing or neurosurgery, "advanced" skills are hard to master, but not so here. You're about to learn a wide range of invaluable skills and practices that are going to make a huge difference to your effectiveness, almost all of which could be mastered by a determined ten-year-old. It isn't hard to grasp the idea that you need to get to your venue early, because the laws of physics govern how long it takes to cool down a warm room, but hardly anyone does it. Nor is it difficult to understand that because laptops don't always cooperate well with projectors, maybe it's a good idea to get it all working before the room fills with a jury of your superiors.

POSTSCRIPT: SHOULD YOU READ THE FIRST BOOK FIRST?

I've already referenced my first book, *The Compelling Communicator,* a few times; and you may be wondering whether, if you haven't already done so, I would recommend that you read it first. Yes, I would, and not just because I want to sell an extra book. It's because without that essential foundation, this book won't make all the difference you're hoping for. Lots of people are interested in presentation delivery skills, hoping to improve their "game day" performance, and there's no doubt that if you study and apply the principles in this book, it will make you substantially better at that aspect of communication. But as we've already discussed, no matter how good you get at delivery, it's never going to be enough to redeem deficient content. If you're hastily throwing together sender-oriented, confusing, illogical material and packing it onto dense and illegible slides, your delivery isn't going to save you. But by contrast, when you build strong, simple, logical, and compelling content, that sets you up to have some real fun when the delivery moment comes. So I do suggest you start with *The Compelling Communicator* and lay the foundation of great communication architecture. However, I'm a realist. Some of you will choose to start right here. Hence, it's incumbent on me to provide an overview of the design process, so that will be our opening chapter.

CHAPTER 1

A Brief Review of Message Design

❧

I f you haven't read *The Compelling Communicator*, that's fine: this foundation will serve you well. But even if you have read it, this chapter will still be a useful refresher. I introduced the main tenets of "brain-aligned design" back on page 4, so here I want to explore them a little more deeply by means of a wonderful case example. If, however, you feel sufficiently familiar with the first book, skip right on to Chapter 2.

THE SEVEN HALLMARKS OF EXCEPTIONAL MESSAGE DESIGN

Rather than re-describe the process of communication design, let's instead look through the lens of outcomes. What does that process create? What does the material look like that you're now preparing to deliver? To illustrate this, we're going to study some donor messaging we at Oratium[1] helped build for Eva Kor's foundation, CANDLES (*Children of Auschwitz Nazi Deadly Lab Experiments Survivors*). This piece was designed to raise funds to help CANDLES develop a roster of speakers who would continue Eva's speaking legacy when she would eventually step off the stage (as has now sadly occurred).

---

[1] Oratium is a company that helps individuals and organizations design and deliver messaging.

On the following pages, I've included the handout that accompanies the presentation. As I walk through the hallmarks of exceptional design, I will reference how these show up in the CANDLES piece. I encourage you to look back at the pages of the handout as we go so that you can see these elements for yourself.

1. Great Messaging Is Crisp, Clean, and Simple

You're trying to create a presentation (actually a conversation) that someone will enjoy rather than merely endure. In order to do that, you must build it with thoughtful consideration of the brain-space of a normal human being, and ensure you don't violate the limits of their working memory. Any secondary material is either gone or demoted to an appendix.

CANDLES: You can easily see the crispness and simplicity here. The whole story is told in one bifold document, designed to be left behind by the presenter. It's the right amount of content to create a conversation that's rich but can still easily be had comfortably in an hour around a dining table without anyone feeling firehosed.

2. It Is Deeply Rooted in an Audience Problem

In a society that is increasingly overloaded with information, we typically engage with only a tiny fraction of the messages that swirl around us. That amounts to perhaps 100–150 of the roughly 5,000 messages that compete for our attention daily—which presents communicators with a serious challenge. (*continued on page 25*)

Pg. 1 – Front Cover

WE LIVE IN A BROKEN WORLD,
WHERE PEOPLE ARE IN PAIN AND SUFFERING...

THE PERPETRATOR MAINTAINING POWER OVER HER LIFE:

*What was most difficult for her was that after her attack, she could no longer dance. She said that **dancing and the rape had become so intertwined in her mind** that she would break down in panic attacks any time she tried to dance. Even though the attack happened years ago, **her perpetrator still had power over her life.***

CARRYING ANGER TOWARD HIS ABUSIVE FATHER:

*He was trying to overcome pain and anger toward an abusive father. **For years, this person carried the pain** of what the father had done and he didn't know how to **free himself.** He was still angry and hurt, even after years of therapy, hypnotherapy, meditation, and healing work.*

CHILDREN GROWING UP WITH ANGER AND RESENTMENT:

*The teacher was trying to help Native American children **overcome anger and resentment** toward their white counterparts and an oppressive government system. She was trying to help the children understand that if they hate a people for what had been done in the past, **they had no room to grow themselves.***

...BUT WE DO NOT HAVE TO ACCEPT THE EFFECTS OF THIS BROKEN WORLD. THERE IS HOPE.

Pg. 2 – Inner Left

HOPE EXISTS WHEN WE **REGAIN** CONTROL OVER OUR OWN LIVES
THROUGH FORGIVENESS.

Eva is a living testament of surviving the most horrific human conditions.

"In Auschwitz, dying was so easy. Surviving was a full-time job."

Eva chose to relive her painful past by speaking about her experiences.

"People must know what happened so that it will never happen again."

Eva released herself from the ties to Dr. Mengele through forgiveness.

"Every person has the human right to live free from pain of the past."

Forgiveness is liberation for the person doing the forgiving. Eva's message provides a pathway of healing to others.

"I struggled with the idea [forgiveness] for a while. It doesn't mean I forget or it didn't happen. But it does give me freedom. It allows me to move past the pain and say he [the attacker] doesn't control that part of my life anymore. It gives me a sense of power, and a sense of peace."

"Making the decision to forgive [my father] in order to free myself was the best thing I have ever done for myself. I know now, that although I cannot control what others do, I can decide how their actions will impact me. I am no longer suffering or a victim. I am at peace and finding my way to happiness."

"I used Eva's documentary Forgiving Dr. Mengele to address this. One young man thanked me and told me that if you [Eva] could forgive the atrocities, then he too could forgive the things that have happened. Thank you for helping me to impart change, forgiveness and empowerment to my people."

BUT WE HAVE A PROBLEM: EVA DOESN'T SCALE.

Pg. 3 – Inner Right

Eva Doesn't Scale, But Her Message Does

Is universal

Spreads across boundaries

Can be taught to others

Can be taught by others

Helps people free themselves

So how do we scale Eva's message?

The Eva Kor Ambassador Program

A group of world-class speakers will ensure that Eva's message and life lessons of healing and forgiveness spread light to every part of the world.

Eva's message will reach people who would otherwise be unable to access it, meaning her message will reach more people than ever thought possible.

The Eva Kor Ambassador Program ambassadors are recruited, trained, and approved world-class speakers. The program consists of two tiers: the master tier will be executive-level speakers, and the premier tier will include a spectrum of speakers who can share Eva's message with schools, civic groups, and other community organizations.

How it will work:

❶ Give in-person presentations with supplementary materials

❷ Receive stipends and scholarships

❸ Learn to identify speaking opportunities and target audiences

❹ Touch hundreds of thousands of lives by sharing Eva's message

What we need to get there:

❶ Hire a program director

❷ Recruit speakers

❸ Train speakers how to present and counsel

❹ Develop marketing materials

❺ Develop supplementary materials

❻ Build presentations

Vision of the Future: Eva's message reaching people

Year 1	Year 2	Year 3	Year 4	Year 5
9,000	36,000	72,000	99,000	117,000

Will You Help Us Spread This Light?

Pg. 4 – Back Cover

Experience shows that the most reliable way to penetrate someone's "content-relevance filters" is to anchor in a problem they care about. Being problem-centric is truly the beating heart of being audience-centric.

CANDLES: This piece opens by discussing the brokenness so evident in today's world, by describing three lives torn apart by the actions of others. One cameo describes a young dancer who was sexually assaulted outside her dance studio and so emotionally traumatized by the experience that she was never able to dance again. The main problem in view here is the prison of bitterness that many people live in as a result of suffering at the hands of others. This is a deeply audience-centric opening. It resonates with everyone.

3. It Pivots on a Small Number of Big Ideas

Ideas matter. As important as facts, data, and illustrations are, ideas are the "currency" of the mind, the chunks of information that the brain will best attach to and remember. But beyond their "stickiness," the right ideas lead people to take action, because a presentation's big ideas lay out your view of how the problem you are discussing can be solved. Hence the central goal of communication should be to *powerfully land a small number of big ideas.*

CANDLES: Eva's story gives rise to three powerful ideas that address the problem of human hurt and brokenness:

1. Hope exists when we regain control over our own lives through forgiveness.
2. Eva's message provides a pathway of healing to others.
3. Eva doesn't scale.

The central thesis is the essence of Eva's lifelong mission, born out of her own excruciating experience: forgiveness is the key to freedom from the bondage of past hurt. Eva eventually found peace and freedom from her hell in Auschwitz only as she forgave the Nazis who perpetrated those terrible crimes.[2]

4. Big Ideas Are Supported by the Right Data, Along with Powerful Imagery

As you seek to support your big ideas, you should use the best facts and data you have, but no more than you actually need. In addition, you should blend "dry" facts and data with story and imagery that bring your ideas to life.

CANDLES: We see this blend clearly and elegantly executed in this donor piece. The presentation recounts the basic facts and details of Eva's Holocaust experience, but it also makes spectacular use of story. Indeed, the wonderful and surprising moment in this presentation is when you learn that each of the three people imprisoned by their pain (as seen on page two) found freedom from that hurt through forgiveness (as seen on page three), as each story is closed out. Their stories are compelling proof of the big idea that forgiveness can truly release a person from bitterness.

5. It Has a Logical Structure (Sequence)

The brain struggles with random information because it can't store, or even necessarily comprehend, information where the individual pieces have no context. In just the same way that Chapter Six of a book makes perfect sense because of Chapter Five, a presentation

---

[2] I can't even begin to do justice to this idea and mission. I highly recommend her book, *Surviving the Angel of Death: The True Story of a Mengele Twin in Auschwitz.*

must flow logically so that each piece makes sense, having been set up by the preceding piece. The real art here is to design a sequence based on how the audience wants the story to flow.

CANDLES: We see a great sequence in this piece. The logical question in the audience's mind following the discussion of the pain stories is, "This is awful . . . is there any hope? Can this be solved?" The presentation takes its cue from that implied question and flows straight into the solution: "Yes, it can . . ." using Eva's insight on the power of forgiveness to break the cycle. This then leads to a new question: "How does this survive when Eva retires?", which opens the discussion of the new team to do the work, and so on. Every great presentation is a designed conversation.

6. It Leads Logically to a Call to Action

Communication is always about action. You want your audiences to do something with what you have presented to them. Maybe you want your team to rally in a difficult season, or in this case, a donor to give generously. You should always remember to ask for the action at the end.

CANDLES: There's a very clear call to action in the "ask" at the end, where the donor is invited to underwrite various aspects of the speaking academy that CANDLES wishes to build. (It's particularly smart that there are different possible levels of participation, reflecting the diversity of the audiences to whom this will be presented. The best presentations often have a fallback action if the audience isn't ready for the main action.)

7. It Has a Leave-Behind Designed for Re-Presentability

Having your message live on after the meeting is one of the single most important outcomes that communicators must strive to create. In sales and donor presentations especially, you need messaging that sticks so deeply that your original hearer can effectively re-present the story in the broader decision meeting that takes place a week or a month later. But given the inherent frailty of human memory, the document you leave behind is going to be the most important driver of this. Scientific research shows that people don't remember much more than about 10 to 15 percent of the material in a typical presentation. The true value of the handout is that it frees you from the limitations of unaided recall and opens up the wonderful world of aided recall. This presents another blow to the traditional slide-based presentation. **It's sobering but true that people do not re-present someone else's slides, which means the traditional slide-based approach fails the test of re-presentability.**

CANDLES: This story has been perfectly captured in a well-designed document that is highly re-presentable. Whether the original hearer is a wife who later discusses it with her husband, or a foundation member re-presenting it at the grant approval meeting, this leave-behind creates a high level of accurate re-presentability.

AND RESULTS FOLLOW

The donor piece I've described is wonderfully crafted, and it's a great example of the seven hallmarks of exceptional message design. However, the design is not an end in itself. Communication isn't intended to be art; it exists to move an audience to a desired action. As in our example, the CANDLES piece is, without apology, designed to encourage supporters to give generously, and it has been extremely effective in that regard. We now have years of data and countless stories demonstrating that communication built in this way is extremely effective at moving an audience toward a desired action, even if you implement the model imperfectly.

A client in the industrial space recently told me about a customer meeting one of their salespeople had arranged where they'd traditionally done poorly with the old PowerPoint approach. Their customer was a manufacturing plant manager, and this time the salesperson went in armed only with a picture of a Van Gogh painting. At one point he poked a hole in the painting to illustrate his single big idea that one safety incident is as destructive to a plant as a hole is to an artistic masterpiece. Not quite the full messaging model, but I've got to give him credit: he went in with a big idea and landed it very powerfully. A punctured Van Gogh print isn't quite the polished leave-behind we generally recommend, but thirty days later, they had a $1.8 million deal. Funny things happen when you change the way you communicate.

CHAPTER 2

Introducing a Model for Message Delivery

Assuming a strong foundation of a well-designed message, we can now pivot to the subject of how that message gets delivered. As you look at the full terrain of presentation delivery, it naturally gathers into three big topics.

➤ **How you prepare for the day,**
➤ **What you do on the day, and**
➤ **Who you are on the day**

Whether your upcoming event is for a ballroom of 5,000 people or a conference room of five, exceptional presentation delivery happens at the intersection of these three "baskets" of skills. The book is organized around the mastery of these three baskets, so let's start with a high-level overview of each.

MASTER HOW YOU PREPARE

MASTER WHAT YOU DO

MASTER WHO YOU ARE

MASTERING THE MOMENT

HOW YOU PREPARE FOR THE DAY

This set of four chapters concerns itself with everything you do ahead of the event—from several days out, right up to the final moments before you take the stage—to give yourself the best possible chance of success. Some practices are obvious, and their connection to effectiveness is quite linear. For example: without thorough rehearsal, you won't be as precise in your language as you need to be, and that's going to hurt you. But there are many other less obvious but equally crucial preparation practices, such as investigating the emotional dynamics of the crowd. The group who just crushed its quarterly goal is in a completely different state of mind from the group who just missed it—and if you're the speaker, you'd better know which one you're addressing. The main value of this section is shedding light on things that most speakers don't realize are important. **Indeed, some of the practices you're going to encounter may at first sight seem "small." But what's easy to miss is how much of a difference these "small" things can make.** The majority of presenters walk in blissfully unaware of the emotional state of the room because it never even crossed their mind to inquire, and then they end up getting badly burned by it on the rare occasion that there's a problem. It's like a cow wandering into an electric fence.

WHAT YOU DO ON THE DAY

Having dealt with the preparation for the big day, we turn to the practical matters of public speaking itself. These eight chapters explore the most important aspects of communication's mechanics. How do you deliver a fabulous opening? How do you mitigate the nerves that attempt to join you on stage? How do you make sure the group discussion is rich, valuable, and inclusive? How do you shut that discussion down in an inoffensive manner when it's not? How do you use humor? And, though I can't believe I'm saying this, what do you need to know about eye contact and body language?

WHO YOU ARE ON THE DAY

Having covered everything that leads up to the day, and everything you do on the day, what could possibly be left? The answer is, there's more to excellence than simply *What You Do*. Beyond the horizon of mechanics lies a more mysterious topic, which is *Who You Are*, and the question of style or persona. There's an infinite range of speaking styles: you can be warm or cold, funny or serious, intimate or aloof, assertive or deferential. Our final four chapters are concerned with the relationship between effectiveness and the kind of person you portray yourself as being. The topic covers some truly fascinating questions: are all these styles created equal, or are some more effective than others? Is your own style fixed, or can you move between different personas while remaining yourself? Does the "right" style actually depend on the presentation setting, and if so, how?

The other main topic in this section is **language**. Language has a majestic power to influence and inspire, whether for Churchillian good or Hitlerian evil. And yet, most presenters leave that tool neglected and rusting in their toolbox, shying away from language that's more "muscular" in favor of a duller and more pedestrian lower common denominator. Can a presenter in today's everyday organizational setting use language and even rhetoric in a way that's both powerful and relevant? Yes, and in this section, I'm on an unashamed mission to reignite both your love for language and your willingness to push your linguistic boat out just a little further.

HOW TO USE THIS BOOK

The three big topics I've just described play completely different roles in your success but are equally important, and you need to master all three. However, it's an oddly diverse terrain. In one chapter, we'll discuss having the right set of laptop dongles; but in another, we'll look at how to use the rhetorical device *epistrophe*. This is simply the nature of public speaking: it spans topics from the mundane to the sublime. To help keep this odd breadth manageable, you have two aids. First, the book is built on short, highly practical chapters. After reading it through, you'll be able to come back and use it for reference, returning to specific topics where you want a refresher. Second, to help with practical application, the appendices contain a vital set of checklists that summarize the most important lessons from each of the three sections. I strongly advise that you copy these "field guides" and keep them with you. Or, better still, download and print the free PDFs from our online resource library, which is found at www.oratium.com/resources.

SECTION ONE
How You Prepare for the Day

You have your presentation built. Now what?

CHAPTER 3

Anticipating the Mindset of the Room

A well-designed presentation is thoroughly audience-centric because it's been built around their issues and problems. This is what creates the intellectual connection to the audience that's so essential. But as you approach the day itself, you'll want to understand where your audience is physically and emotionally, because that's the context in which you'll be working. A recent experience illustrates this well.

My wife works with children in the foster care system, and sadly, almost all these kids have seen things no child should ever see. Some time ago, she attended a seminar to learn how witnessing traumatic events like domestic violence impacts a child's later behavior, and how to determine whether those past experiences are now affecting them. One test in particular caught my attention: kids are shown various pictures and asked to tell a story about what each picture is saying. The stories their minds conjure up are extremely revealing of their state of mind.

Here's an example they used in the class: if you show a young child a picture of a man working under a car, the child from a stable background is likely to describe a dad working to fix the car, and that when it's fixed, he'll be taking the family on a fun trip or vacation. Quite an optimistic construct. But in contrast, a child from an abusive background will often see a much darker story. The car has run over the man. It was driven by someone who was very angry with him, probably some enemy, or even his wife. It's the same information, but the interpretation is vastly different.

This is an extreme example, but it makes the point exceedingly well. People's perception and interpretation of new information is *always* influenced by their prior experience and current emotional state. Life would be so easy for presenters if audiences were simply emotionally neutral, blank canvases upon which to paint a story. But they aren't. Your audience's canvas is a complex, pre-painted Picasso of unpredictable patterns and colors. We all interpret information based on a wide range of personal lenses and filters that emerge from our prior life experiences.

Several years ago, I was presenting to a room of about forty executives from various companies, and it was a lively meeting with a great discussion. We passed out evaluations at the end, asking them to grade the session from *terrible* to *excellent*. I recall receiving thirty-nine out of forty *excellent* ratings, which felt wonderful. But lurking in the stack was one final assessment, and it wasn't rated *excellent*, *good*, *fair*, or even *poor*. It was marked *terrible*, and that sheet, anonymous of course, had some scathing and personally hurtful things to say about both the presentation and me personally, including words like "arrogant," "know-it-all," and "condescending."

If this has ever happened to you, you know that no matter how irrational that lone evaluation may be, it still hurts. But what was really going on there? I'm certainly capable of being an arrogant know-it-all, but when thirty-nine of forty reviewers go the *other* way, you have to conclude that this was more about the hidden issues that one individual had carried into the room that day. This problem will show up from time to time for most presenters. The trigger might be your gender, accent, title, or skin color—I've seen all of them. Strangest of all, sometimes it's simply resentment of the fact that you were up there speaking, and they weren't the one enjoying the limelight of making the presentation. The point is, people bring into any meeting a range of preconceptions that is often more about emotion than intellect, which will almost always be, at first sight at least, unseen.

The Strange Case of Being Evaluated

If your presentation is being evaluated, which is common for conference speakers, pay careful attention to the overall body of feedback. Take that feedback seriously, because it's valuable to your growth as a communicator, but don't get unduly worked up about individual outliers—especially strange overreactions like this one that may have their roots in race or resentment. As I'm sure you realize, they're much less about you than they are about the person filling in the form. Hard as it is, just shrug and move on. Remember: any time you're in front of an audience, you've put yourself in a position where someone can take an anonymous potshot. It's an occupational hazard.

While it's unlikely you'll root out any deeply held prejudices, there are some discoverable issues that are well worth mining for. The best way to do that is by asking the organizer a few intentional questions on the day of the event itself, or very close to it. You probably won't ever uncover the individual who's going to hate you for simply being British (and yes, I've had that), but you can find out whether there are any particular issues the group is dealing with, either individually or communally, of which you should be aware.

Usually, on the day of the event itself, or very close to it, I'll ask the organizer if there's anything going on with the audience, anything they're dealing with that's worth my knowing about. By asking this question, I'm looking for two things.

PHYSICAL CONDITION

I'll always explore whether the audience is tired or fresh, based on what they've been doing up to the point of my presentation. Quite often I'll hear, "This is the end of a four-day conference, and we've been working them pretty hard," or "Last night's awards banquet ran pretty late," both of which are code for "They're exhausted and running on fumes at this point." Having learned this, what's critical is now to make some adjustments . . . because that's why you asked.

> A hallmark of amateur communicators is not changing the plan in light of changing events. You *must* respond to and make use of this priceless information.

In this case, knowing my audience isn't coming in with a full tank of mental energy, I would a) trim out any secondary content; b) make sure the session is high energy and fun; c) add more breaks if it's a longer session; and d) truly bless them by finishing a little early. This is a perfect example of "advanced is not complicated," because these course corrections are simple to execute but will have an enormous impact on the effectiveness of the session. Imagine how miserable it would be if you didn't make these adjustments, and instead deluged a group who was already running on empty. Everybody loses in that scenario.

I would also make the session less interactive. While this might seem counterintuitive, a highly fatigued group is often happy to sit back and learn, while being less willing, or even able, to do the hard work of engaging in a debate around thorny or difficult questions. I wouldn't necessarily jettison group exercises, as they can inject energy (they'd have to be comatose before I'd do that), but don't press tired individuals into participating in questions or tasks they don't have the mental capacity to complete.

The other physical issue to check for is jet-lag and time-zone blues. There's nothing harder than when someone from the West Coast of the US has to be in an 8:00 a.m. meeting on the East Coast. Unless they had a recovery day (incredibly rare), that's a 5:00 a.m. start for their body clock and probably a 4:00 a.m. wake-up call. Coffee will get them through the morning, but by the afternoon they're going to be dragging. Transatlantic or trans-Pacific is even worse. If they're fresh off the plane, they're going to be struggling mightily at some points across the day. If it's the majority of the group, adjust for it by simplifying your content, but if not, at least give those struggling individuals a break. When Heinrich and Marie-Claire's eyes begin to close, it's not their fault and it's not a problem. Don't call on them; simply let them be and check in with them later to see if they missed anything that you can re-explain. The main lesson here is simple: ask questions to specifically check for the audience's physical condition.

EMOTIONAL MOOD

In addition to physical issues, you need to find out about any emotional issues that may be circulating. Many years ago, I was presenting research findings to a group who had just learned that, courtesy of a recent merger, some major layoffs were coming. But they hadn't yet been given the details of specifically where the ax was going to fall; that little ray of sunshine was a few days away. In a perfect world, this research briefing should have been canceled, because no one was in any mood to engage . . . but of course, life doesn't work that way. Forty-five of the fifty attendees were going to escape unscathed, and for them, this was valuable information they were going to need. But that didn't matter. The professionalism the group maintained was truly admirable, yet they were still detached and distracted. And that was fine: having been in that position myself, I knew the agony of their uncertainty firsthand. But from a presentation standpoint, once again, something needed to change—specifically, all the planned joviality and humor were now absolutely off the table, because **in these situations, you have to match the mood of the room.**

As you make your inquiries, it's also common to learn that a specific individual is working through some personal challenge or tragedy. It may not affect the overall meeting (although it may mean you'll need to ditch some example or illustration), but it's important for you to know. Fate often decrees you will be sitting with them over lunch. That's how the universe works.

I can't paint this kind of situation only as negative, because unless you're particularly ill-fated, you'll be blessed with an equal number of days of highly positive situations that counterbalance these darker moments. If the group just beat their quarterly target, nailed a massive product launch, or saw some other success, everything now works in reverse. Rather than being dejected, they will be looking to have fun, be playful, tease each other, tease you, and generally let off steam. And again, your job is to respond—in this case, by rising to match their lightness of mood. Don't get uptight about the rambunctious atmosphere. Yes, control any excesses, but most of all, relax, have fun, and enjoy the bumpier ride.

In sum, it's vital to understand where your audience is, both from a physical and emotional standpoint, and to make appropriate adjustments in style and tone. The investigation itself only takes five minutes and a couple of questions, and most of the time there's nothing to be found. But when there is, the knowledge is more precious than gold.

CHAPTER 4

The International Audience

THE CHALLENGE OF COMPREHENSION

Most of the time, presenters and their audiences share the same mother tongue, which is great, because it's one less thing to think about. However, if you're about to present, and yours is the second language for some or all of your audience, you now have a whole new set of challenges to manage. This is another key preparation moment.

In the not-too-distant past, this was only an issue if you were presenting to a group who was genuinely "international," or where you had physically traveled to present to your Italian distributor. However, in today's global and multicultural society, it's far more common for a regular corporate meeting to contain a meaningful international contingent. Whatever the reason, when some of your audience members have a challenge with language fluency, this brings an important issue into view. For the sake of this discussion, let's assume that you have an English as a second language (ESL) group as your audience.

When addressing a partially or largely ESL group, the rules change. The challenge is now one of basic comprehension, and it's made harder by the nature of oral presentations. When you read a book, if you don't fully grasp a particular paragraph, it's not a problem. You can read and reread it as often as required until you do. But oral presentations don't work that way; the audience can't go back and re-listen to a phrase that has already passed, and if you lose them, you may never get them back. Hence the presenter has a particular burden to make certain they get it the first time, and that requires some deliberate adjustments. It's actually a difficult moment when you learn you have an ESL issue, because several frustrating limitations have just been placed upon you, and you have no choice but to accept them. For example, as we'll discuss in Section Three, language is a powerful tool, which the best communicators use to their great advantage. But in an ESL situation, that tool is essentially taken away. Depending on the audience's level of fluency, you could be heading back to frustratingly basic vocabulary.

When to Adjust

Deciding whether the situation merits a change in approach is a tricky call, with significant consequences if you get it wrong. In a room of 500 people with ten ESL attendees, you probably aren't going to modify your approach to meet the needs of those ten. Is that going to diminish their experience? Yes, but there's really nothing you can do about it. As Mr. Spock famously said, "The needs of the many outweigh the needs of the few." However, as that number rises, you reach a tipping point when the decision changes. When about 20 percent or more of the audience has an English fluency challenge, that's about the point at which you need to start considering making adjustments. But be certain that you have no choice, because there's a painful tradeoff here. When you deliver material slowly and with less imaginative language, it may work for the ESL contingent, but the presentation will feel lumbering and pedestrian for the native English speaker. I've had to do it many times, and it's a horrible trade.

How to Adjust

When the audience makeup leaves you no choice, the way you boost ESL attendee comprehension is by making three significant adjustments:

> ➤ **Language and idiom:** what you say
>
> ➤ **Speed and enunciation:** how clearly you say it
>
> ➤ **Length of segments and breaks:** how long you ask them to focus

LANGUAGE AND IDIOM. The first and most basic change you need to make is in your use of language. Speakers generally forget how hard it is for an audience to take in new material, and a presenter's familiarity with their subject can easily blind them to how complex it can be to the listener. This is why—for any audience—you have to carefully root out technical terms, acronyms, and jargon that can creep in unnoticed. But when addressing an ESL audience, the problem is multiplied a hundredfold. Now, even the most apparently ordinary English word can become a serious barrier to communication.

Consequently, your linguistic choices are now highly restricted. While you don't necessarily "simplify" the argument itself, linguistically that's *precisely* what you're doing. There will be nuances within ideas that you simply may not be able to express. Obviously, how far you need to go depends on the audience. If your ESL contingent comes from an organization where English is the working language, they will operate at a much higher level; but if that's not the case, you're probably coming down closer to the level of language that people learned in high school: simpler nouns, verbs, and sentence structure.

I recently saw a wonderful example of this principle in practice. Eddie Izzard is a brilliant (but shockingly irreverent) British comedian. Looking for YouTube videos of his shows I hadn't seen, I came across a gig he did in a club in Stockholm. The routine contained his hallmark razor-sharp wit, but the show itself felt subtly different. And then I realized why: I could sense several moments where he both slowed down and intentionally simplified his vocabulary and syntax, almost like he was talking to young teenagers. It was so subtle you could easily have missed it, but when I checked it against similar material he had delivered to native English audiences, the language differences were clearly discernible. Izzard is truly a genius. Even though the level of English is fantastic in Sweden, he still recognized the issue, and this almost imperceptible adjustment was a masterful example of deliberate adaptation to an international setting.

Closely related to language is the idea of idioms, or figures of speech. Idioms are such a part of everyday life that we barely notice when we're using them. They're simply *par for the course* (there's one). But they can be problematic for an ESL audience because idioms are almost invariably culturally defined. When an Englishman talks about being "as sick as a parrot" or an American speaks of needing to do an "end run" around some obstacle, these phrases have no meaning outside their original cultural context and can be incomprehensible as a result.

Obviously, stripping out any culturally defined idea, illustration, or example is the answer. But if you can, the best solution is to "internationalize" your material with illustrations that relate to your audience. For example, I recently presented in Sweden (business, not stand-up comedy), and I wanted to depict the danger of getting design wrong. My usual example is that of an odd building in the US that was so poorly designed it had to be abandoned, but that illustration wouldn't have worked in a Scandinavian setting. However, a quick Google search gave me the example of the *Vasa*, a medieval Swedish battleship. She was a monster, designed to dominate the seas for decades, but, in an odd blend of comedy and tragedy, she capsized and sank moments after being launched, a direct result of some disastrous design decisions. The same point, supported by a good visual, became an infinitely better example for that audience.

The Vasa, now on display in Stockholm, finally retrieved from the bottom of Stockholm Harbor 325 years after her short but spectacular three-minute naval career.

The main lesson is this: in most presentations, your general goal is to use language that is richer and a little loftier than that of everyday speech; but with an ESL crowd, you need to go the other way. Your primary goal becomes that of ensuring comprehension, and the only way to achieve this is to make sure your language is precise, clear, simple, and not culturally bound.

> **In an ESL setting, the standard is not to be so clear that you can be understood. That's easy. The standard is to be so clear that you cannot be misunderstood.**

SPEED AND ENUNCIATION. When you have your language sufficiently simple, you now need to slow it all down. As any of you who speak a second language know, even if you're relatively fluent, performing real-time translation requires an enormous amount of brainpower and is impossibly difficult to do at full speed. You have to help your audience out, and the way you do that is to speak at about 70–80 percent of normal speed. Unfortunately, this will feel painfully slow for your native English hearers; however, I've always found that if you make it clear you're going slowly for this reason, you will be forgiven. They won't love it, but at least they won't blame you for doing it.

Closely related to speed is enunciation. In addition to speaking more slowly, it's important to speak extremely clearly. Translating between languages is hard enough. If you give the audience the extra challenge of having first to figure out what a word actually was, then it's game over. Returning to Eddie Izzard, this was the first thing I noticed. When I went back and checked that particular stand-up event against his US routines, I found that he was performing his material noticeably clearer and with more careful enunciation. If you want to know how to do this, we'll discuss improving enunciation in Chapter 8.

LENGTH OF SEGMENTS AND BREAKS. Finally, if you've ever tried to follow a presentation in a second language, you will know that the sustained concentration makes it utterly exhausting. How exhausting will depend on the level of fluency, but if it's an issue, the way to compensate is by shortening the segments. My working rule is to deliver in segments of no more than thirty minutes, and then give the audience a decent break to "reset" their mental energy.

The Rule of Half: Implications for Your Quantity of Content

Speaking slowly, with more breaks and shorter segments, is key to winning with an ESL audience; but the aggregate effect is that you will only be able to present about half of your normal content. We regularly teach our full-day workshop in ESL environments, and we've learned that in those settings we must use our *half-day* workshop content. This material takes four hours when taught to a native English–speaking group, but it fits the full day perfectly for the ESL crowd. When you need to trade off comprehension with content, comprehension always wins.

DIFFERENCES IN DISCUSSION

When you are presenting in a truly international setting, it's worth noting that questions and discussion work very differently in varying regions of the world, and the differences are maddeningly complicated. For example (and please forgive the generalization), it's typically true that North American and British groups will have a boisterous discussion style, where people just dive in without too much regard for politeness or politics. However, Asian cultures tend to be different. Questions can be perceived as a sign that the listener is either ignorant or wasn't paying proper attention. They can also be seen as an insult because they imply that the speaker wasn't clear enough. For cultural reasons, junior people may avoid asking questions if they have more senior leaders in the room. For these reasons, in Asia—depending on the country—you will often get far fewer inbound questions than you would typically expect. And if you try to solve this by throwing questions out to the group, that doesn't work either. You typically won't get an answer, because answering can be seen as arrogant. But if you ask the same question of a specific individual, you will get a robust response, because being selected is seen as an honor. The broader point is that this topic is ridiculously complicated, and many a presenter has crashed and burned through not understanding the cultural rules of the rooms they are in. The issues here are as diverse as the number of countries and cultures in the world, hence the principle is: *Google it.* As far as you can, find out about the local "rules" and respond accordingly.

THE POWER OF THE HANDOUT

As you've read, one important aspect of the presentation model we've set forth is the use of an audience handout. We've already discussed how much it drives comprehension and re-presentability, **but its incremental value for the ESL audience cannot be overstated,** because it gives them an additional opportunity to make sense of the words that are coming at them. It's the benefit I described earlier, whereby a book gives you the luxury of rereading a line of argument until you get it. We've had many non-English speakers take our class, and you can tell by the way they attach to the handout that it was the true key to learning for them.

PRESENTING IN THEIR LANGUAGE

When the entire audience speaks a single other language, if you have the ability to present in that language, it will always be well received. However, be careful. If you can pull it off, that's great; but if you can't, the thud of the fall can be spectacular. We all remember John F. Kennedy's famous "*Ich bin ein Berliner*" comment, which does not actually mean "I'm a Berliner," but rather "I'm a beloved German doughnut." Funnier still, many years ago, I was working for a British multinational company and was part of a team that went to visit our French distributor. There was a dinner, and our British CEO, being reasonably fluent, chose to address the group in French. Okay so far. However, while he was talking, it was clear that he was in a little physical discomfort, and when someone asked him if he was okay, he replied, "*Oui, j'ai mal au rognons.*" Which he thought meant, "Yes, I'm fine. I just have some pain in my kidneys."

However, while "kidneys" is one translation, the word *rognons* is more literally translated as "sweetbreads," and given that word's typical use, what he actually said to the audience was (and there's no easy way for me to say this): "Yes, I have some pain in my testicles." This would have been bad enough, except for the fact that, sensing the audience's very evident puzzlement, his lovely wife then chimed in to help out, and in perfect French added, "Indeed he does, I have to massage them for him every day."

True story.

The lesson? Don't present in another language unless you're perfectly bilingual or have an excellent lawyer.

CHAPTER 5

Rehearsal

Due to its importance, rehearsal is the one delivery topic that appeared, as an epilogue, in my earlier book on message design, *The Compelling Communicator.* If you read that, you will recognize this discussion. This chapter covers essentially the same ground with some further development of the big ideas. If you want to skip the chapter here, that's fine, but please do read the new section "Cementing the Storyboard" on page 71.

I n this chapter, we return to one of the central themes of excellent presentation delivery, which is precision in language. When you've taken the time to design a great presentation and made these important final adjustments based on the audience's physical, emotional, and intellectual status, it's critical that this presentation, and none other, is what shows up on game day. For this reason, rehearsal—the practice that "grooves" the argument into the speaker's mind—is a high-ranking driver of success.

THE PROBLEM: RECOGNITION VERSUS RETRIEVAL

I have a good friend who in his "retirement" leads a nonprofit that works to relieve extreme poverty on a small island in the Philippines. Last summer, I was helping him put together his presentation for their upcoming fundraising banquet. He was planning to talk about a much-needed water sanitation program, and together we crafted the three main points that he would present. However, my friend is significantly more comfortable driving into the jungle looking for sick kids than he is onstage, even when the crowd is comprised of his oldest and dearest supporters. (Note that paradox; for many people, presenting to a crowd of friends is actually far more intimidating than presenting to a room full of strangers.)

Unfortunately, as the evening arrived, he hadn't rehearsed his remarks as carefully as he should have, and they were not "grooved" and ready to trip off his tongue. Plus, he was nervous. As a result, on the night, while the three points were present in his presentation, they were so obscured by eddies, minor details, and personal anecdotes that they were essentially lost on the audience. The points had been clear in his mind a few days earlier. **The problem was, his lack of rehearsal meant that when he stepped up to the microphone, he was asking his already nervous mind that night to create the right structure and language on the fly while staying away from points he didn't need to make. And in that high-stress moment, that was just too big an ask.** It was still solid and utterly authentic, and the fundraising goal was achieved. But from a communication standpoint, the message was unclear, and a long way from what it could have been.

This story teaches an important lesson. It's extremely common for presenters to build a great argument, only to deliver something substantially different on game day. Crucial points get missed, transitions fall by the wayside, data is poorly explained, and by far the most common problem is that riffs that were tight and punchy in the mind become long, rambling, and disjointed when they come out of the mouth. The main cause of this problem is one specific misunderstanding of the way memory works, which then leads us to prepare in the wrong way.

Most people prepare by running through a presentation a few times in their head, skimming their notes visually, and concluding, when it sounds about right (in their heads), that they know exactly a) what they're going to say and b) how they're going to say it. But they're wrong; they don't know either of those things at all.

> There's actually an enormous difference between having a general idea of what you're going to say, and having "grooved" the specific language so well that *that*, and *only* that, is what comes out on the day.

And, of course, by the time you discover you didn't know it, it's always too late. We've all lived in that painful moment when you realize it isn't as clear in your head as you thought it was, and there's a sea of puzzled faces in front of you who've realized exactly the same thing.

In order to solve this problem, you have to dig down to the root issue, which is the difference in human memory between **recognition** and **retrieval**. When you leaf through your slides and, recognizing everything, say, "Okay, I've got this," only to later discover that the crisp, clean narrative wasn't there at all, that's the recognition versus retrieval trap. You knew the material well enough for your brain to recognize it, but not well enough to fully recall it. If you really want to understand this distinction, consider a dollar bill. If I showed one to you, you would instantly recognize it. But if I asked you to draw one side and get the main elements correct and in roughly the right place, you probably wouldn't be able to do it at all. That's the difference between recognition and retrieval.

Compounding this problem is the fact that you need your brain to be on its best game to summon an argument correctly from memory. But of course, most presenters are both nervous and distracted by the other aspects of the moment ("Why is that guy texting?" "Is that leaf-blower distracting?" "Do these pants make me look fat?"), and the higher-stakes the setting, the more this will be true. Nervous, distracted minds do strange things. They will often blurt out unintended phrases or freeze up altogether. Some time ago, I actually saw a speaker who was momentarily unable to name all four of his kids. This is a genuine problem; if you don't know the material well enough, you are relying on your brain to rescue the situation when you're going on stage. But be warned: the nervous mind is like a beloved but unreliable friend. He's probably not showing up at the moment you truly need him.

UNPOPULAR BUT TRUE: REHEARSAL CLOSES THE GAP

If you want to create the smallest possible gap between plan and execution, you need to prepare in a different way. The first real "gap-closer" is easy to miss: it's the design of the presentation itself. If you have poorly organized material, it isn't merely a problem for the audience; it's a huge problem for you. It'll be extremely difficult to get it all straight in your head, so you'll be wrestling to deliver it just as much as your audience is wrestling to understand it. In contrast, if you have crisp, clean, logical material, it won't be fighting you nearly as much, and you're already well on the way to it coming out just right.

As important as the design is, however, the principal way you get there is through rehearsal. **Exceptional communicators invariably use rehearsal to achieve complete mastery of their material by reaching the "point of perfect retrieval," not merely the "point of perfect recognition."** Such preparation not only gives presenters the precision they need, but it also frees them up to be much more present in the room, allowing them to stay on top of other important aspects of delivery, such as reading the signals the audience is sending, managing the clock, and dealing with unexpected disruptions.

Rehearsal gives you the fluency you need, but it's important to note that this does not come because you have *memorized* your material, but because you have *learned* it. Most people can't memorize material, but in truth, they don't need to try. Rehearsal is about learning. When you have your material safely tucked away in your long-term memory, you're free to just talk naturally and conversationally and enjoy the day.

SO . . . WHY DON'T WE REHEARSE?

Given the enormous gap-eliminating value of rehearsal, why don't we do it more? It's a lively discussion in our workshops, and the reasons are varied and interesting, including:

➤ I don't have time.

➤ It feels weird/people are watching ("Dad, he's doing it again!").

➤ I think I've got it/ I've given it before.

➤ I don't want to sound wooden; I want to be spontaneous and really be "me."

➤ I don't want to hear how bad it is. (Seriously, when I first heard that in a workshop, I laughed because I knew it was a joke, and that I'd never hear it again. I was wrong. It actually shows up about one in three times.)

➤ I don't know how to do rehearsal.

Most of these reasons are legitimate, with the exception of "I don't want to hear how bad it is." (That's just crazy. Do you *really* want to hear how bad it is when you're up there giving the presentation?) But the true root reason is deeper, hiding behind this list. Knowing that people will always make time for the things that are truly important, the real reason is that they don't actually understand how much of a difference it's going to make, and that's primarily because they don't appreciate the distinction between recognition and retrieval. Most people simply have no idea just how much better rehearsal is going to make things. If they did, they'd take the time and get over the weirdness.

THE CASE FOR REHEARSAL

Let me make the case by outlining the four extraordinary benefits that rehearsal provides.

1. Final Content Refinement

In one of his more famous speeches, when reporting on the Battle of Britain, Winston Churchill delivered what is probably his most memorable recorded phrase: "Never in the field of human conflict was so much owed by so many to so few." This phrase is breathtaking in its beauty, but what most people don't know is that right up to the moment when he delivered the speech, he had a different phrase planned, which was the wholly less impressive, "Never in the history of mankind have so many owed so much to so few." In fact, it was a pretty close call, because he actually fixed it while rehearsing in the car on the way to deliver the speech. That's the amazing thing about rehearsal. It's often when you do some of your clearest thinking regarding the argument you're trying to craft. You won't be doing any radical rework at this stage, but those final refinements, particularly in language, will make your argument noticeably better.

2. The Language Gets "Grooved"

The second big benefit of rehearsal is that it *cements* that final language you have just found, making sure that those perfect words are what actually come out of your mouth. Those words matter because even the most powerful idea can be robbed of all its strength through sloppy, imprecise, or clichéd language. The problem here stems from the enormous complexity of spoken language. How many different ways are there of wording even this one simple paragraph? If you think about all the possible combinations of vocabulary and syntax, mathematically speaking there's an almost infinite number of alternatives—and it's the same with any idea you're trying to convey. If you only reach a place of "recognition" of your material, giving you a "pretty good" idea of what you want to say, what's the likelihood your brain is going to pull the single cleanest and most perfect phrasing from this *near-infinite* range of possibilities? Not a chance. And yet, that's what the unprepared speaker is asking their brain to do. As good as your point may be, if you only have a vague idea of how you are going to deliver it, the chances of getting it exactly right in the moment are almost zero.

Of course, this doesn't mean you'll simply stand up there with your mouth flapping if you're less than fully prepared. You're going to say something, and your brain will generally still pull good, solid language out of the ether in the moment. But is that what you want? Of all the ways an idea can be expressed, many will be weak, some will be good, but only a few—maybe even only one—will be fabulous, and that's the one you want to make sure you use. Only rehearsal gets you to that point of perfect retrieval of "grooved" language. I call this "muscle memory of the mouth": the point when those key phrases are so embedded that they still come out right, even when your brain has momentarily wandered off to wonder whether that odd draft in your nether regions is the legendary unzipped fly you were warned about in traditional training.

3. It Stops You from Saying That Thing You Really Shouldn't Have Said

All speakers embellish. They add in phrases, words, and thoughts they hadn't planned, and except in the case of scripted presentations, every speaker does it every time they get up to speak. Much of the time, you'll add valuable new thoughts as they come to you in the moment, but that's not always the case. The question is, how far off-script are you going, and how much damage might you do if you stray too far? The risk here is real, as I can demonstrate with two questions.

Question One: In a presentation, have you ever said something you didn't actually plan to say? Of course. Question Two is similar but subtly different: In a presentation, have you ever said something you planned *not* to say? Yes! And we've all done it. It's a shocking truth that again demonstrates our onstage brains have a dangerous tendency to turn to mush. In the calm sanity of your office, you had a good reason for deciding to leave out that horribly off-color joke, but then, with a crowd in front of you that you want to please, your brain suddenly decides that this is the funniest thing ever. It's not. Undisciplined embellishment is perilous.

The Three Deadly Landmines of Undisciplined Embellishment

BLOWING UP YOUR TIME. If you planned a tight thirty minutes but start embellishing content, you're reopening the door to the deadly problem of firehosing. As I'm sure you've noticed, presenters frequently run long, especially at conferences. But how many of them rehearsed to run long? None. What happened? They embellished the extra content in the moment, either by adding additional points, restating and clarifying ideas that came out wrong, or exploring eddies that would have been better left alone. None of these by themselves are especially malicious or evil, but running long is a major presenting *faux pas*, and even more important, there's no point building a presentation that stays within your audience's limited working memory if you're going to abandon those boundaries on game day.

BLOWING UP YOUR FLOW. Imagine you've designed exactly the kind of logical narrative flow that is greatly helpful for audience comprehension and retention. What happens if you're up on stage and you utter the immortal words, "Now, I know this is a little off-topic, but let me quickly . . .?" **No!** By introducing your own rabbit trail, you destroy the flow you worked so hard to create. Whenever I hear a speaker utter the phrase "Okay, where were we?" as he or she seeks a way back from some self-inflicted detour, that's a rage-inducing moment for me. If *you* don't know where we are, how am *I* supposed to? The less-rehearsed speaker is always more prone to introducing these flow-destroying digressions.

BLOWING UP YOURSELF. This point is an odd combination of seriously funny and deadly serious. As you probably know, in many ways your brain is a connection engine, and whenever you're presenting, in some dark backroom behind the scenes of your conscious mind it's constantly making connections. Some of these are inappropriate, rude, or brutally hurtful. And here's the scary thing: they're trying to get out of your mouth. You've probably heard of a Freudian slip; that's what we're talking about here. Of course, Freudian mistakes can be really funny. Until they're not.

Here's my worst transgression. Many years ago, I was making a presentation to a leadership group at Disney, where I was discussing a way to improve sales effectiveness. The audience, however, didn't like the idea and they were pushing back pretty hard. The discussion became animated in a perfectly good-natured way, when I, for reasons known only to my subconscious, uttered the immortal words: "Guys, I don't see why you're not getting it! This is not a Mickey Mouse idea." There was a dull thud as the words landed and, after a pause, a dear friend, Randy Garfield, said, "You know, Tim, we don't say that around here."

"I'm sure you don't," was my timid reply. It's a funny story, but within it lies a serious point. To my knowledge, I've never used that phrase in conversation before or since, but there I was, surrounded by the legendary mouse, and his name was trying to get out of my mouth. Executives at Disney are genuinely the most gracious (and as it turns out, forgiving) people you will ever meet, but can you imagine how serious this gaffe could have been?

You don't have to imagine it because I can show you exactly what that looks like with a far graver story.

I know of one US company where a senior executive went to visit their German subsidiary, with the goal of getting them to comply with some new internal policy. He was pressing them in the meeting, and they were expressing their dislike for the change. In the heat of that moment, he said, "Look, guys, I don't want to be a Nazi about it, but we really need you to do this."

There's nothing remotely funny about this story. There really is such a thing as a career-ending comment, and this came awfully close. That executive is still not permitted by his company to travel outside the US, and it wouldn't surprise me if his career trajectory has been permanently affected. We live in a highly sensitized world, where even innocent mistakes in language (as this was) may not be readily forgiven. I know this man. He had no prior intention whatsoever of summoning that phrase, and he was mortified when he did so. But the lesson is clear: when you're in Germany, surrounded by all things German, never underestimate what naughty little things your connection engine is doing, and just how much those things are trying to get out of your mouth.

Regarding embellishment, it all comes back to rehearsal. The clearer you are on what you want to say, the less you're ad-libbing in the moment, the less likely one of these three deadly landmines is going to go off.

Defeating Excessive Embellishment

There are three rules that will particularly help you win this challenging battle:

1. **Trust your instincts on "leave-outs."** As a matter of discipline, if in rehearsal you made a conscious decision NOT to say something, *under no circumstances* should you say it. You had a reason for leaving it out during your preparation. Leave it out.

2. **Stick to the plan.** Plan what you're going to say, and then, within reason, say only what you planned to say. With sufficient rehearsal, you will hear yourself deviating from the plan, which is half the battle. The other half is having the self-discipline to stop when you sense you're drifting too far.

3. **Rehearse with a buffer.** If your rehearsal runs to exactly your allotted time, be careful: you're allowing yourself zero room for even a single word of embellishment, and that's just not practical. You're going to embellish a little, so for the typical presentation your rehearsal should run no longer than about 80-85 percent of your allotted time. That creates the buffer you need to make room for the legitimate (and high-value) points you're going to embellish in. Just don't take this as license on the day to explore every little tangent that comes into your mind.

4. *It's the Key to Recovering When a Presentation Gets Derailed*

If you think about it, 100 percent of presentations get derailed in some way. There's always something like a late start, an unexpectedly long discussion, or a temperamental projector that throws a wrench in the plan. Whenever I speak at conferences, about half the time I start late because they're running behind schedule (and, as unfair as it is, there's often a tacit request for me to get them back on track). There are a thousand things that can snip ten minutes off your time, and how you respond speaks volumes about how well you've prepared. Under-rehearsed presenters are frequently caught off-guard by the sudden change in plan, and they often respond by flying through their original material and by implicitly—or explicitly—shutting down conversation. This is a horrible response to losing time. In contrast, the prepared presenter will calmly and imperceptibly trim out ten minutes of secondary material and seamlessly stitch it all back together.

Taken together, these four reasons, plus the fact that rehearsal is a wonderful cure for nerves, create an overwhelmingly compelling argument to rehearse to a much greater extent than we normally do. So, how do we do it?

THE HOW OF REHEARSAL

"Just Do it." The good news about rehearsal is that it isn't intellectually hard; it's merely a matter of self-discipline. However boring, the discipline to turn back to the first page and start again is a marker of greatness. That said, the rules of rehearsal are worth knowing.

Conditions

As far as you can, physically replicate "game conditions." If you're to present standing up, rehearse standing up. This will mirror the lung capacity of the real event, and help you develop your breathing/speaking cadence as well as the inflection, modulation, and hand and body movements you'll use on the day. You want the actual event to feel so much like rehearsal that your mind just slips into it like a comfortable jacket.

I don't rehearse in front of others, because I generally already know what I'm looking for and they may not. That's a personal view, but it's true for many speakers. That said, if you have someone you trust, and you want those untainted eyes, then go right ahead, as long as they know how to pitch their comments at the right level. You can end up in an asylum if your helpful mock audience either aims too high, as in, "Maybe you can lose that whole first half," or too low, as in, "You said 'and' where I think you meant 'but'." (True confession: in a long-ago consulting role, I actually had a junior analyst removed from a rehearsal for saying that.) Regardless of whether you choose to work solo or with a test audience, always do your last rounds alone. You don't want any external distractions in your final preparation.

The one exception to going it alone is humor. Try that on everyone. It's never quite as funny in rehearsal as it is on the day because testing it is artificial, but that's okay. If it's pretty funny in rehearsal, it will generally work well in front of an audience. But if you're about to unknowingly drop a career-ending bomb, it's best for someone to tell you, and they probably will.

And finally, if you decide to leave that joke out, I'm begging you: Under no circumstances whatsoever change your mind on stage. I have never in my life seen that decision turn out well.

Amount

There's no single, correct answer for the "how much?" question here because it depends on the setting. The right amount of rehearsal for you will depend on length, complexity, familiarity, and most importantly, stakes. However, as a working rule, I recommend three to four full run-throughs of any new material where you're reasonably familiar with it, and when it's a moderately important setting. But if you're less familiar and the stakes are high, don't hesitate to do more. TEDx speakers will commonly do thirty or more run-throughs, and I've done the same for critical keynotes. Heavy rehearsal is for those rare, truly high-stakes moments, where nothing but your absolute best will do. The idea of rehearsing that much probably feels like bad news—but there's good news.

In any presentation, is all the material equally important? No, which means you don't need to get everything perfect. Small delivery glitches in your secondary content aren't going to be an issue. What you want to do is make sure you're flawless on your most critical content. I call this "proportional preparation." Within any presentation, there are a small number of critical moments you definitely want to get right, which are:

> - Opening
> - Closing
> - Critical insights
> - Transitions
> - Complex points
> - Humor
> - Planned questions to the audience

If you nail these but have a few minor misspeaks on the rest, you're going to be fine—and given that this subset is probably only about 20 percent of your total content, this is good news. Focus the extra rehearsal on those key moments, but remember that anywhere you're trusting your mind to find the words in the moment, you run the risks of embellishment, which is why you always rehearse the whole thing a few times.

You may be wondering: within this 20 percent, what is the most important? Clearly, your insights are right up there, but topping the chart is your opening. This is the moment when you're being most carefully scrutinized, where you're setting the stage for all that's to come, but where your brain is at its most unreliable. For this reason, Chapter 7 is entirely devoted to the specific topic of "conquering the opening." No matter the setting, I will always rehearse my opening the most, and it's always the thing I do last. Right up to the moment when I stand up, I will be silently mouthing those first few sentences.

FINAL IDEA: IMPRINT YOUR "MENTAL STORYBOARD"

There's a presentation behavior I truly despise, and we've all seen it far too often. A speaker is working through their material when they click to the next slide and pause to look up at it, orienting themselves to what they're going to talk about next—and then, turning back to the audience, they launch into this new chunk of content (usually making no connection to the content that preceded it). At its worst, they even give the game away by saying, "Okay, what's next?" as they click and look up. **What they're revealing here is that they don't have the storyboard of the argument clear and imprinted in their own mind, so they fall back on the tried and tested "let the slide be your guide."** At first sight, this may seem rather innocent, but it's not. If you don't have the storyboard clearly in your own mind, a lot of other things are about to go wrong.

The lesser issue here is that this is disrespectful of the audience: you owe it to them to know your own material. But the greater issue is that of audience comprehension—and please stay with me while I take you through it. For a presentation to be fully comprehended, a logical narrative flow is one of the few truly non-negotiable elements. But if you as the presenter don't have the storyboard clear in your mind ("Okay, what's next?"), you are, by definition, unable to reveal the structure to the audience. Transitions are the way that structure is revealed, as in, "Okay, this new system will solve our data security problem—how easy is the migration going to be? Let's look at that." But it's impossible to deliver those if you don't have the story clear in your own mind. The inevitable result is that the audience will see the chunks of content in an episodic, disconnected way, but they won't see the bigger story. Presentations like that don't make a ton of sense, and they certainly don't stick. But it's what happens most of the time. You need to reveal the story, and for that, you must *know* the story.

Cementing the Storyboard

This crucial piece of preparation is a specific type of rehearsal, done very late, with the goal of **specifically and intentionally cementing the storyboard in your own mind.** I will, without exception, do this before every presentation to ensure that I have the whole argument mapped out, from beginning to end, so I always know where I am and where I'm going. This way, when I get to the conclusion of any point, I'm not looking for a slide or new section of a handout to prompt me, nor am I scouring my brain for what comes next. I know exactly what comes next, and more importantly, I know why. As a result, that all-important transition isn't only possible; it's inevitable. This is one of the most important pieces of final preparation. Most people don't do it, because they don't see why it would matter. But it *does* matter—because it's the single biggest key to your presentation flowing properly as you move between sections.

Cementing the storyboard is extremely easy to do, and it's not time-consuming. What you do is this: verbally or in writing, re-create your argument at the level of the storyboard, by which I mean your main points, your big illustrations, and your transitions. Or, put another way, walk through the chapters of the story. Scribbling it on a piece of paper is perfectly acceptable, **but doing it out loud is actually better because this expressly tests and proves that your mind can retrieve the argument.** For a one-hour presentation, this should take less than two to three minutes.

An illustration here is essential. There's a module in our live class where we teach the doctrine and practice of simplifying an argument. We talk about our tendency to pack too much in, explain why this is so toxic, and show how to fix it. Every time I prepare to teach that section, I'll lay out its high-level structure. I can't show you verbally, so let me show you what the cocktail-napkin version looks like (though this is actually more detailed than I would do in real life). I filled it out here so it would make more sense, but my actual shorthand would be gibberish to another reader. That's fine, though, because I'm doing it for me. For clarity, I'm giving you my points, "P," and my transitions, "T."

> **P** – Intro. Even with the right content, we still have a tremendous tendency to pack too much in.
>
> **T** – Why do we do that?
>
> **P** – Several powerful and well-motivated reasons (completeness, need to look smart)

T – What's the problem with that?

P – Terrible outcomes. Firehosing people is irritating, but more important, it violates brain's bandwidth: "working memory."

T – What is working memory?

P – The part of the brain that takes in new information. Very limited. Violate that, and it shuts down.

T – So . . . it's serious. Can it be solved?

P – Absolutely. Disciplined defoliation. Pull out everything you can.

T – How do you do that?

P – Manage down quantity.

T – But complexity is equally toxic, so:

P – Manage down complexity.

As you read that through, I'm quite certain you could discern the entire cadence and flow of the argument, even from those few short clauses. It's that powerful, which is precisely why you want it in your mind as you stand up to present. This is one of the single most important disciplines of preparation. **When I have the story laid out end to end in my mind, I never find myself presenting an independent idea or thought: I'm always presenting a chapter of a larger story. And the way you know you've got it is that your transitions are flawless every time.** You should do this storyboard exercise a few times as you're rehearsing ahead of the day, but you should also do it one last time, close to the time when you're going to speak. It'll be two of the most valuable minutes you've ever spent.

Audiences love (although usually at a subliminal level) a well-structured argument. In the design phase, you built just such an argument. The final part of the job is to make sure the "road map" is clear in your own mind before you get up on stage.

PROMPTING YOURSELF: SCRIPT OR BULLETS?

With rehearsal finished, how are you going to prompt yourself when giving your presentation?

Getting Practical

When it comes to prompting yourself, you have three possible options. First, take your cue from the slides on the screen. Second, use abbreviated note cards. Or third, fully script the presentation.

This is a narrow, secondary, and slightly more technical topic. Hence, you will find a full exploration of the relative merits of these three options in Appendix III.

First Principles: To Prompt or Not to Prompt?

Our discussion of rehearsal brings an obvious question to center stage. **If rehearsal helps us to "cement" the flow and language we want, does that then give us the freedom to stand up and just talk without notes?** In other words, does a great speaker use or refuse notes?

It isn't even a debate. Use notes. I've seen countless speakers attempt to deliver their remarks without notes, and it rarely works out well. The problem is our old friend: *precision.* If you want to make sure you deliver every point you've planned—in exactly the right sequence, flowing smoothly both within and between each one, and using exactly the right language throughout—you're asking your brain to do too much if you try to do all this entirely from memory.

Our brains don't hold recordings at that level of detail. And without help, even the best-rehearsed speaker will miss something at points, especially across a longer presentation and even more so when fielding questions from a lively room. If the central thesis of this book is making sure that this great message you've designed comes out exactly right on game day, then it's truly playing with fire to ask your brain to perform the Herculean task of doing it all from memory.

Why is it, then, that so many speakers choose to go without notes? Simply put: because it looks cool. Most of the time when I see a notes-free speaker, I sense that the underlying motive is the desire to impress, as though it's somehow cleverer to be up on the stage talking from the heart than it is to be using note cards. But that's a dangerous motivation that can land you in a lot of trouble. It only works if either a) you truly have it down cold through having given the exact same talk multiple times, or b) you're blessed with that rare gift of perfect memorization.

But most notes-free speakers I see don't have either of those things. They get up there, too cool for notes, and even though they "know" their material at some level, it's not enough to perfectly nail it. Consequently, the cool image comes at the cost of sloppiness, imprecision, and repetition as they follow the train of synaptic connections wherever it leads them—and it's a seriously bad trade. Perfect notes-free presenting can be done, but generally only for the shortest presentations. As a rule, notes are a speaker's best friend.

This may leave you wondering about the popular world of TED talks, because these talks are usually delivered without notes, and are often quite good. In fact, the TED model is driving some of this notes-free behavior, because people see this "talk from the heart" approach and want to emulate it, sensing that it's a key element of this highly successful presentation model. But there's a flaw in that logic. It's important to understand what you see when you watch a TED talk: for most of these speakers, that moment on stage is the high-light of their professional careers, and in some cases, of their lives. That sets these talks so insanely far apart from the norm that you have to be very careful when you try to import the approach into everyday life. Our team has coached a range of TEDx speakers, and it's common to see *thirty or more* rounds of full rehearsal. That's a crazy number, but it makes perfect sense given the enormity of that particular setting.

Most everyday presentations don't merit that degree of prepara-tion—they don't have the importance, and you certainly don't have the time. Here's my point:

> **You absolutely do want to be as precise as the best TED speaker, but because real-life doesn't afford the luxury of thirty rounds of rehearsal, that's exactly why you're going to need notes.**

There are many principles of TED speaking that are worth emu-lating: brevity, no dependence on slides, etc., but notes-free speaking isn't one of them. (And by the way, in some of the very best TED talks, the speakers wisely use note cards and are clearly the better for it.) The best news is, no one's going to care. There are no prizes for pacing around like an uncaged tiger, doing it all from memory; your audience won't think less of you for using notes, if they even notice at all.

CHAPTER 6

Beware: This Venue May Bite

⌒⊗⌒

WHEN VENUES ATTACK

At the time of this writing, I'm delivering at least one major keynote presentation per month, because that's how we both reach new customers and expand within our existing customers. Our keynote content is highly engaging, and I know exactly how to deliver it—my reward for frequent repetition. But whenever I show up to present, as well as it should go, I know that one grave danger still lurks in the shadows . . . the venue.

I'm writing this on a flight home after speaking at a tech company's sales conference in Texas, where I addressed a group of 180 software engineers in the after-lunch slot. The venue was, curiously, a Maggiano's restaurant, and while I was surprised at the choice, the room itself was fabulous: bright, airy, cool, decent acoustics, and the lunch that preceded me was marvelous, or at least it appeared to be. I'll never know because you should never eat before you speak (see Chapter 10: Energy).

But two venue gremlins were lurking. First, the group was running a bit late, so to get them back on track, the host innocently asked me to begin while the food was still being cleared and coffee served. Beware! This is not the harmless request it seems to be. It is a gilt-edged, razor-sharp, world-class presentation killer. There is almost nothing more destructive to a presentation, and especially its opening, than fifteen servers moving through the room, clearing and clattering plates. It's like fingernails across a chalkboard, making it almost impossible for you or the audience to concentrate. Plus, I was going to work from a handout, and it's hard to make that work when the audience has an array of dirty dishes to compete with. I've seen this plate-clearing movie before, and it never ends well. So, politely, but even more firmly, I declined, carefully explaining my reasons. We would delay the start until everything was clear. It was an easy decision: we had a two-hour session planned, and losing ten minutes was no great hardship. If my time had been an hour, this would have been a bit trickier, but I'd likely still have made the same call.

The second gremlin was genuinely bizarre. The room we were in is generally used for large banquet functions, and for those events, Maggiano's pipes Italian music through the ceiling speakers to create the right ambiance. That's a lovely touch for a wedding reception, but a Frank Sinatra accompaniment is hardly suited to a discussion of technical messaging with 180 software engineers. And, guess what? In this particular Maggiano's, the ceiling-mounted speakers can be turned down, but they can't be fully turned off without silencing the music for the whole restaurant. So despite our best efforts, the entire presentation was accompanied by "Old Blue Eyes" crooning surreally in the background. Fortunately, it wasn't quite loud enough to distract, but it was close. And it messed with my head the whole time.

You may never find yourself competing with Sinatra, but the deeper point is this: the final big act of preparation is to seek and destroy all the venue vampires that are waiting eagerly to mess up your day. Most venues weren't actually designed with presentations in mind, and that includes, oddly, a shocking number of office and hotel conference rooms. (What else are they for?) While the good speaking venues are amazing, the bad ones create huge problems. Great speakers are obsessive about this because they've all been bitten too many times. And every time I think I've seen it all, some new venue finds a bizarre new way to ruin my day.

The "Four Horsemen" of a Vicious Venue and How to Deal with Them

Let's establish the four most common ways the venue can sabotage you.

1. **NOISE DISTRACTIONS.** Whooshing air conditioners (turning on and off randomly), traffic noise, roadwork chaos, leaf-blowing, weed-whacking, servers clearing tables. Especially common are loud groups next door where the venue has turned a ballroom into several breakout rooms using paper-thin sliding room dividers. It's good for their profits but bad for your sanity and deadly for concentration.

2. **LOUSY ACOUSTICS.** Some rooms reflect sound as perfectly as the Sistine Chapel, while others absorb and deaden the sound like the padded cell of a lunatic. You should learn to love hard, reflective surfaces; they might echo a bit, but it's rarely too much, and they mean the sound will travel. I get nervous when I see fabric-covered walls, sound-deadening ceiling tiles, or cavernous, high-ceilinged ballrooms. Presenting is hard enough without your audience having to strain to hear every word.

3. **TEMPERATURE AND DISCOMFORT.** An excessively warm room, especially in the afternoon, can take down the legs of almost any speaker, no matter how good they are. I've never felt the afternoon slot is a problem; in fact, I like it and will often volunteer for it. But it's a big deal if it gets too hot. The biochemistry of tropical-greenhouse warmth at 2:40 p.m. after a heavy lunch can create a hill that's almost impossible to climb. For this reason, my "spider-sense" is exceptionally finely tuned to the temperature of a room I'm going to speak in. Similarly, other sources of physical discomfort are an issue. For example, if people have insufficient legroom or are too tightly packed around too few tables, it will seriously impact attention and focus after only a few minutes. And it's even worse when it's those "modern" minimalist chairs that look cool but were actually designed with the sole purpose of inflicting maximum pain on the victim.

4. **LIGHTING AND SCREEN VISIBILITY.** It still baffles me how often a room designed for presentations will have downward-pointing floodlights placed directly above the screen, and worse still when they can't be turned off independently. This one's tricky. You need the screen to be visible, so you'll want to kill those lights; but you can't darken the room too much, because the audience needs light to work and for you to see them. That balance can be hard to achieve. And we've all been in the crazy room with a big bright window placed directly behind the podium, partially blinding the audience and turning the speaker into an eerie silhouette for the length of the presentation.

If you were surprised to see a whole chapter on managing the venue, now you know why. Even if you get everything else right, every one of these venue issues has the potential to seriously damage a presentation, and some can completely demolish it.

The good news?
It's much more in your control than you realize.

Having understood the importance of venue problems, the second thing you need to understand—which inexperienced presenters tend to miss—is that **it's only out of your control if you let it be.** It's easy to think that the venue you're given is simply the hand you've been dealt and that you have to just battle through, but that's completely untrue. Great speakers are inveterate venue tinkerers (Steve Jobs was famous for it, and he was especially obsessive over lighting); they know exactly how to deal with all these challenges, and it's important to remember that as the speaker, you do carry some genuine authority to ask for things to be changed. Exercise it. Do it politely and graciously, but exercise it nonetheless.

This idea of control might seem surprising, so let's break it down. The first principle is that you cannot manage these issues at all if you don't have the time, which leads to the cardinal rule: **You must show up early enough to make the changes you need.** If you walk in ten minutes before you're due to speak, you are one hundred percent at the mercy of the venue, and shame on you for being that speaker. But if you show up an hour early, almost everything can be fixed or mitigated. What follows are some priceless tips and workarounds, from moving furniture to adjusting lighting to the nuclear option of changing rooms (and sometimes that's a real and viable option), but all of these need time to execute, and the more time the better. Whenever anyone from our team is presenting, we always aim to get into the room the night before to set up. Not only is it a lot less frantic to move furniture around in jeans and a T-shirt with a nice adult beverage in your hand, but you don't want to be dragging tables, dripping sweat in your best suit, as the audience begins to drift in. It looks incredibly unprofessional. So, having put time on your side, let's tackle the four horsemen of a bad venue.

SOLVING FOR NOISE

Most noise distractions can be managed. I arrived at the Maggiano's venue well over an hour before I was due to speak. We used that time to find the (always hidden) controls and turn the sound down, at least as far as we could. And as we talked through the event, I had enough time to calmly explain how big a problem the noise of the servers was going to be, which they understood, and which led us to agree to set a new start time. Indeed, giving the group a stretch break as the room was cleared meant that the event actually started with a certain ceremony, rather than being a blurry and noisy overlap with dessert.

We typically send two speakers to any event, and if there's any distracting noise, such as a loud corridor conversation happening right outside, the second speaker will head straight to the door to deal with it without even being asked. If you have a colleague, you can do the same, but even if you're presenting solo and can't leave the stage, you still have an option. Everyone in the audience is noticing the distraction, so don't be afraid to ask for help. "Hey, folks, would somebody mind trying to quiet those guys down outside?" Someone is always happy to help (former football players are always keen), and don't miss this: audiences love it when a speaker shows the strength and authority to take charge of the situation, a topic we'll return to when we talk about managing overly boisterous audience members.

Even though you can't win every battle, the limits are farther out than you think. Many years ago, we held an event at a prestigious hotel in Sydney, Australia. The attendees had made a considerable investment to be there, and we had made a considerable investment to host the event in that particular hotel. As we got started, our worst nightmare began: the bone-shaking noise of jackhammering started coming in from a street repair happening directly outside, which threatened to completely derail our event. This is where you get the hotel involved. We found the banqueting manager and made it clear that if they didn't somehow get it stopped, there were going to be some very serious repercussions of the "we won't be paying our whole bill" kind. And, miraculously, they somehow managed it. Not only was the event rescued, but once again the audience loved that the speakers took it on, rather than standing passively by while this annoyance was happening outside. Of course, we got lucky there, but you'll never know until you try. Ironically, if you try to fix it and fail, you still look great in the audience's eyes. It's when you don't try that you look weak.

The bottom line? You have much more control than you think. The hotel doesn't need to leaf-blow directly outside your meeting room. They can do your part of the property later, and usually they are perfectly obliging when you ask. *You simply have to ask.* If you can stop an Australian road crew, moving a leaf-blower is a piece of cake.

SOLVING FOR ACOUSTICS

Acoustics problems are a little trickier. Obviously, you don't get to rip out the ceiling tiles, but there are three things you can do if the acoustics are truly horrible. First, if possible, move to another room. If there's an equivalent room available, the switch isn't necessarily that hard. You can't always do it on the day, but if it's an event you're organizing/hosting, that's the kind of planning you should be doing ahead of time. Even if it's someone else's event, if there's a big problem, it doesn't hurt to ask.

Second, if you have a "dead" room, consciously project more and speak a little louder. This can solve the problem for shorter presentations where the problem is marginal, but not when it's particularly bad and certainly not for an extended period. Your voice won't survive.

Hence, the third answer is to get a mic. Amplification is the only effective solution for poor acoustics, and while almost all venues with larger ballrooms have them, it's worth checking ahead. I don't worry about a microphone for groups of under fifty, but above fifty it starts to become a valuable option. As soon as you know you're presenting to a larger group, start thinking about sound amplification. Make certain it's a lapel mic ("lavalier") and not a handheld or a podium mic; both of these completely limit your movement, yet the hotel will often not perceive the difference.

SOLVING FOR TEMPERATURE AND DISCOMFORT

Because people work substantially better in cooler rooms but become comatose when it's warm, do everything you can to get the temperature down. About 68 degrees is the target (20 degrees Celsius). But this is the place where time truly matters because physics dictates that chilling down a warm room takes time—plus, finding the darn thermostat in the first place can be a treasure hunt in itself. If you're speaking at a hotel or conference center, pre-warn them. Their meetings/banqueting department will create a work order with the details of the event, so make sure your temperature request is on it ahead of time. Of course I don't want frostbite, or indeed any real discomfort, but a slightly chilly room will make a lot of other things go better. I'll trade "warm and cozy" for "engagement and learning" in a heartbeat, especially in the afternoon. It's a terrible thing to confess, but if people complain, unless it's genuinely freezing, I'll listen sincerely and then ignore them. If I feel pressed, I'll even pretend to fiddle with the thermostat. I'm sort of kidding but sort of not, because this is a surprisingly big difference-maker. If it's after lunch and someone turns the temperature up to 75 degrees, it doesn't matter how good you are. You've lost.

Regarding other sources of physical discomfort: Very often, the organizers will set up too many chairs for the tables, making it all too cramped. So, if you can, thin it out to give everyone some leg and elbow room, adding tables if necessary. As crazy as it sounds, it's also common for tables to be set where several folks have their backs to the speaker, which results in an awkward, twisting, notes-on-lap experience. Hotels specialize in this mistake, and you have to fix it by removing those place settings altogether. Make sure every chair has a front or side-on view of the show.

SOLVING FOR LIGHTING

There are several answers for lighting problems, and in my experience, you can almost always manufacture the balance you need, where the screen is visible but the room also has enough light to work and to allow you full engagement with the audience.

Start by checking the room orientation. You want natural light if possible, because it's scientifically proven to be the best for learning and creativity, and it won't wash out the screen; but that light needs to be coming from the side or the rear. Don't let there be a strong natural light source directly behind you or in the stage area you're going to stake out. If you can reorient the room so that you're speaking from the unlit wall, that's the best. But if you can't do that, you're going to need to draw the curtains or blinds.

When you're working with artificial lighting (which is most of the time), if that light is washing out your screen, this often leads to a rookie mistake. Most speakers are so slide-driven that they automatically lower the lights to honor their slides. But aside from the fact that the audience now can't see their handout or take notes, you've lost all connection with them—and if it's the afternoon, you just set up nap time. To achieve the balance you need, your first job is to play with all the light switches in an effort to kill the offending bulbs while bringing other lights up to compensate, and this is usually the answer. However, if this doesn't work, and your screen is still washed out, you have two final options.

First, you can often move a mobile (floor) screen forward, back, or sideways to minimize the washout. If a light is directly above a screen, it's surprising how often moving that screen a foot back or forward solves the problem. Second, when the screen is fixed (coming down from the ceiling), your final option is to have some of the offending bulbs removed or slightly unscrewed by maintenance professionals. While I have done this myself dozens of times, it's certainly best for safety and liability reasons to leave it to the professionals.

WAIT . . . ISN'T THIS ALL JUST A BIT CRAZY?

"Unscrewing light bulbs? Are you mad?" Looking back over these four areas of problem and resolution, I suspect that some of you are thinking that paying this level of attention to the venue is unnecessarily obsessive. It's not. In many fields, it is precisely this level of attention to detail that is a hallmark of greatness. The golfer Nick

Faldo used to cut his fingernails to the same length before major tournaments so the weight of his swing would always be the same. Crazy, right? Or is it? Michael Jordan was likewise legendary for staying late after practice to shoot an unreasonable and obsessive number of free throws. It's the same with presenting; it's no coincidence that Steve Jobs was a world-class presenter who was also manic over these kinds of details. The two were tightly connected. I urge you to be like that. In any presentation there's a lot you can't control, so give yourself the best possible chance of success by controlling everything you can.

Truthfully, paying attention to these details isn't crazy at all; the difference between a good meeting and an amazing meeting might just be the difference between an audience who's cramped, warm, and squinting, versus an audience who's cool and comfortable, with ample light. It's your job to make that happen.

OTHER ESSENTIAL IN-ROOM PREPARATION

In addition to solving the "Four Horsemen" problems laid out above, there are two other venue issues you will need to take care of.

Layout for Learning

We've talked about layout from the lighting and comfort standpoint, but you should also make sure the layout is good from a learning and participation standpoint. You want to bring people in as close as you can, which will improve your intimacy with the audience and increase their interaction (as well as helping with acoustics problems). You also need to ensure that everyone has a clear view of the podium, screen, and whiteboard/flip chart. Typically, the best way to achieve these two things is to speak from the long wall in a rectangular room. If you think of the room as a tennis court, you should present from the umpire's chair. There's nothing worse than presenting from the "baseline" in a long, thin room where the back row can only be seen with a telescope. I prefer separate tables with six to eight attendees each rather than classroom or theater-style seating, if you have that option. This facilitates far better group ("table") exercises and discussions, but also allows each audience member to feel some sense of community, which you lose in a college lecture theater layout. For a smaller group where you want a lot of interaction, consider the horseshoe setup. This creates a highly interactive feel. The chart below is the chart we send ahead to all meeting organizers regarding set up.

Example Room Setup

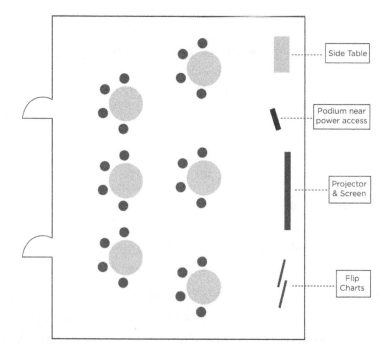

Slay the Technology Dragon

It's a symptom of a society that has become too dependent on its technology, but almost nothing seems to unglue today's presenters faster than discovering their laptop isn't talking to the projector, or that they can't make sound happen, right before—or more terrifyingly, right *after*—they stand up to speak. I'm sure you've witnessed—and probably experienced—the horror of frantically searching for that one mysterious and miraculous laptop setting that will make it all work, while the clock ticks your time away and your audience looks on in stern and silent disapproval.

There are three ways to effectively slay the technology dragon.

1. **PRE-TEST EVERYTHING.** I'm not a harsh person, but shame on you if you walk in five minutes before the bell, plug your laptop in, and hope it works. You cannot take that big a risk, but most people do. Get in early and pre-test it all, including images and sound, and if you can't get it to work, there is usually some AV wizard around who can. Technology varies by location, and there are multiple adapters for computer connections. Never assume the venue will have the adapters you need; make sure you have the ones you need with you.[3] There are currently three types of dongle to connect a laptop to a projector. Carry them all. Of course, meeting rooms or hotels should have them, but to quote a brilliant idea I picked up from the way Disney teaches customer service: "It's not my fault, but it *is* my problem." Yes, the venue *should* have the adapters, but what

---

[3] Not to be too geeky, but you need to know what output your laptop has and have the appropriate adapter for that output. You can know what your computer's inputs are, but you can't always know what the venue's projector will need. Projectors use a range of inputs (like VGA or HDMI), so you should carry an adapter for both types of connection.

if they don't? Sure, it's their fault, but it's still your problem. And, remember that low-tech is still tech, so as obvious as it sounds, test your marker pens. In my experience, 98 percent of whiteboard or flip chart markers lying around the world's conference rooms died about five years ago. Best of all, bring your own. And if you're using a flip chart (which I prefer to the whiteboard because you don't have to erase it and you can go back and revisit something you drew earlier), make sure there's enough paper for your session and that you have a spare pad on hand. Ridiculously obvious, vitally important.

2. **BACK IT UP.** *Always* back up your technology. In ultra-high-stakes situations, I still travel with two laptops, each loaded with identical presentation files. That's extreme, but for a presentation that could be worth hundreds of thousands of dollars, it's no great hardship, and it makes perfect sense. I read once that the great thing about being paranoid is that you only have to be right once. It's the same here. Have I ever needed that backup? That's not the point, but actually, yes, courtesy of me stupidly placing my water near the laptop, then knocking it over. (That's another amateur mistake. Never place coffee or water anywhere near your technology. Fate finds that too tempting.) The simpler approach to backup is a flash drive with your visuals on it. You're almost always guaranteed that someone else will have a laptop.

3. **HAVE YOUR "NO-TECHNOLOGY" PLAN.** In the movie *Apollo 13*, there's a great cameo moment where the mission controller, Gene Krantz, played by Ed Harris, pulls his team

together to discuss how to get the ill-fated astronauts back home. He fires up the overhead projector (remember those?) and the bulb blows. He snarls, pushes it away and grabs a pen, then turns to the whiteboard. I love that. He had a message to deliver, and the technology was a tool, but he wasn't in the least dependent on it. Few people are like that today, and presenters who can function independent of their technology are an increasingly rare breed. It's far more common to see a speaker reduced to a pile of smoking rubble when their technology crutch gets pulled away. So, you need to be like Gene Krantz. How do you do that?

If you've followed the doctrine I've outlined across this and my prior book, you'll know that I place high emphasis on the audience handout. It's a better teaching device than slides, and it's a better record of the conversation, especially for re-presentability. But in case you didn't notice, **one of the huge added benefits of the handout is that it makes you immune to an irrecoverable technology problem**, and that's pure gold. I was in Berlin several months ago and was the second of two "over-lunch" keynotes at the end of a conference. We were both given twenty minutes, but the first presenter ran horribly long and there simply wasn't time for me to set up my laptop. Everyone was royally ticked at the first guy, as we all knew the schedule, but it wasn't a problem. I ditched the projected visuals entirely, and it was just me, the handout, and a little extra work on the flip chart. And as I learned from conversations after the event, the audience really noticed, because a speaker who is centered on substance but agnostic to technology isn't the norm these days.

Practically speaking, develop your no-technology bailout plan by thinking through how you would deliver your content from the handout alone. It's such a powerful and refreshing presentation technique that recently (following Berlin!), I've ditched the screen altogether, working with the handout and flip chart alone. Not only do I find it gloriously liberating to be altogether free of technology, but at conferences where the audience does evaluations, there are always a handful containing the "I loved the no PowerPoint" comment.

PSYCHOLOGICAL CALIBRATION: THE OTHER REASON TO GET INTO THE ROOM EARLY

As we've seen, from a purely logistical standpoint, there are priceless benefits to arriving at the venue ahead of time and getting everything set up just right. But there's also an intangible, psychological benefit, as another film reference illustrates.

In the movie *Gladiator*, there's a moment where the hitherto provincial gladiators are brought to fight in Rome. As they're ushered into the Colosseum for the first time, their bravado is replaced by paralyzing awe as they gaze around, soaking in the enormity of their insanely impressive surroundings. It's a beautifully observed moment in the film, but the point isn't fictional; any contemporary athlete will tell you that seeing a big arena ahead of time makes a huge difference with nerves on game day. So if you find yourself slated to speak on a particularly big stage, you don't want the first time you walk onto that stage to be when five hundred pairs of eyes are watching you. Get into the room when it's empty to calibrate your mind to the venue and its dimensions so that the surroundings feel familiar when the big moment arrives.

Wimbledon, the spiritual home of tennis, is a pretty intimidating sports venue. When a player is scheduled to play on center court for the first time, the ground staff will quietly usher him or her into the empty arena the night before to get a feel for the stage in the hopes of mitigating their initial "gladiator" moment. They may still get annihilated, but at least they do it with a bit more dignity.

RESTATING THE BIG IDEA: GET THERE EARLY

A venue problem can take an otherwise fabulous presentation and put a huge dent in it. And that's if you're lucky. If you're less fortunate, it can completely demolish it. Most venues issues can be solved, but only if you're there. **So show up early.** If everything's fine, what a blessing; you've just been given some extra rehearsal time. And if there are some things you couldn't fix, and you still find yourself presenting with a little soft Sinatra in your ears? Relax, you did what you could.

SECTION TWO

What You Do on the Day

The Big Day Comes

To this point, we've looked at everything you can do ahead of time to give yourself the best possible chance of success on the big day. That day is now here: the time has come to stand up and start talking. In this section, my goal is to provide a deep study of the mechanics of presenting, and it's all going to be within your reach: once again, advanced isn't complicated. The place we naturally begin is with the opening.

CHAPTER 7

Conquering the Opening:
A Disproportionately Important Moment

⌒∞⌒

As we've discussed, not every element of a presentation is equally important. Some sections are more pivotal than others, but by far the most critical is the opening, for three reasons. First, it's the moment when the audience is most highly attuned to what's going on. They are looking at you, metaphorical pens poised, with hopeful expectations for the time to come. If you nail those first few minutes with calm and poise, there's often a silent, collective sigh: "Oh good . . . in a world of garbage presentations, this is actually going to be worth my time." They relax, and the resulting empathy and enthusiasm play an important role in setting you up for later success. In contrast, a botched opening can have the opposite effect, sending a chill through the room. People want their time to be used well, and if they sense it won't be, that can bring on unsettling feelings of hesitancy and concern.

The second reason is something we introduced in our discussion of rehearsal. This moment, when the audience's scrutiny is at its highest, is also the moment when your usually brilliant brain may decide to abandon you, courtesy of those pesky opening nerves. I vividly recall a presentation I once made that had a complex opening that I hadn't perfectly "grooved" in rehearsal. Compounding that error, I hadn't tidied up my notes after making some late modifications, so those notes, rather than being a clean set of sequential points, were a tangled mess of lines and scribbles. In the nervous fluster of the opening moment, my mind lost its grasp on the structure of my remarks, and my mouth completely dried up. As I looked down for help, the spaghetti on the page was no help in getting me back on track, and I felt my neck reddening and sweat beading as I went silent, a bare thirty seconds in, desperately trying to find my place and jump-start my iced-over brain. After what seemed an eternity, I eventually spotted the point I needed and picked the story back up—but a decade later, I still remember that moment with a chill. The opening is paradoxical: at the very moment you need to be at your best, your brain can be at its worst.

Winning Your Battle with Nerves

This is a logical point to talk about opening nerves because it's hard to start strong if your demeanor is hesitant and you're shaking like jelly. If you struggle with this affliction, you're not unusual; some fear of speaking in public besets almost all speakers, from the least to the greatest. Churchill and Lincoln both wrote about the great battles they fought with paralyzing nerves.

The first thing to say is that there's nothing irrational about this fear. We all have some regard for what others think of us, and that's not simply pride or vanity. There are good reasons why we don't want to look foolish in front of our customers, colleagues, leaders, or peers—not the least of which is that whenever we present, we're implicitly evaluated on more than just our communication. Attributes like intelligence and leadership ability are also squarely under the microscope. As a result, quite apart from the immediate sense of shame and foolishness, we know that serious, even career-ending consequences can flow from laying a total egg, and this perceived risk increases arithmetically as the crowd gets larger and more senior. It's little wonder we get nervous: it would be odd if we didn't. Psychology teaches that while some fears are unique to individuals (spiders, enclosed spaces), all people share five common fears—and one of the big five is public humiliation. Fortunately, except in extreme cases, nerves can be controlled. They can't always be fully eliminated, but they can be mitigated to a point where they won't be a problem. In order to unpack this, we need to understand the two different types of nerves.

"Opening" nerves: your friend and ally. Opening nerves have many names: jitters, stage fright, or butterflies in the tummy (very English). These nerves aren't psychological, but physiological: they're the body's reaction to the adrenaline coursing through your veins just before you get on stage. These nerves are normal, natural, and ultimately beneficial because they pass quickly. And once gone, that same adrenaline is the fuel you need for the rest of the presentation. In a moment, we'll walk through techniques to mitigate their impact, opening the door to their positive effect.

"Crash and burn" nerves: your enemy and tormenter. People don't actually fear the act of speaking in public; they fear the humiliation and rejection that may result from saying or doing something stupid. These nerves are more psychological, and they can paralyze you. Fortunately, there are two solid cures. The first is great presentation design. When you hastily throw material together at the last minute, the knowledge that it isn't great and that it might get a negative or even hostile reception can torment your soul. In contrast, there is something wonderfully stabilizing about knowing you have great material that the audience is going to love. Never underinvest in your presentation's design; it underpins everything else that happens. The second cure is rehearsal. If you have great material, your only other fear is that it won't come across properly on game day, and that you'll somehow fumble and butcher it. Rehearsal eliminates this concern, and combined, these two remedies dethrone paralyzing fear, replacing it with the speaker's most desired state: underlying confidence. All that's left to deal with is "jitter mitigation," which is central to the discussion that follows.

The third reason the opening is so crucial is that the way it goes determines how quickly you transition from your initial nervousness to the open ocean of confident flow. It's like a large ship leaving a small harbor—the initial moments of departure are difficult and dangerous, so your goal is to get out into the safety of open water as soon as you can. It's the same with a presentation. If you nail the opening, the nerves evaporate, confidence takes over, and you can move forward calmly as planned. But if you fumble the opening, you are highly aware that you haven't started well, and rather than evaporating, the nerves begin to reassert themselves, which can put you into a downward spiral. It's rare, but I've seen speakers so rattled by a bad opening that they never recovered. **Your presentation opening is vital. If you are smooth and accomplished in those first few minutes, you pour confidence both out into your audience and back into yourself, and everything can proceed calmly and according to plan.** The way you get there, knowing you are compensating for an unreliable brain, is to 1) seriously over-manage the details of the opening, and 2) make sure you open with exactly the right tone of authority.

OVER-MANAGING THE OPENING

Over-Manage the Final Minutes Before Show Time

The last few minutes just before you go on can be used productively if you know how.

1. REWIRE YOUR THINKING: the reality is that your presentation isn't going to go as planned, and that's okay. Mike Tyson, the former heavyweight boxing champion, isn't one of the world's great philosophers, but one of his quotes has proven extraordinarily insightful: "Everyone has a plan until they get punched in the face." Whenever you present, you have a plan in mind. But for many speakers, if they get "punched in the face" at the opening and the plan gets derailed, even by something minor like a late start, it can seriously unsettle them. The solution here is a simple mental adjustment that makes a huge difference. You have to embrace the incoming "punch," and you do this by

rewiring your thinking, but not in the way you might expect. I'm not saying you should prepare for the possibility that your plan might be derailed; that's not nearly good enough. **You need to go a sizeable step further and embrace, as fact, that it is unquestionably going to be derailed in some way: you just don't know how.**

You might think this is pure paranoia, but it's not. I'm quite serious. Whenever I walk into a room in which I'm going to present, I already know something won't be right, and I'm simply waiting to see what it is. When you mentally recalibrate in that way, when the problem inevitably hits, it will have little effect, because you were genuinely expecting it. Again, recalling the movie *Apollo 13*: the spaceship had a small problem on takeoff when a booster rocket shut down early, but they fixed it and moved on. At that moment, Commander Jim Lovell calmly says to his crew, "Well, gentlemen, I guess we just had our glitch for this mission." It's an intentionally cute moment in the movie because what the audience knows that Lovell doesn't is that in about half an hour, his whole ship is going to blow up . . . but in that moment, at least, it's a perfect example of the mindset I'm talking about. He didn't assume everything was going to go right; he assumed something was going to go wrong, so when it did, it didn't faze him. This practice is entirely mental, but it's real and it's truly important.

2. **WALK OFF THE BUTTERFLIES.** The higher the stakes, the greater those jitters—and if you're really feeling them, then it's a great idea to walk off the adrenaline before you get up to speak. A little physical activity will push the blood

around and help settle things down. Don't go for a jog around the parking lot; just walk, swing your arms if it's safe to do so, and take a few deep breaths to loosen yourself up. Always take a final bathroom break right before you go on, even if you don't think you need it. Not only will the walk do you good, but you don't want to be distracted by messages from your bladder while you're presenting, and the bathroom mirror is an effective cure for cabbage in the teeth or a misbehaving zipper.

3. **MUTTER LIKE A LUNATIC.** The other invaluable practice in the last moments before you go on, literally as you're about to get up, is to recite your opening lines under your breath. Keep doing it until you know you have it absolutely imprinted. It is a wonderful feeling to stand up there and deliver that first couple of sentences calmly and smoothly, with nary a glance at your notes. Sometimes that's all you need to put the ship out into open water.

OVER-MANAGING YOUR PERSONAL INTRODUCTION

Obviously, in settings where you're presenting to peers and colleagues, you won't be introducing who you are. However, in many cases—especially conferences and workshops—the audience doesn't know you, and an introduction is necessary. In these cases, there's one ironclad rule: don't get stuck with your own introduction.

Get Someone Else to Introduce You

The more you ponder this idea, the more powerful it becomes. You want to be introduced by someone else for two reasons. First, the introducer gets to say, and probably *wants* to say, a bunch of positive, affirming things about you, **which, thanks to the traditional rules of social behavior, are things you can't say about yourself.** You can't stand up and say, "Hi, my name's Dennis, and I'm a remarkable combination of genius and speaking talent." But here's the strangest thing; if *someone else* stands up and says those words, it's perfectly acceptable. Research shows that favorable introductions raise both the respect of an audience for a speaker and their expectations for the session—and what's surprising is that this is still the case when the introducer is known to have a relationship with that speaker. That's the power of the third-party testimonial. However, while you do want them to say nice things, don't let them go over the top about you, which brings me to the second, more subtle reason. The third-party introduction can create a powerful initial connection between you and your audience, but only if it's done correctly. **The key is to get the introduction to focus primarily on the audience problem you are going to solve, and not on you as the speaker.**

The independent endorsement of the importance of the problem and your ability to solve it will heighten the audience's interest in a highly valuable way. For this to work, you almost always need to change what the introducer was planning to say because most introductions go down the path you don't want, which is the dry recitation of speaker credentials. Even though it's customary, an introduction that focuses too much on the speaker will ignore the audience and steal this opportunity for connection. So, how do you manage this redirect? **NO BIO!** Because most people have no clue how to do a good introduction, they'll usually ask for a bio or will have pulled one from somewhere, and then when they read it aloud, it's invariably stilted and awkward, especially if they end up reciting the names of your kids. Don't let this happen. I never give an introducer my bio; and if they've pulled one off our website, I always (quite seriously) tell them to ignore it, because there's a better way to go. Work with your introducer on the introduction. Ask them to mention the problem the audience has, the one you're going to be discussing, and to indicate that you know how to solve it. You aren't going to offend them. No one loves the dry bio reading, so introducers always welcome something to help them with this high-profile task. You serve them—and yourself—by creating an introduction that sets up the session better.

An example will bring this to life. Last year, I was speaking at a conference of CEOs. The CEO who'd invited me was going to do the intro, so I planted the seed about staying away from my bio and actually wrote out a few notes for him, which he readily accepted. I'm going from memory, but this is almost exactly how the introduction went:

> "Ladies and gentlemen, we all run medium-sized companies here, and I know for a fact that like me, most of you truly struggle to get your messaging right, especially when you're out in front of the customer. [There's the audience problem.] And we've all got some marketing people or some agency trying to help, but they never seem to be able to get it right. [That's even better—a bolder statement that I wouldn't have been able to make for political reasons.] Well, I'm delighted to introduce Tim Pollard of Oratium today. I've seen the work they do, and it's pretty incredible. It's made a huge difference for us and for many other companies, from start-ups to the biggest corporations, and I guarantee, you're really going to love this. Please welcome . . ."

Sun Tzu, the ancient Chinese military leader who authored *The Art of War*, famously wrote: "The battle is won or lost before it even takes place." With that introduction, my battle was largely won before I even stood up. If you manage the introduction correctly, the audience is already disposed to believe that this is going to be a great session that will solve a significant problem they have. When you do finally stand up, all you have to do is not mess it up. Of course, the person who introduces you matters; you can't go and grab someone off the street, but generally you don't have to. There's almost always some senior manager, conference organizer, or interested/informed attendee who can do this.

Understanding Speaker Credibility

This question of the presenter's introduction sits at the heart of a critical issue, which is, "How does a speaker establish credibility with an unknown audience?" Establishing credibility is vital, but as we've just seen, there's a trap. By tradition, most speakers lead with their credentials (i.e., their bio) in order to establish credibility. But the self-serving nature of credentials and achievements can be a real turnoff to audiences, especially in cultures that place high value on a self-effacing humility (e.g., Japan or Sweden). It's truly ironic—when you lead with all your great accomplishments, it's easy to tear down credibility in the name of creating it. The solution is this pivot to the audience problem. While the primary goal of leading with the problem is to create engagement, this is also the best source of credibility you have. If I show that I truly understand the pain my audience is experiencing, and that I have some insight on how to solve their problem, there is no greater source of credibility.

That may leave you wondering whether the genuinely valuable experience you have is banned from the discussion entirely. Not at all. Credentials absolutely matter, but they're always best woven into the fabric of the presentation itself. If I'm presenting on how to fix messaging, the examples I show from different corporate clients or TED speakers scream out credibility, but because they come out in context, these credentials never connote arrogance. If I opened with our client list, the same information would be much less well received, courtesy of where it was placed. Your credentials can speak powerfully, but only if you weave them into the body of the argument itself.

The special case of "Qualifications"
While you should avoid opening with your credentials, there may be cases where your *qualifications* to speak need to be established, and that's different. You tend to see this more in academic, highly professional settings. If a person were speaking to a group of neonatal oncologists, for example, it would be important for them to state up front that they've run the neonatal oncology department of Denver Children's Hospital for eleven years, because this establishes the factual basis for their qualification to speak. But it would still be better to have a third party do it.

Introducing Yourself

There will be times when the audience doesn't know you, and with no convenient third party around, you have to introduce yourself. How should you do that? As you would expect, in largely the same way as I've already described. Avoid reference to yourself, and dive right into the audience's problem. They will be pleased and surprised—both by the orientation to their interests, and the implication that this will be a good use of their time. Aim roughly for lines like this: "Good morning. Thanks so much for the time today—my name's Andrew Jones, and it's a pleasure to be here. Time is precious, so let's dive right in. We're here to look at—and more importantly solve—an intriguing problem. Why do we have so much trouble getting our manufacturing plants to the level of productivity we want, and how do we fix that without compromising safety?" It's exactly the same as the third-party introduction without the added "and the speaker is wonderful" comments.

Over the years, there have been a handful of times when people have said they would have actually liked to hear a little bit more about me during the introduction. What that tells me is that I'm getting it about right.

> If you want to be an audience-centric communicator, something has to be different about you. Taking the spotlight off yourself and putting it on them is a very audience-centric thing to do.

LEADERSHIP PRESENCE: THE TONE OF AUTHORITY

One important and recurring theme of this book is the need for presenters to accept the authority that the audience grants them, and nowhere is this issue more vital than in the opening. Many years ago, I worked for a woman who was the most impressive researcher I've ever met, and who routinely spotted trends in the healthcare industry that would only reveal themselves to ordinary mortals months or sometimes years later. As the head of a major research organization, she was regularly called upon to present these findings, but as brilliant as her insights and intellect were, she was shockingly hesitant when she got up to present. It's a little difficult to capture the style of her openings on the page, but they would go something like this (imagine a nervous smile and faltering tone as she addressed a room full of hospital leaders getting settled for their day):

"Er hi . . . Hello? Can we maybe make a start? Er . . . Okay, then . . . okay . . . okay . . . well, let's start in a minute . . . thank you."

This was so strange to witness. The woman is an intellectual powerhouse, but that was not being communicated by this extremely timid opening. And audiences noticed. There's a paradox here: **Everyone understands that speakers are nervous before a session, but what we often fail to realize is that audiences are nervous too. People want a well-run, well-controlled event, and they worry when a speaker appears to be weak and unable to deliver it.** This is almost always implicit; only in rare cases will the audience ask a speaker to take charge, but it's what they want nonetheless.

There are three keys to calming your audience by establishing the proper "presence" at the opening.

Presence Key #1—Pre-Announce Your Authority

There's a priceless technique that sends the perfect signal of authority: "Speak before you speak." If that sounds odd, the idea is this: whenever the setting allows, before you officially begin, walk up to the mic or to the front of the room and issue a two-minute warning to the group. Your tone should be polite, firm, and above all, poised. A simple, "Hey folks, good morning . . . we'll be starting here in about two minutes. If you'd like to start shutting down email or grab a final coffee, that would be great, thanks. Two minutes." Then walk away from the mic.

It's a simple practice, but not only does it serve the practical purpose of getting the room off email and ready for the presentation, more importantly, it also has the almost magical effect of informing the group in no uncertain terms that you are in charge—the very thing they want to know. Think about how different this feels compared to the opening of that hesitant researcher. The unspoken reaction will be, "Oh good, someone's running this show." And there's an invaluable byproduct of this drill: it means you've already spoken when you do formally begin, and this significantly dampens your nerves. Your big opening is now the second time you speak, and they already know you. It's an invaluable technique that sends the signal you want, with a little nerves management thrown in for free.

Presence Key #2—Mitigate the Final Jitters

Even if you've walked them off a bit, there will still be some final residual jitters as you literally take the stage. They'll miraculously vanish after you start talking, but until they do, you don't want to be dancing around like a cat on a hot tin roof. The answer is to still your movement by restraining yourself physically, and the best way to do this is by having one hand in your pocket (admittedly easier for men), and the other on your notes. Most traditional training tells you *not* to have your hands in your pockets, but that's nonsense. The audience either won't notice or won't care, and having your hands safely anchored quiets your nervous movement rather well; in fact, I think it exudes a certain confidence. If there's a podium, which there will be for the bigger keynote, a good alternative is to gently place both of your hands on its sides for those first few seconds. It's not a death grip—you aren't trying to squeeze resin out of the wood—but it looks good and will keep you still and centered as you get started. A few moments in, relax and let your hands loose to do whatever they want. Once the initial nerves have passed, you will welcome the boost in energy **and especially the heightened mental sharpness that the adrenaline provides.** You simply need to keep it all under control until you're settled in. And remember, if you issue the earlier two-minute warning, you will have already gotten most of these opening nerves out of your system. It's like a magic trick.

Presence Key #3—Set the Rules of the Room

After the introduction of the topic at hand, conclude your opening by graciously establishing the rules of the day. Not only are these rules important to the success of the event, but they also send another important signal of your authority. Tell them about timings, breaks, and your right to move conversation forward if needed. In an ever more distracted society, it's worth fighting the "cellphones off" battle with your audience. With this issue, the fundamental question of learning is actually more important than the authority signal you're sending; society's growing tendency to multitask has been well documented, and it's now common to see people trying to follow a presentation while simultaneously answering the siren call of their email. The problem is, they're fooling themselves. It's long been proven that the brain isn't neurologically wired to parallel-process two simultaneous streams of attention, and multitasking in a presentation severely limits learning. There's such irony here; many of the people sitting in your audience are also parents who will, rightly, press in hard with their kids to stop them from texting and driving. Yet they somehow feel that the exact same cognitive limitations don't apply to them. Tempting as it is, don't use that argument on your audience. (I've tried it, and it doesn't work. Shaming people by pointing out their hypocrisy is rarely a good motivator.)

Address the issue, but stay polite, as in: "Folks, please do turn email and your phones off. We'll take plenty of breaks, and you aren't going to get as much out of this session if you're distracted." Almost anyone who's heard me speak has heard me tackle this topic humorously with: "There was a study in the *British Medical Journal* that said if you're distracted by your phone while performing another task, you experience an 11 percent loss of intelligence . . . and interestingly, that same study said that if you smoke marijuana while performing another task, you only lose 7 percent. So—faced with a choice, I'd truly rather you smoked dope than be on email." It's a fun moment, but you get your point across. Feel free to use it. And of course, if someone else in the room has some real authority over the group, take them aside and ask them to cover it. You will help yourself by explaining the breaks. If people know they'll have a chance to get caught up on the other things going on in their world, they're less likely to self-distract.

Understand that this isn't about pride, ego, or winning some psychological battle with your audience. This distills to a real issue. If they allow themselves to be distracted, it will genuinely diminish what they get out of the session, and that, not the presenter's feelings, is what makes it a battle worth fighting.

PRACTICAL APPLICATION

Most presenters don't open strongly enough because they don't understand all the moving parts. To help you apply these lessons, in Appendix I (and also downloadable) you'll find two applicable checklists (of five total). One lays out the elements of a good opening, and the other summarizes the main practices of this chapter.

CHAPTER 8

The Basic Mechanics of Exceptional Presenting

~∞~

Having sailed through those delicate opening moments, you're now simply presenting the body of your material. Assuming you were a successful two-year-old, you probably know how to speak, but there remain several things that can move the dial either for or against you as a speaker—everything from the lies you're tempted to tell but mustn't, to the temptation to fake a British accent when you were born and raised in Cleveland. Mastering these mechanics won't redeem weak material, but it will add a wonderful final flourish to good material—while getting them wrong can introduce some problems you'd rather not have. The ten things that follow are small, important, and easy to implement.

THE TOP TEN OF BASIC SPEAKING MECHANICS

1. Your Speaking Voice: Be Yourself

The larger question of presentation style will be discussed in the final section of this book, but I have one basic point to make on your literal speaking voice, which is this: just be yourself. Unless you're dealing with horrendous acoustics (amp it up) or a largely ESL audience (slow it down), speak normally. I frequently see speakers affecting some voice that clearly isn't their own, as if they're trying to be some bigger, better version of themselves—and it never works. Just be yourself, entirely. You are perfect as you are. The tone you want to shoot for is *conversational coffee shop,* and you should sound exactly as you would if you were having a relaxed talk with old friends. Even in a room of three thousand, each audience member should feel like you are chatting personally to them. In the words of the old quote, "Be yourself, everybody else is taken." (While traditionally attributed to Oscar Wilde, this quote's actual origin was a flyer from a long-forgotten US hardware store. But it's still true.)

2. Speaking Clarity and Enunciation

Many people have been told that they speak too fast, but if that's you, that's probably not what's actually going on. The more likely issue is that you don't speak clearly enough. People can actually process the words of human speech at a surprisingly high rate, which is why it's possible to listen to podcasts at 1.5 times the recorded speed without the slightest difficulty. So when people tell you that you speak too fast, what they're more likely observing (though they often don't realize it) is that there's an issue with speaking clarity. This is a serious issue, made worse whenever you're presenting in a room with dodgy acoustics. If people are struggling to understand what you're saying, that can be a game-ending problem. The good news is, unless you have an impediment that requires speech therapy (and that's outside the scope of this book), the problem can probably be solved. The best way to improve your diction is to think of consciously forming your words at the very front of the mouth: think lips, teeth, and tongue. This is an incredibly effective remedy for unclear diction, and there's a way to practice that I learned from a friend who is completely deaf. *Whisper.* When a deaf person has trouble lip-reading a friend or family member, that person is told to enunciate better by forming their words at the front of the mouth, and the way they are taught to do this is to whisper, which naturally forces their words forward. Try it and see.

Of course, you may still need to watch your speaking speed. Most people speak at between 140 and 160 words per minute. If you're the rare person who is flying much faster than average, improving your enunciation will help people with your words, but they'll still have difficulty with your ideas. You need to practice slowing down, and truthfully, the best way to do this is pretty obvious: write "SLOW" all over your notes.

3. Protecting Your Voice

If you present on a regular basis, and especially if you talk for long periods, you need to keep your speaking voice in good shape. First, avoid milk or cream directly before you speak. Lactose coats the throat, and more than once I've seen speakers end up sounding like Gollum thanks to the three lattes they had that morning. Black coffee is better, but the energy boost comes at a price: coffee dehydrates you, and the larynx works better when it's well hydrated. As boring as they are, cool water or tea (green or chamomile) will help your voice be in top form.

At some point in your life, you will be called to present with a heavy cold or cough, or with a throat that's seriously challenged for some other reason—and for those occasions, God gave us slippery elm bark. This shredded bark can be bought from most tea shops. When you chew it, it releases mucilage (basically a slime, but not as disgusting as it sounds) that coats the throat with near-miraculous results. I learned this trick from my daughter Grace, who was a vocal performance major in college, and it really works. I carry a little pouch with me everywhere I go, and on the rare days I need it, it's an absolute lifesaver. (Legal disclaimer: I don't know if you can be allergic to it, but like anything, you need to check.) You'll likely carry it for years and never use it, but when that day comes, you'll be digging out my email address to thank me. By the way, slippery elm bark is a mild laxative, as you'll discover if you experiment with it excessively, or if the dog gets into it. That doesn't mean you should stay away from it; it's fine in regular quantities. But just remember, they didn't call it "slippery" for no reason.

4. "Ums" and "Ahs" and General Speaking Idiosyncrasies

Despite the fact that these verbal tics get an absurd amount of airtime in traditional training, it's hardly ever a real issue. Most people have some of this in their speech, but unless it's weird or excessive, audiences don't notice. The thing to know here is that most of the time, "ums" and "ahs" are what your mouth does while your brain is figuring out what to say next, which is probably why the technical term for these is "filled pauses." You're pausing, so your brain is filling. The cure is therefore . . . rehearsal! When you genuinely know your material and it's flowing smoothly out of long-term memory, most of these critters will go away.

One delicate variant I need to mention is that if you're one of those (likely younger) presenters who inserts "like" between every other word, for the love of all that's holy, stop it. It makes you sound horribly uneducated. These forms of speech are also fillers that your brain inserts when momentarily looking for the next phrase, but this is trickier to fix because it's not about inadequate rehearsal: these will have become a core part of your everyday speech. The way to tackle this is to audio-record yourself and **listen, correct, listen, correct** until you've driven every trace of the evil habit out of yourself.

5. The Power of the Strategic Pause

There's a big difference between those pauses that creep in while you're fumbling for words, and deliberately pausing for effect. Most advanced writers on rhetoric note that the strategic pause is a powerful tool that speakers will use when they want particular emphasis or dramatic effect. It's a skill worth cultivating because a carefully chosen pause can add tremendous weight to an otherwise mundane statement. Imagine you're introducing a keynote speaker. Read the following lines, and ponder the difference to the hearer when these lines are delivered with and without four critical pauses.

"Ladies and gentlemen, the woman who has led us safely through a tremendously difficult season, Mrs. Jane Doe." (Polite applause.)

Or:

"Ladies and gentlemen . . .
The woman who has led us . . .
Safely . . .
through a tremendously difficult season . . .
(hold . . . hold . . . hold...) . . . Mrs. Jane Doe." (Crowd goes wild.)

The pauses in that latter narrative are *not* the random pauses of the underprepared speaker; those are moments carefully crafted for emphasis. You should use these pauses when you get to your most critical thoughts and ideas. Owing to the dramatic effect, use them sparingly and wisely, and not: "Ladies and gentlemen . . . (dramatic pause) . . . the bathrooms are . . . (dramatic pause) . . . out on the right." That's beyond weird.

6. *Humor*

The most wasted day is that in which we have not laughed.
—NICOLAS CHAMFORT

THE POWER OF HUMOR. Humor is a wonderful thing. It relaxes people, it increases affection and respect for the speaker, and it restores energy to a sagging room. When properly used, humor will make almost any presentation better—but be careful. The problem with humor is that it's like a gun with the safety off. It's much trickier to use than it appears, and when it goes wrong, it can go spectacularly wrong. All this is made worse by the fact that there's a frighteningly fine line between hilariously funny and deeply offensive. Fortunately, these risks can be mitigated. Here are some simple rules to guide the perfect use of humor.

Making humor work.

1. **CONGRUENCE.** The most important thing to remember about humor is the need for "congruence," by which I mean it should be fitted to the occasion and to the moment in the presentation. Certain presentations are serious in nature (in whole or in part), and if you use humor in the wrong place, it can be deeply inappropriate. You clearly shouldn't joke around when announcing layoffs or discussing a team's missed goals, but I've still seen both done.

   Unfortunately, the question of congruence is maddeningly complicated by unwritten rules of culture and context. Imagine you've been asked to deliver a funeral eulogy. Would humor be appropriate? That depends. For a long life, lived richly and well?

Absolutely, within limits. But for a life cut short in tragic circumstances? Almost certainly not.

2. **STICK TO WHAT WORKS FOR YOU.** Congruence isn't only about what's fitted to the occasion, it's also about what's fitted to you. You are much safer using the humor that fits your natural personality. One guy on our team, JD, is hilariously funny in a very head-on manner, while my humor is naturally more sardonic and dry (i.e., British). We're both funny but in very different ways. Use what works for you, and be careful stepping away from your natural brand of humor. Don't be that guy who ignores reality in the face of tradition and opens his presentation by saying, "People tell me I'm not funny, but here goes anyway." Don't go there. People tell you that for a reason.

3. **NEVER USE SPONTANEOUS HUMOR. EVER.** Flowing directly from the above, unless you have spectacularly good humor instincts, never, ever trust spontaneous humor unless you're comfortable spending a night in the county jail. The joke that just came to you and is now trying to get out of your mouth may sound funny in your head, but you have no idea how it's going to play. You have only one way of knowing, which is to put it out there and see what happens, but that's a risk you simply can't take. As Churchill once said, "We are masters of the unsaid word, but slaves of those we let slip out." The golden rule is inhibition. DON'T say it.

4. **NEVER USE HUMOR AT THE EXPENSE OF YOUR AUDIENCE.** A few years ago, I was walking a group through a rather complex diagram. I was discussing Point 7

when an audience member asked me, "Sorry, where is Point 7?" It was a completely reasonable and legitimate question, but without thinking, I smartly answered, "Right there between Points 6 and 8." It sounded hysterical in my head, but out of my mouth it came across as harsh and insulting, because it was. (There's the spontaneity problem.) The room laughed, but the questioner didn't. I knew I had insulted him, so I immediately apologized, which is the only course of action (never ignore it as though it didn't happen; you have to own it and apologize), but the damage was still done. **Never laugh at your audience** unless you have a deep relationship already established, and even then, be careful. It's perfectly fine to laugh at yourself: that's both safe and endearing. But be careful as you start pointing your tongue elsewhere. Stay away from sarcasm for the same reason. Sarcasm is nothing more than rudeness made permissible by a thin veneer of humor, as in, "It's between Point 6 and Point 8." The problem with sarcasm is that it always has a victim. It's cheap humor, and it can galvanize the whole audience against you.

5. PRE-TEST . . . ALWAYS. Planned humor should be your rule. But given that most people aren't quite as funny as they think they are, it's a good idea to test it as well. One of our clients has a senior executive who is insanely smart and who oversees a multibillion-dollar line of business. He also thinks he's hilarious. He isn't. He was recently assigned a big keynote at a company meeting, and as the day drew near, he was proudly bragging to his team about the three hilarious jokes he had baked in. Knowing his challenges in this area, they literally begged him to run these jokes by

them first, but he didn't want to; he wanted them to get the same laugh as the audience. Eventually he caved under pressure, and the team later recounted the "jokes" to me. It was sobering: two of the three were simultaneously racist and sexist and were so offensive that they would have probably led to a lawsuit and/or his immediate dismissal. The third was the dubious "winner" in that it was only mildly off-color. **Most people don't have great humor instincts.** Testing with others is the only sure way to know.

6. **REHEARSE IT.** Numerous articles written by comedians ranging from Woody Allen to Jerry Seinfeld all say the same thing: when it comes to humor, the difference between not funny, funny, and hysterical can come down to one word, or a heartbeat's difference in timing. However spontaneous it may appear to be, the best humor is excruciatingly planned and rehearsed. This is well understood by comedic professionals, and it's a lesson every speaking professional needs to learn.

7. Be Careful About Apologizing

Sometimes presenters feel the need to apologize to their audience, and that's fine, as long as it's something you should legitimately apologize for. "I do apologize, I'm fighting a cold, and my voice is a bit scratchy. I hope you'll forgive me." That's totally okay. In general, feel free to apologize for things that aren't within your control. What's absolutely NOT OKAY is apologizing for an egregious error on your part that you should have fixed ahead of time, and where all you're doing with the apology is trying to obligate the audience to release you from any responsibility. In that case, the apology is insincere, insufficient, and will probably infuriate the audience even more than the initial offense. As crazy and reckless as this sounds, it happens constantly, and most commonly with slides. Hands up if you've heard some variant of: "I'm sorry you can't read this slide," or "I'm sorry you're drinking from the firehose today." The problem is, you're *not* sorry, because these are your slides and this was all completely within your control. If you really cared, you would have fixed it.

A colleague told me he was in a company presentation once where the speaker actually said: "I'm sorry you can't read these slides. I just put this together this morning and I didn't have time to do it properly." That baffles me. How could someone be so unaware as to not understand how deeply insulting that "apology" actually was? I'm passionate about this, so discount it if you want, but in my view **it is unacceptable to disrespect an audience with poor preparation, and then think you can make everything right by simply apologizing for it. People's time is precious, and whatever the setting, speakers have an obligation to honor and respect the gift of time they are being given. Don't apologize for your miserably illegible slides. Respect your audience enough to fix them.**

The Particular Apology You Should Never Make

Please make a mental note to never again say, "I'm sorry. I know I'm the only thing standing between you and lunch/cocktails/the bar/dinner . . . yuk yuk yuk." Trust me, it's not funny; everyone's heard it a million times before, and it wasn't that funny the first time. More importantly, why on earth would you deliberately plant such a thoroughly negative idea in your audience's heads? This apology comes dangerously close to implying that lunch is going to be more interesting and rewarding than your presentation. Presenters do weird things when they don't think them through, and this is one of them. Your head should be in a completely different place. Believe that your material is extraordinary, that they're going to benefit hugely from it, and that compared to what you're serving, lunch is going to be a bitter disappointment. I don't care if the kitchen is busy preparing roast ostrich in a kumquat sauce, I'm not apologizing for my session. As long as I don't run late, lunch will still be there when we're done.

8. Be Careful About Lying

Continuing with the theme of low moral character, there are two outright lies that speakers constantly employ, and both will equally infuriate your audience.

1. Do not put up some lengthy list of points, and say, "Okay, I'm just going to go through this briefly," or "Okay, I'm not going to cover all of these . . ." and then labor through the whole thing in excruciating detail. I see it all the time; **it stems from the speaker realizing that the list is irritatingly long, correctly sensing that this is a problem, but then not having the moral courage to actually follow through and limit himself/herself to the few things that are actually important.** Know ahead of time which points matter, and cover only them—or better still, kill the long list altogether. Shorten it to only the things that matter.

2. Closely related is the second whopping fib, which is the "false close." Speakers will often promise, "Okay, this is my last point," or "Okay, we're almost done," when they're not even close to being done. Similar to the above, the reason is fascinating—the speaker is again sensing that the audience is getting restless, and out of fear, they throw out the promise of finishing soon in the hope it will somehow pacify the crowd. But it's revealed as a hollow promise when they don't follow through and actually wrap up, which ends up making things far worse. Great speakers never get caught in this blatant lie. They see the signs and legitimately cut to the close . . . well, actually, that's not true. The great speaker never presents so much content that this is even an issue. The solution here is one simple rule. You get to say, "Okay, we're drawing to a close here," or "Okay, let's close with this . . ." **once and once only,** and then you sure as heck better close. The existence of this lie suggests that there's one additional skill to discuss that is as important as it is usually absent. Time management.

9. Manage the Clock

The idea of a speaker running long is a genuine cliché. It happens all the time and is one of the more serious problems on this list of mechanics. Running over your allotted time messes with other people's schedules, other presenters, other meetings, conference timings, travel arrangements, food planning, etc., etc., and it irritates everyone. That's if you're lucky. In the worst case, someone will embarrassingly order you to close or your audience will start walking out as you're wrapping up.

> **But running long never need happen if you know how to manage your time properly, and that all starts by having a deep appreciation that the clock is not your friend.**

You're in a life or death battle with a ticking menace and only one of you will prevail.

There are multiple ways your timing can be derailed, but regardless of cause, by far the most important thing is spotting that it's happening early. Once you've fallen terribly behind, it's essentially impossible to recover, because past a certain point you have only four options, and they're all bad. You can cut out big gobs of content, you can ban questions, you can speak super fast, or you can run long. Audiences hate all of these, and yet in many presentations, the time has been so poorly managed that the speaker is forced to use several of these toxic tools in combination. Sometimes your time is cut by an external force, like a change in schedule that slices your hour down to thirty minutes. That's just life, and the time management response is to know how to cut your content to fit. Generally, audiences don't like skipping content (they always feel they're missing the good stuff), but in these cases they'll be tolerant because they know it was out of your control. However, there are three big ways your time can get blown up that you absolutely *do* control, and if you let one of these happen, your audience will be far less forgiving.

1. **FIRST TIME THIEF: EMBELLISHMENT.** As we saw in our discussion on rehearsal, your mind is going to add in content that you hadn't planned for. Remember, the fix is to self-govern when you sense yourself embellishing beyond a reasonable point, and always allow that 10–15

percent buffer. Never plan to use all your time; leave room for a permitted amount of embellished genius.

2. **SECOND TIME THIEF: UNCONTROLLED DISCUSSION.**
    Everyone's been in that meeting where there was a lively, vibrant discussion that felt great at the time, but came at a heavy price when important later topics couldn't be discussed or possibly even presented. Discussion is unfailingly good because it means people are engaging with the material. But like so much in life, what's good in moderation can become a real problem if it gets out of control. The full scope of "managing your audience" will be discussed in a chapter to come, but for completeness here, it comes down to two basic time management rules. First, plan enough discussion time. This always feels hard, since presenters worry that if they bake in that time and the discussion doesn't happen, they'll be faced with the boogeyman of finishing early. Don't worry about that. The discussion IS going to happen, especially if you know how to trigger it, but even if it doesn't, people love meetings finishing early if the topic has been covered. Have the courage to bake discussion time in. Either way, you're going to make people happy.

    Second, manage the discussion as it's happening. You can usually let a lively discussion go for a while, but there will come a point when you need to graciously shut it down, knowing that it's beginning to eat into other things. I've always found that if I say, "Hey, folks, this is a great conversation, but we've got a lot of other important stuff to cover, so if you don't mind, let's move on," or the less subtle but equally effective, "Okay—let's take one more question . . .", then I can get it back under control.

3. **THIRD TIME THIEF: SELF-INFLICTED EARLY RELAXATION.** The third time management mistake is so common that it's on full display almost every time someone presents. It happens when the speaker is far too relaxed about their time at the beginning and moving far too slowly as a result. We've all fallen prey to this, because it's so natural to relax when your full hour is stretching out before you—but it's a total trap. We fritter away those early minutes, and by the time we wake up to what we've done, it's almost invariably too late to recover. Solving this requires another profound reboot in your thinking. **You have to treasure every minute you have, and embrace the idea that a minute at the beginning is worth precisely the same as a minute at the end, even though it doesn't feel that way.** When you've truly internalized this, you begin to feel the healthy pressure to get into your material quickly. Audiences like it when speakers avoid the fluff and dive right in, but the main reason to do so is to get out ahead of a clock problem.

Then, once you're into the presentation itself, always know your "timestamps": where you need to be by what time. Write these on your notes and stay as close to those timestamps as you can, because the key to finishing at 11:30 isn't what's happening at 11:20, it's what was happening back at 10:17 when you chose not to tell that extra joke, or at 10:52 when you politely closed down that discussion that was threatening to get out of control.

10. *Falling Walls and Falling Water: Responding to the Unexpected*

I shared this anecdote in my earlier book, but it bears repeating here. It was an unremarkable Thursday in early November 1989, and I was teaching a multi-day seminar in Heidelberg, Germany. I recall being somewhere in the morning session when a woman burst through the door sobbing uncontrollably, although it was evident from her face that these were tears of joy. Through those tears, she was shouting in German, and a moment later, everyone else in the room started crying. Of course, I'm the idiot at the front who's completely clueless as to what's going on, but eventually one manager in the room turned to me and, holding back his own emotions, said, "The Berlin Wall has just come down." I've only rarely worked in Germany, and I still deeply appreciate the miracle that put me there on that particular day. People were pouring through the newly torn-down gates from East Berlin, grabbing the nearest phone, and suddenly everyone in the West was getting unexpected calls from their much-loved but long-estranged relatives. Setting the history aside, it set up a fascinating moment for me as the presenter, because the entire group was now looking at me for direction. I considered our various options for about five seconds then made the call: "Okay. Class dismissed. We can come back and do this another time." The group erupted in happiness and headed for the door *en masse.* That was that. We arranged a lovely do-over a few months later.

Normally it's not that dramatic, but here's my point: Sooner or later, every presenter is confronted with something totally unexpected that they need to respond to. It might be something external, like a power failure or an audience member having a medical problem, but more commonly it's some mistake you've made, like knocking over a water glass or dropping your notes. If you've ever witnessed one of these moments, you'll know that everything suddenly gets exceedingly quiet and intense in a slow-motion kind of way. All eyes will be on the speaker because how they respond reveals everything about the real person behind the presenting mask. If you sail through the incident calmly and with humor, it speaks volumes to your true presence; but if you fold up like a cheap suit, then something very different is revealed. Presentation mistakes are unusual in that the public setting amplifies them to the point that they feel genuinely catastrophic. There's a vast difference between messing up in front of my wife and messing up in front of two hundred of my peers. And the deep fear that people have about public speaking often stems from this very real possibility of public embarrassment and humiliation—which is why we need to talk about it. You have to know how to handle these moments.

The first thing to say is that this is all about perspective. If you've ever been to Disney's property in Florida, it seems monumentally huge while you're in it. But in truth, it's not. Last year I was flying out of Orlando, and on the climb out, I noticed a distinctive white pyramid shape beneath us, hardly more than a tiny dot on the landscape. It was the Space Mountain ride at Walt Disney World, and having apprehended that, I rapidly recognized the whole Disney property, including all the parks, resorts, lakes, and even offices that I know so well. On the ground, the property is a gigantic labyrinth, but from the air, it literally shocked me how absurdly tiny it actually is when compared to even the small fraction of Florida I could see at that moment. Here's the photo to prove it. If you can't make out the parks, that's kind of the point.

Presentation mistakes contain these two competing perspectives. When something goes wrong onstage, it feels like Disney on the ground, monumental and therefore crushing. But it's really not. It's nothing. It's Disney from the air. The audience knows you're human, they don't expect you to be perfect, and they will often view these glitches with warmth and sympathy because they all know how hard it is to be up on stage having things go wrong. So here's the mental adjustment we need to make. As horrifying as it feels, relax; and if you can, draw out the funny side of it. "Whoops, that's not good . . ." is the perfect reaction as the water gurgles into your laptop, and if you laugh it off, you take the tension out of the situation for everyone. And curiously, when you take it in stride rather than folding up, the group's respect and affection for you will grow substantially.

CHAPTER 9

Teaching to the Handout

❦

R.I.C.E.

Of all chapters in this "What to Do" section, this one might be the most unexpected. It's short, but it contains one of the most important of all delivery skills, and possibly *the* most important if you present in a sales setting. "Teaching to the handout" simply means referencing where you are in the handout at all times and making sure that the presentation is always tied to it. The handout is the "campfire" that you and your audience are gathered around, and teaching to it correctly will unlock the full value of the shared experience it can create. (By the way, the handout can be one page or several pages, as long as its focus is on your most powerful takeaways.) For context, it's worth considering exactly how the handout helps you, which is best explained through the acronym "R.I.C.E.": Re-presentability, Intimacy, Comprehension, and Engagement. They are most logically explained in reverse.

E = Deeper Engagement

People need something on which to focus their attention. Slides tend to have a distant feel, and they're transient, which can cause the mind to wander. In contrast, the handout is tactile and contains the full argument, which people can see unfolding. Furthermore, its focus on an audience problem (a key architectural feature) contributes to its natural ability to draw people in.

C = Increased Comprehension

Presentations are about a transfer of learning, and learning is hard. Your audience is processing everything for the first time, and the handout improves their learning outcomes. It helps keep them in the flow of the argument, and hearing your points while simultaneously seeing them in print greatly boosts their comprehension. In addition, learning is boosted by the handout's ability to minimize the distraction caused by note-taking. In a recent experiment, we presented the same material to four groups, two using slides and two using a handout. When tested on content retention, the PowerPoint slide groups made nine mistakes in total, the handout groups, only one.

I = Raised Intimacy

Some time ago, we filmed a technology firm's sales presentation for training purposes, in which I role-played as the customer. We had a small audience for the filming, and afterward we asked for their thoughts on the role-play. I was fascinated when several observers noted that as we shared the handout, it created an observably greater sense of intimacy than that seen in a typical sales conversation. They added that this seemed to be the opposite of the distancing effect you often see with slide-based presentations, when people become separated from each other by the screen that metaphorically sits between them. Interestingly, these observers had not been through our training and had no idea that this was part of the purpose behind our approach.

R = Improved Retention and Re-Presentability

By far the most important value of the handout is that it raises your audience's ability to retell the story. If you want your customer to represent your argument effectively a week later in a room you aren't invited to, walking them diligently through the handout is key. **The dirty little secret of teaching to the handout is that you're essentially training your audience to re-present your story.**

R.I.C.E IS REAL

If you want evidence for these R.I.C.E. attributes, here you go. In partnership with cognitive neuroscientist Carmen Simon, we recently conducted scientific experiments in which we measured the brain activity and focus of an audience in a simulated sales meeting where either slides or a handout was used. (This experiment gave us the content-retention data I mentioned earlier.) The following picture is remarkable. It is the presentation seen through the eyes of the audience member, with the presenter in the upper left. The shading indicates where the focus was being directed; the darker the shade, the greater the focus.

As you can see, this participant engaged deeply with the handout, and it's worth noting that the left side of the handout contains the customer problem, which reveals the particular focus the problem discussion will create. You can also see how their attention moved seamlessly between the presenter's handout and their own copy (with very little wandering elsewhere), which is a good portrayal of the intimate, shared experience that's being created. If you want to get on the same page as your audience, this is literally what you're seeing the handout deliver. Finally, the visual "toggling" between the two handouts is strong evidence that as the presenter is teaching the material, the audience is learning it. That's the foundation of re-presentability.

HAND IT OUT AT THE BEGINNING

At every workshop, we get asked whether the handout is given at the beginning or end. It should be obvious that it has to be the beginning. If you wait until the end, not only do you lose all the effects I've just described, but for good measure, you tick off your audience, because they will have worked to take notes that they now see they didn't have to take. That is seriously infuriating. Some of you may have been told to give handouts at the end to avoid people reading ahead, and I recently taught at a college where that had been the specific guidance of a prominent public speaking professor. That's absurd advice whose logic collapses under a moment's thought. If people are actually disconnecting and reading ahead, it's because the material/conversation isn't interesting to them. Withholding the handout doesn't solve the underlying problem: if they're bored, they'll simply find something else to look at. That advice is like telling people to smash their plates if they've run out of dishwashing detergent. It completely misses the real problem. If your content is relevant, engaging, and worthy of their attention, you won't have an issue.

When you pass out your handout, it will help if you position it correctly. Make it clear that you're going to go through the whole document and that they get to keep it. That way, the audience feels less pressure to read ahead, because they know you're going to get to everything. And finally, even if you get a little leafing ahead, who cares? Given the value of the handout both for immediate comprehension and subsequent re-presentability, the gains significantly outweigh the disadvantages. The eye-tracking study I just described actually sheds some light on this whole behavior. It showed that people will typically take a few moments to scan the whole document as you give it to them, getting a feel for the overall content, which is no bad thing. Once they've oriented themselves to it, they focus back on the presenter, tracking with the right sections as they're presented. In short, it's a non-issue.

Teaching to the handout is one of the most important delivery skills you need to master, but that shouldn't be of concern, because you're probably doing a version of it already. Almost all presenters know how to orient an audience to their slides, or "teach to the screen," as in, "Okay, look at Bullet 3," or "Look at the pie chart on the right." This is no different; you're just doing it in reference to a document instead ("Okay, look at the graphic on the lower left of the page."). From a practical standpoint, teaching to the handout is about following three simple rules.

Rule #1

In the opening, explain that you will be walking through the whole handout "as the basis of today's discussion," and that this will both save them from taking notes and give them a useful takeaway, especially if they later want to share the material with others. You want them to see it as valuable so you should treat it as such. Position the handout as vital to the conversation, not some throwaway piece of paper.

Rule #2

Teach to it diligently, just as you would currently teach to the slides on a screen, but more intentionally. Reference it often, indicating where you are on the page, and be very clear when you are moving between sections.

Rule #3

Draw special attention to the critical words, phrases, and ideas you most want them to remember (which should therefore be prominent in the handout). Don't be afraid to read these verbatim: this helps the ideas stick and actually rewards the hard work you will have done of designing a good handout in the first place.

When you're done, make sure there are extra copies for them to take if they wish. In most sales settings, the hope is that they will re-present the story to a broader group, and extra copies are extremely valuable for supporting this. When they take them, as they commonly will, you can leave the meeting happy, knowing they only took them for one reason.

A VIDEO SUPPLEMENT

Because this is a less familiar skill, follow the link below for a short video that demonstrates how to teach to a handout correctly.

www.oratium.com/resources

CHAPTER 10

Energy

THE VALUE OF ENERGY

Have you ever been in a room where a presenter was working through their material, but for some reason, at some point, the energy level started dropping and dropping and dropping, until a moment came when for all practical purposes, the meeting was over, even though it wasn't actually finished? Nothing was being learned, nothing was being discussed, and nothing was being retained, and silently but politely, people were waiting for it to end so they could pick up and move on. I'm sure you can visualize it, because the scenario is all too common.

Energy matters. Everyone engages better in, and feels more rewarded by, a lively event. When an audience stays energized, they leave positive and enthusiastic about the whole experience, and more importantly, they will have learned and retained much more. But when the energy level sags and the meeting limps toward a forlorn conclusion, people detach. They learn and retain very little, and they leave deflated. The energy level of an audience is a complex thing to unravel: on one level it's definitely tied to a blend of physical factors, like biochemistry, ambient conditions, and time of day, and as such it's tempting to think that this is mostly out of the speaker's control—

and some of it is. If, for example, your audience includes a woman who's deeply jet-lagged or a man who was kept up all night with a teething baby, their energy challenge is primarily flowing from them. But here's the big idea: most of the time, energy is about the presenter, and the job of cultivating and protecting the energy level of the group falls squarely on their shoulders—even when the conditions are hard. In fact, *especially* when conditions are hard. Many people believe you should avoid presenting in the after-lunch session, because of the legendary energy challenge it presents. But have you ever noticed that great speakers can carry that slot without the slightest difficulty, while other presenters can take a perfectly lively group and create mass narcolepsy by 9:05 in the morning? Energy isn't about what the clock's doing, it's about what the speaker's doing. So, how do you maximize an audience's energy level?

IT STARTS WITH MESSAGE DESIGN . . .

When it comes to energy, the root issue is clearly the design of the presentation itself. There are two critical errors that most presenters make in their message design that have equal potential to completely suck the life out of the room: content quantity and content density. When you "firehose" people with too much material, it isn't simply irritating; you overload the part of their brain that takes in new material (their working memory), and past a certain point, they simply give up and shut down. Similarly, when you serve up incredibly dense and complex content, especially in the form of overloaded slides, it has the same effect. The audience may stay with you for a while, but when that seventh slide comes up that looks like the electrical wiring diagram of an oil refinery, they aren't coming with you.

And this can actually be demonstrated scientifically, if we return to our study of the brain activity of audiences exposed to different presentation types, the picture below is a "heat map" that shows where the eyes and attention went of someone viewing a complex slide in the midst of a run of complex slides. (The darker the shade, the more the attention.) It's truly fascinating. As you can see, their eyes scanned multiple elements trying to find something to attach to, but after a certain point, they settled and focused deeply in the upper left—**over an area of pure white space!** In other words, unable to decipher the complexity, their minds wandered, and they completely checked out. This was only slide four in the run, and we made sure that the slides were professionally and expertly presented. That's the problem when the twin mistakes of quantity and complexity show up.

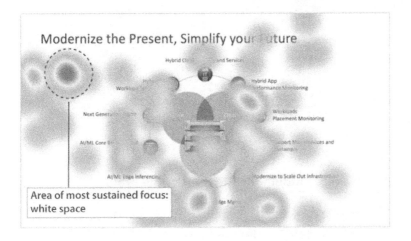

In contrast, a well-architected argument will, by design, tend to boost energy and engagement. When your message is deeply rooted in an audience or customer problem, it will be engaging. When you keep the material crisp, simple, and logically ordered, it will be engaging.

Here's a picture of how the audience viewed the same essential material when it had been more carefully crafted and embedded in a handout. You see clear focus on the key elements, and while it's a little obscured (middle left), the deepest focus went to the most interesting aspect of the problem. This demonstrates a completely different level of engagement, resulting in higher levels of retention and re-presentability.

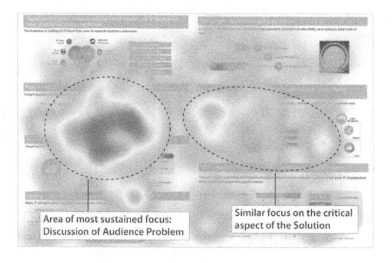

Area of most sustained focus: Discussion of Audience Problem

Similar focus on the critical aspect of the Solution

Riding the Rhythms of the Brain

There's something else about good message design that supports the quest for energy. We know that people don't "lean in" continuously throughout an entire presentation, and recent scientific research shows that they tend to lean in and out on a cycle of about ten to twelve minutes. Wouldn't it be helpful if presenters could synchronize with that cadence? They can. A well-designed presentation will discuss an important audience problem, flow through three to four big ideas, and end with a powerful close. Perhaps more by luck than anything else, this model creates the natural "high-water mark" of a new idea or thought, about every 10-15 minutes—exactly what you would want to align with an audience's natural cognitive rhythms. Many presentations hit a sort of turgid flat spot in the middle where the energy sags and the audience is lost, but a well-structured argument inoculates you against this particular disease.

AND THEN, IT'S ABSOLUTELY ABOUT THE PRESENTER

With the content properly constructed, the game-day piece of the energy puzzle falls solidly on what the presenter is doing. You've already made sure the room isn't too warm or uncomfortable, but the larger truth is: most of the energy in the room flows from the presenter, and the golden rule is:

> **Your audience will never be more excited about the material than you are.**

Your energy matters because they will rise or sink to *your* level of enthusiasm. If you bring a level of evident passion to the conversation, the audience will tend to come along with you, because the wonderful thing about enthusiasm is that it's highly contagious. People like passion in others, even when they don't fully agree with their position, and audiences especially like passionate presenters. But if, as so many presenters seem to do, you subtly communicate that the material isn't that interesting, or even worse, that you don't sincerely want to be up there presenting it, then the audience will be infected by that attitude and sink to a similar level of apathy. This is another reason why you should never apologize for "standing between you and drinks." Do you see the energy-sucking potential of suggesting that drinks will be better than the conversation that's about to come? That's a deflating signal to send.

LIFT THE ENERGY VERBALLY

As a presenter, one of your goals is to convey that your material is interesting, unusual, fascinating, striking, curious, or even shocking. And one of the best ways to accomplish this is with your language itself. You want to routinely see phrases like these in your narrative:

> ➤ "Look at this chart, this is really interesting."

> ➤ "That story is just fascinating in what it reveals."

> ➤ "This data still surprises me."

> ➤ "There are marriages that are alive today because of this one practice. That's incredible." (A line from a conflict-resolution presentation)

> ➤ "What that means is, this isn't just a fundraising banquet: you're actually saving kids' lives tonight. How cool is that?" (From a recent banquet "ask")

Phrases like these radiate energy into the room, and audiences notice and respond to the speaker's passion for their material. One of the highest compliments a presenter can ever receive is, "Wow . . . you really love this stuff, don't you?" Yes. Hopefully you won't need to fake your enthusiasm, because if you aren't excited by your material, then why are you up there presenting it at all?

LIFT THE ENERGY PHYSICALLY

In addition to getting your language right, you want to make sure your own physical energy level is as high as it can be. For a bigger event, your adrenaline will often carry you through the whole thing (although when you finally wrap up, the crash can be pretty spectacular). But for the regular presentation, where you aren't amped up on adrenaline, here are some great practices to ensure that you have plenty of energy to share with the crowd.

Get Enough Sleep

This is almost too obvious to mention, but it's vital, and one of those places where small adjustments can make a big difference. When relevant, never take the last flight in, because problems there can be catastrophic; speaking well on three hours' sleep requires superhuman effort. Be especially careful when you're dealing with different time zones—crossing the US or the Atlantic is rough, especially when you're moving west to east, so give yourself sufficient recovery time if you possibly can. I'm pretty obsessive about protecting my sleep. When it comes to hotels, I always request the highest floor, and the room farthest from the elevator, because that's the most protected from three a.m. drunken revelers. I likely won't fare well in a hotel fire, but at least I'll be well rested.

Eat Lightly or Not at All

If you have a heavy meal sitting in your stomach, it's a huge energy thief, so never eat any kind of big meal before you speak, and ideally don't eat anything at all. I limit myself to a light snack about an hour before, which gets my blood sugar where it needs to be without weighing me down. If you're the lunch or dinner speaker . . . it's a trap! Let the food pass you by; their eating time is your rehearsal time. Your speaking will be much better for it, even though you'll be so hungry afterward that you may actually eat the scraps off other people's plates. While my team has never agreed with me on this, I view this as perfectly acceptable behavior.

Do a Light Workout

It's often a good idea to do a light physical workout a couple of hours before you're on, especially for a bigger presentation. A swim or a good, long walk will boost your metabolism, which is what you want, and it will also help to burn off that nervous energy. Don't overdo it, and don't do it too close to show time: "Post-Gym Flop Sweat" isn't the look you're going for.

Visualize Your Perfect Sparkliness

Many years ago, Jessica—a dear friend and one of the finest presenters I've ever known—taught me a brilliant trick. I've never forgotten it, and it's never failed. Before you get up to speak, and especially if you feel sluggish and fear that you might not have your "A" game, visualize yourself up there being lively, witty, and sparkling. This may sound crazy, but there's robust science behind it, because your brain actually does visualize most of the things you do before you do them. As strange as it sounds, if you've visualized standing up there, being wonderfully effervescent, when you do step up, you can often slip on that persona like a garment.

Movement

When presenting, don't be afraid to move around. Physical movement energizes both you and the audience. I often have two flip charts placed on opposite edges of the stage area, and shifting between them creates a nice element of movement. Rehearsal plays an important role here, because when you're fully comfortable with your material, you can be less tethered to your notes and more able to freely move around. But keep it within limits—and don't move out into the audience under *any* circumstances. Some speakers think this is the coolest thing ever, but trust me, it's not. It freaks people out. It's like the comedian who comes off stage and moves out into the crowd. Suddenly a thousand people who, a moment ago, were having the time of their lives are now terrified they're going to be called on and embarrassed. Remember, your audience "paid" for you to be on stage. Stay there.

Encourage Real Breaks

This is important for longer sessions, where you give people a break in the middle. People don't actually take breaks anymore. The moment you dismiss them, they jump on email and try to clear as much as they can before you call them back. The problem with that seemingly innocent habit is when they do come back, they're more exhausted than when you dismissed them. This is a peculiar new phenomenon, and one you want to curtail if you can. Encourage them to take a real break, and within the bounds of politeness, point out that if they only spend it on email, they're killing their own energy reserves in the name of productivity.

POSTSCRIPT: IT ISN'T ALWAYS YOUR FAULT, AND THAT'S JUST FINE

Several jobs ago, I was asked to go and speak to the board of a major bank in Venezuela. The board hadn't actually invited me; McKinsey had told them that our research was worth looking into, so someone had called to arrange it, and I was dispatched. I entered the auditorium slightly before two p.m., and shortly thereafter a group of about fifteen elderly gentlemen wearing identical black suits filed in, accompanied by the ominous aroma of a recently imbibed liquid lunch. As they took their seats, the scent of disaster was also in the air, and this was soon confirmed when several of them fell asleep before I'd even started. Moments after I'd begun, the rest of the room followed—every single one. And impressively so, including loud snoring and some graceful sliding off of chairs.

At this point, I found myself living inside philosophy's greatest existential dilemma: "If I'm talking but nobody's hearing me, am I really talking at all?" I could have stopped speaking with no ill effect; indeed, I could have quietly tiptoed out and no one would have been any the wiser. Of course, I didn't. I soldiered on through the whole presentation, heroically completing the most surreal hour of my life. As I drew to a close, I raised my volume a bit and coughed pointedly, at which point a small contingent woke, thanked me, and wished me farewell, while the remainder finished their nap in peace.

Sometimes it really isn't your fault. I left and went fishing for bonefish on the coast. It was amazing.

CHAPTER 11

Eye Contact and Body Language

❦

Have some.

Don't be weird.

That's it.

CHAPTER 11A

Eye Contact and Body Language, Part II

～⋙～

W hile I'm sorely tempted to leave this topic exactly as per the previous page, it's worth a couple of pages. But let's not get it out of proportion. I believe that tradition, rather than reason, causes this to remain at the center of modern presentation skills training, and I laugh whenever I see ever more ludicrous variants on the tired old theme. One recent gem in the eye-contact space is that the speaker should fix their eyes, hawk-like, on one person while completing a phrase, then move on and fix their eyes on another person for their next phrase. This is absolute madness.

This whole topic reminds me of the famous question, "What's the only man-made object that's visible from space?" Answer: "The Great Wall of China." Everyone knows that, except there's a problem: *It's absolutely and verifiably untrue.* The wall is so narrow it's utterly invisible from even an ordinary airliner flying overhead, let alone from anywhere in space. So why does everyone believe it? Because we've all been told it's true. And until someone calmly tells us it's *not* true, we'll keep believing it. Eye contact is like that. It's not as big a deal as you've been told. Even so, there actually are a few things worth knowing.

EYE CONTACT

Yes, have some. Eye contact is normal between people, so look at your audience, but no differently than you would look at someone in any everyday conversation, and that's the rule. Fixing them with such a creepy, intense stare that it screams "psychopath!" is a bad idea. Also, don't look over their heads. Some speakers do that, and it's annoying.

Interestingly, you don't want to make too much true eye-to-eye contact at all. Scanning the room, looking toward the audience, is sufficient to create that connection you want; but looking people directly in the eye is something most of your listeners will find slightly unnerving.

Ironically, the main purpose behind scanning the crowd isn't actually the connection at all—it's to see what the crowd is telling you. You should be looking for facial expressions indicating agreement, puzzlement, or restlessness, which are all important signals you need to read and respond to. As you scan the room, don't favor one side. Scan equally. We'll discuss this in Chapter 13 on managing audience dynamics.

BODY LANGUAGE AND MOVEMENT: BE NORMAL

When it comes to body language, don't overthink it. Basically everything is okay, and again, simply being normal is the golden rule. Don't get worked up about the traditional bugaboos. Having one hand in your pocket is fine. Indeed, it makes you look thoughtful; Churchill did it all the time. Because audiences are primarily evaluating your content, minor physical idiosyncrasies pass well under their radar screen, so it's only an issue if you're doing something truly weird and distracting.

Last year, I was watching a marvelous speaker presenting on the topic of how to liberate Native American communities from the paralyzing cycle of drug and alcohol abuse. While he was speaking, the fingers of his left hand were moving continuously, as though he was playing the piano. Initially, it didn't bother me, but after a while, I found myself drawn to those magical digits, first trying to figure out whether they somehow matched the cadence of his speaking (they didn't), and then trying to discern exactly what the tune was that was playing somewhere in his head. Discerning any physical oddities is the only reason I'd recommend videoing yourself, although truthfully if you've got a really good, weird one, lots of people will have told you about it. In general, being aware of the problem is 95 percent of solving it. In this case, Mr. Rachmaninoff needs to put that hand in his pocket.

The one physical posture I would try to avoid is one where you're closed off, with your arms folded low across your body in an obviously defensive way. Protecting your bodily organs from impending inbound spears doesn't exactly exude confidence. Other than that, you are your best visual aid, so err on being expressive: use your arms and hands liberally. Yes, empty your pockets of keys and change if you feel strongly about it, and it's always a good idea to check that your fly is securely closed.

One final point on body language: When presenting graphics onscreen, don't turn your back fully to the audience. It's a little rude, and more importantly, you miss their reaction to what you're discussing. Hopefully we've already disposed of the hated practice of reading text slides; if you don't have them, you can't read them. But even when describing legitimate graphics, do it from one side.

CLOSING THOUGHT:
"CONGRUENCE" AND A PLAY WITHIN A PLAY

Congruence was a key idea we discussed in humor (match your humor to the setting), and it's similarly vital when applied to eye contact, body language, and all things physical. In fact, it's the most important thing to be said on the whole overblown topic. Congruence means that your general physicality should match the content of your message. If your point is serious or grave—think of a funeral eulogy—your body language should be still, quiet, sober, and reflective, with little movement or energy. However, if your setting and point is upbeat—think of an award presentation—your body language can be far more animated, expressive, and buoyant.

In addition to writing plays, William Shakespeare was both an actor and a director, and in his most famous work, he finds a clever way to share his thoughts on how plays should actually be acted. Within the story of *Hamlet*, a play is to be staged, and the character Hamlet is directing it. In one scene, the play is being rehearsed, and Hamlet gives advice to his actors about how it should be performed. This short speech is widely regarded as the one and only time Shakespeare chose to make his views on acting known, and as such it's intriguing. The full scope of this speech would take up several books, but in addition to hammering his crew on the importance of truly learning the material through rehearsal, he adds a fascinating single line on how actors should make use of their physical bodies. He basically says, "It's all about congruence," but puts it this way:

"Suit the action to the word and the word to the action."

Eye contact and body language in twelve words, courtesy of The Bard.

CHAPTER 12

Delivering Insight

❧

"If everything's important, then nothing's important."
—ANONYMOUS

W e now reach one of the most important of all delivery skills, but as I began to write this, I quickly realized an important fact: this can either be a long, bad chapter, or a short, good one if accompanied by an explanatory video, because the skill I'm going to discuss is much easier to understand through visual demonstration. Hence, I'm going to keep the text explanation fairly short and let the video bear most of the load. Read the chapter first. The link is at the end.

THE PRINCIPLE OF SIGNAL

Why do we hate monotone speakers? Obviously it's because they're boring, but there's a more subtle and important reason: it's because they're sending no signals regarding the relative importance of the material they're presenting, and that's a huge problem. When speakers have little variation in their delivery, they're either implying that everything they're saying is equally important, which is nonsense, or that they expect the audience to distinguish the *genuinely critical* from the *merely supporting* without assistance. But after everything we've learned about the cognitive limitations of the brain, what's the chance that an audience can take in new information at presentation speed, and do that level of in-the-moment interpretive analysis? Zero. **It's almost impossible for the first-time hearer of new information to pull key insights out of that material if it's being uniformly delivered. But without apprehending those big ideas, the listener has ultimately gained nothing from the experience.**

Coincidences can be uncanny. I just recently attended an electrical industry conference. The final speaker had a slide containing six identical-looking bulleted points, which he argued were the six most important success factors for electric utilities moving forward. As he walked through the slide in somewhat of a monotone, his words actually suggested that Point Three was the most important of the six; but nothing in his delivery drew attention to that fact, and while a few people picked up on it, it was quite clear that most people didn't. In other words, he did have a big idea, but it never landed. Remember this story, because we'll come back to it.

Great speakers don't make this mistake. Knowing what's most important in their material, they are deliberate in their delivery in order to make sure the audience knows when to lean in and listen. And similarly, by different use of their delivery, they also let the audience know when they're on something of lesser importance, and that it's okay to lean back, relax, and conserve energy. In other words, whether to emphasize or de-emphasize, they **signal** the importance of their material.

ACHIEVING SIGNAL THROUGH MODULATION

The delivery skill that creates this signal effect is called **modulation**. I define modulation as **variation in delivery with the goal of heightening or reducing emphasis.** It involves a range of techniques, and when used properly, it creates invaluable signposts for your audience.

The technical word for modulation is "prosodic variation," but if I'd named a chapter Prosodic Variation, you probably wouldn't have read it. Prosody isn't complicated; it's about how your speaking tone varies, or as Merriam Webster defines it: "the rhythmic and intonational aspect of language." In other words, it's the variation you create in your speech by using different combinations of pitch, volume, pace, rhythm, and intonation. To keep it simple, think of modulation as the way you set your Degree of Emphasis, or DE. When you want to make a particularly important point, you go for a high level of DE. When you're making secondary points, you shoot for a low level of DE. The goal is to modulate in a reasonably wide range, so there's a big difference between your high and low DE, thus making it easy to spot when you're on more or less important material.

When you use modulation well, it's exciting to watch. You increase the impact of your material by drawing attention to your more important ideas, but at the same time, you also reduce overall audience effort by giving them permission to lean back for the secondary material. More impact for less effort: quite a trick.

THE VALUE OF VARYING SPEED

Let me bring this to life by looking at one aspect of modulation, which is speaking speed. Imagine that your normal speaking speed is 100 percent. For me, this is about 164 words per minute, which is a little higher than average but nothing unusual. When I deliver material at this brisk and breezy speed, that's low DE, and the pace is essentially signaling that while this content is still important (if it wasn't, it wouldn't be there in the first place), it's not the most critical stuff we're going to talk about today. I call this type of material "simple description." Now imagine that I'm making a point that's a little weightier; perhaps I'm explaining the layout of a complex chart or using a phrase that needs a little thought to untangle. For that, I'll slow down to about 75 percent of normal speaking speed, which creates more emphasis; that is, the DE is getting higher. In Oratium's live workshop, we use a quote from French author Antoine de Saint-Exupéry to describe the core principle of simplifying a presentation:

"The designer has achieved perfection not when there is nothing more to add, but when there is nothing left to take away."

This is a thoughtful moment for the class: not only does the idea itself need a few seconds to process, but given that most people take the opposite approach to presentation design, packing in as much material as they can until they run out of tiny fonts, this quote raises important questions: "Have I been violating this rule?" "Should I change my approach?"

You can see why you can't blast through that at 164 words per minute, because the slower delivery is needed to give listeners that extra time both to process and ponder. (If you want to prove it for yourself, say the phrase at full speed, and then say it again more slowly. I guarantee that as you do this, it becomes clear that the brain wouldn't be able to process the idea properly at full speed.) Material like this is called "complex description." Now, imagine that within my presentation lie a few truly critical ideas that I definitely want you to retain and re-present. When it gets to the moment to deliver these, I'm going to slow down even further. The exact number doesn't actually matter, but this might be 30-40 percent of normal speaking speed, and that is exceptionally high DE.

The biggest idea we teach in our class is that a presenter's goal is to **"powerfully land . . . a small number . . . of big ideas,"** and I will deliver this phrase exceedingly slowly, providing even more time for my listeners to process the idea and to ponder its implications. But the slow speed also impacts them in another interesting way. The human brain is essentially a guessing engine. It's constantly anticipating what's going to happen next, and even as you're reading this sentence, your brain is already considering how it's going to . . . end. Your brain filled in the word "end" before you read it because that's what guessing engines do. If I'm presenting to you, and we're trucking along at 164 words per minute, your brain will get comfortable with that pattern and expect that I will continue that way. But when I suddenly drop the speed down, the change presents a jolt to your brain, because it hates being surprised. Desperate to figure out what's going on, it responds with massively heightened attention and focus, which it gets from opening up the senses (which, incidentally, is why surprised people have wide eyes).

This all happens because brain wiring is tied to survival. In fact, scientific research reveals that a surprise will heighten an audience's focus for about thirty seconds. As a presenter, that's a fact I can really use. **And what that does is "trick" the brain into dramatically raising its focus on my big idea.** When the still grass on the savannah suddenly starts moving, that's a change that demands your fullest possible attention, because it might be the wind . . . or it might be a leopard waiting to strike. This is easy to demonstrate in a live environment. If I'm talking to a group at my normal speed, some people will be looking at me, some at their notes, and some elsewhere as they listen. But if I suddenly drop to a much slower pace, regardless of what I'm saying, it's extraordinary: every single eye will suddenly dart back onto me, intently focusing on what I'm saying. Why? Because the brain wants to understand what's changed. And here's the value of all this to the presenter: dropping speed leads to raised attention. **Raised attention leads to raised retention. Thanks to the brain's heightened focus, it becomes more likely that this idea is something the audience will take away.**

THE MAGNIFICENT SEVEN: THE COMPLETE MODULATION TOOLBOX

As powerful as varying speed is, it's only one of seven tools for raising and lowering audience attention, and the greatest effect lies in using these in combination. You can see them in the following table, which also explains how you use each to emphasize (high DE) or de-emphasize (low DE) what you're saying.

The Fine Art of Modulation

Tools of Emphasis	High Degree of Emphasis on Critical Points	Low Degree of Emphasis on Secondary Material
Speed	Notably slow and deliberate	Quick, brisk, and breezy
Tone	Serious, "flat," with gravitas	Upbeat, casual, and relaxed
Volume	Doesn't need to be louder, but don't whisper	Normal volume
Eye Contact	Deliberate, intense, and piercing (without being scary)	Looking towards the audience without specific individual engagement
Body Language	Still, quiet, leaning in, and focused	Relaxed, casual, and animated
Language	Specifically naming importance: "This is my big point!"	No signal language
Supporting Materials	Use of icons, boxes, and bolding to highlight big ideas	Only text on the page

In the table on the prior page, two things are worthy of note. First, the top five tools are about your actual delivery. If I want to make a supremely important point, I'm going to slow down, adopt a tone of greater gravitas, and align my physical demeanor to that moment. That's using all five tools at their high DE level. Eye contact and body language do become important here, because both play an important role in signal. For those serious points, I would absolutely quiet my body and look more intently and directly at my audience. But *only* on those important points, which is why the general advice to have continuously piercing eye contact is so wrong. You don't actually want it all the time; most of the time you'll be on secondary material, which calls for far less intensity in your eye contact and body language.

You may be thinking that mastering so many separate aspects of signal is too much to ask, but in fact, using them together actually happens automatically by itself. Imagine you want to make that highly important point. It is perfectly natural to slow down . . . and adopt a more serious tone . . . and become more still . . . and have slightly more intense eye contact. Try it, and you'll see how familiar it is; most people actually modulate quite well in real life. The key is to bring that natural ability back into the presentation arena.

Second, the other two tools aren't changes in your delivery at all, but I can't overstate the importance of both the language you use and your written materials in helping you signal a point's importance.

SIGNAL IN YOUR LANGUAGE

It seems obvious, but many speakers miss the fact that telling an audience how important a given point is, is probably the most powerful tool of all, as in, **"This is my most important point."** You want to hear yourself using language like:

- ➤ "Here's the big idea."
- ➤ "That's really important . . . let me say it again."
- ➤ "This is one of our top three ideas of the day."
- ➤ "This is the most important five minutes of our day."
- ➤ "I suggest you underline or highlight this in your handout."

"Signal language" is extremely powerful. If you remember my bulleted slide gentleman, imagine he'd said something like: "Listen, there are six key things here, but Point Three is the one you've really got to master." Even if he had done nothing else with his modulation, it would have largely solved his problem, even though his slide wasn't helping him. Which brings me naturally to the final tool.

SIGNAL IN YOUR SUPPLEMENTARY MATERIALS

In the above example, given that Point Three was so critical, why did the presenter design a slide that made no attempt to draw attention to it? That was a mistake, and probably the result of late preparation. (It's a common problem with bulleted slides—they're almost always too uniform.) He needed to visually emphasize Point Three, which is one of the most important roles of your written materials. In our presentation handouts, we use two icons. "Critical concept" is for an important point, and "Big idea" is for a load-bearing idea.

> We need sequence of a particular type. It must be THEIRS, not yours. The presentation (conversation) should arrive at a question the exact moment that question arrives in the customer's mind.

CRITICAL CONCEPT

You must anchor in an audience problem, or you are highly likely to lose audience engagement and action.

The two written devices we use for emphasis.

These are invaluable tools for two reasons. The obvious one is the in-the-moment learning reinforcement you create. If you say to your audience, "This is a big idea," and down on the page is that exact idea in a box labeled "Big Idea," it's like having a triple-redundant system, and the audience would have to be unusually dull to miss the point. But the second reason is **re-presentability.** If, a month after our class, someone wanted to re-present the story to a colleague, the Big Idea signals would be invaluable. To get it wrong, they would have to deliberately ignore those icons and dive into something secondary on the page. In that sense, it would actually be harder to get it wrong than right. Contrast that with trying to re-present a typical slide deck. How could you navigate to the big ideas if those ideas had never been highlighted in the first place?

Finally, this is also where the flip chart or whiteboard will particularly help. Write the big idea on the flip chart, even if it's in the handout (and if you know you will come back to it, stick it on the wall). It further reinforces that this idea matters.

Our biggest idea, always reinforced on a flip chart—and once written, stuck on the wall for the entire day.

MODULATION: GETTING HELP FROM YOUR NOTES

Getting modulation right can be difficult, especially for people who don't naturally modulate in a wide range. To give yourself some help, annotate your speaker notes. A simple system of three notes in the margin works well without overcomplicating things:

> ➤ HIT: Meaning, these are points you want to hit hard, but you find yourself under-hitting them in rehearsal. It means go slowly, get the wording right, and "land the punch."

> ➤ QUICK: (as in "move quickly here") Meaning, this is low importance, but I seem to overemphasize it. Breeze over it. Don't take "too much club."

> ➤ CARE: Meaning, this paragraph/phrase contains some tricky wording that you couldn't otherwise iron out. If you tend to turn "best practices" into "breast practices" and you can't avoid the phrase (a common problem in my previous company, which was a best practices research company), "CARE" in the margin is a lifesaver. George W. Bush would have benefitted from this when he famously fumbled the quote, "Fool me once, shame on you, fool me twice, shame on me" by instead saying, "Fool me once, shame on you. Fool me . . . you can't get fooled again." I don't blame him; that's a notoriously tricky phrase. If you have to use it, "CARE" reminds you to watch out, and that it's probably safest to simply read it.

TESTING YOUR MODULATION

Since modulation is a critical skill, you want to know if you're doing it well. There are two simple ways to test it. First, audio-record yourself; the presence or absence of variation in your pace and tone will be perfectly evident, and you can work on widening the DE if the difference isn't clear enough. Second, do a run-through with a friend or colleague, and simply ask them, "What were my biggest points?" Since the whole purpose is to draw attention to those points, that's clearly the right test. If they get them largely right, you're done. If they don't, you still have work to do.

A SKILL WORTH MASTERING

Communication is about the transfer of ideas. Even if you've thoughtfully engineered these ideas into your presentation, your listeners' brains will have difficulty spotting them without a little extra help from you. When you combine a high Degree of Emphasis in your delivery with a well-signaled handout, you put those big ideas on full display. To see this demonstrated, the video link is here:

www.oratium.com/resources

CHAPTER 13

The Delicate Art of Managing Your Audience

"There can be no settlement of a great cause without discussion."

—WILLIAM JENNINGS BRYAN

THE LIVING, BREATHING PRESENTATION

Communication would be so simple if there wasn't an audience out there to disrupt the proceedings, but unfortunately that's never the case (although a webinar does allow you to act like it is). With the exception of the larger ballroom speech, pretty much every presentation is more of a conversation, and as such, it's truly a living, breathing thing. It's a chess match of moves and countermoves between speaker and audience, and the quality of the interaction will often have a significant influence over the meeting's outcome.

A highly interactive group is generally a wonderful thing, but it's also a bit like having a tiger on the loose. I'm sure you can remember some presentation where a lively discussion got so out of hand that the meeting descended into chaos, and whatever the speaker's plan had been, that's not the way things turned out. For this reason, many people fear the audience dynamic, and presenters frequently tell me that they're nervous about questions in general and especially fearful of a turbulent or hostile discussion. Speakers will frequently tell audiences to hold their questions to the end (a horrible idea), often in an attempt to prevent a potentially disruptive discussion from breaking out. But hiding from the issue is not the answer, and muzzling your audience is *most* definitely not the answer. Managing a living, breathing, sometimes friendly, sometimes hostile crowd is a critical skill that all presenters must learn, and when you get good at it, it's actually fun.

BEFORE THE DAY ARRIVES . . .

As I mentioned earlier, you should do everything you can ahead of the event to find out who you're going to have in the room and what dynamics you can expect. We were recently engaged to do a workshop for a client shared between two locations. A little digging had told us that Cincinnati had a senior individual who was likely to be highly disruptive, so we swapped out two team members to put our most seasoned diplomat in that room to manage the dynamic. This was unusual, but it speaks to the applicable point. Find out what you can about the audience makeup. Who are the more senior voices? What is their position likely to be on the material you're presenting? Are there any "characters" you need to watch for?

MANAGING YOUR AUDIENCE: READING AND RESPONDING TO THE ROOM

The Easy Part: Reading the Room

When you're giving the presentation, effective audience management begins with a keen awareness of what the crowd is doing because you can't respond to something you haven't seen. Whether it's fifty or five hundred, the audience is constantly sending you signals you need to read. Sometimes it's so obvious you can't miss it, like an angry question. But, like tremors before an earthquake, the signals are an early indication of a problem, and it's important to spot them so you can get out ahead of that problem. Red flag signals include things like confusion, skepticism, disagreement, disengagement (checking phones), discomfort, needing a break, and especially a certain restlessness that screams a readiness to move on. The way you tune your radar to what the room is "saying" is to continuously look out, actively scanning for the facial expressions and other signs that reveal these underlying thoughts. This is yet another big reason why you need to be fully rehearsed. I've seen numerous speakers with their heads down, wrestling so hard with their notes that they're barely aware there's even an audience out there. There could be people naked or on fire in the crowd, and the speaker wouldn't even notice. Reading the room requires you to be fully present in the moment, and only rehearsal gets you there.

The Hard Part: Responding to the Room

Learning to read the room is the easy part, because scanning faces is simply a physical skill. Now comes the hard part, because responding to the room takes true moral courage. Having spotted the signal, the great temptation is to pretend it isn't there, especially if it's something scary, like disagreement or boredom. We've all been there; we sense the group is resistant or disengaged, but instead of doing the hard thing, which is stopping to investigate the problem, we put our head down and just plow on. You can't do that. If you choose to ignore the signal, you lose your connection with the audience and probably some of their respect. Conversely, when you pull up and act on it, you both fix the broken connection and receive some bonus admiration in the process. As hard as it is, you need to get comfortable with these terrifying phrases:

➤ "You look confused—did I lose you somewhere?"

➤ "I'm thinking some of you disagree with that. Can someone tell me—what's the issue?"

➤ "Okay . . . I can see that makes some of you nervous—let's talk about that."

➤ "Okay, I think it's time to move on."

➤ "You know what? It's a bit earlier than planned, but I'm sensing it's time to take a break."

The prize for this little bit of bravery is huge, because these speakers elevate themselves into an entirely different class of communicator. It is genuinely rare to see a presenter who doesn't merely have their radar tuned to the crowd, but who also has the self-confidence and fearlessness to respond to the signals that the radar picks up. As scary as it feels to "run at the signals," try it, and you'll fall in love with it; it's a moment of power and poignancy. Of course, not all signals are negative. Much of the time, your audience will be sending important positive signals, like smiling, nodding, and leaning in, and responding to these is equally valuable, especially as you are looking for allies to your argument. The big one to watch for is the vigorous signal of agreement, usually an exaggerated nodding or smiling. While I ordinarily don't "cold call" on people, I will in this one case with complete confidence, because this particular signal is the adult version of the little kid raising their hand in class saying, "Pick me, pick me!" You never lose by calling on them in that moment: "Melinda, I can see that issue resonates. You want to share that with the room?" She always does.

INITIATING THE DISCUSSION: OUTBOUND QUESTIONS

Effective discussion management is a critical skill for communicators in most business settings, and unfailingly so in sales meetings. However, while audiences generally want to discuss the topic at hand, the first challenge is that they may be hesitant to initiate that discussion. Asking well-designed questions is the solution to this problem, but it's dangerous to assume the perfect question will pop into your head in the moment. The best way to design these questions is to look at your material ahead of time to consider where the best discussion moments lie and then plan your questions accordingly. One sales presentation we built with a client discusses five interesting effects of getting lighting wrong in a hospital (things like nurse productivity, patient satisfaction, and clinical errors). The discussion moment here is so obvious it's almost impossible to miss. As you wrap up the section, ask, "So, which of these five have you seen? Which are a concern?"

These are classic "outbound" questions, and this ground has been so well trod in other books that I won't overelaborate it here. Suffice to say, open questions invite a longer narrative and are generally better than closed questions, where a one-word answer can be given. However, closed questions can still play a useful role in drawing more people in. The table below provides some examples of easy planned questions:

On Shared Problems	On Facts/Data	On Presented Solutions
"What are you seeing out there?"	"Does this line up with what you're seeing?"	"What do you like about this idea?" "What's hard?"
"How is this showing up in your world?"	"Would your own data tend to support this?"	"What else have you tried here?"
"By a show of hands, who's seeing this problem?"	"Does this look different in your world?"	"How does this compare to what you're doing now?"

The virtue of outbound questions is that they can be precisely crafted. Identify the provocative moment or controversial idea, design the question carefully, and trigger the discussion. Be careful, though, not to ask compound questions, which is easily done because it feels like you're creating more chances to snag an answer. But it's a disaster, as in: "So, hands up if you're seeing this problem . . . or not seeing this problem . . . or maybe a different problem?" I guarantee no hands will go up, and as a bonus, they'll think you're an idiot. Ask clear questions.

Pre-Wiring Your Audience

Sometimes you particularly want discussion to happen, but you know you'll need a little help getting it started. This will often be true early in a meeting with a mixed audience where the individuals don't know each other. In this case, your most valuable tool is the "pre-wire." A pre-wire is simply asking an audience member, ahead of time, to respond to a question or offer an observation at a predetermined moment, with the deliberate goal of opening up the discussion. The pre-wire gets the conversation started, and once one individual has spoken, the floodgates normally open from the rest of the room. Find someone in the audience who has some experience on a point you're going to make and tee them up to talk about it. Then, when the time comes, say, "Pete, we were talking about this over coffee, and you had an interesting insight. Can you share that with the group?" Make no mistake: aside from igniting the room, Pete loves this. He feels like he's on the inside.

HANDLING INBOUND QUESTIONS IS AN A.R.T.– AFFIRM, RESTATE, AND THINK

Inbound Q&A is a completely unique element of a presentation. It stands alone because while you're fully in command of all your own remarks and outbound questions, this is the one moment where by definition, you are *not* in control. Questions and questioners can go anywhere, and because you're less prepared, this is often where ill-advised comments can slip out. Inbound Q&A is almost always where the great "crash and burn" happens, so be warned and be careful.

That said, inbound questions are to be warmly welcomed. They signal interest and engagement, and they also—vitally so—allow the audience to clarify any points of confusion.

> **For this reason, never, ever ask for questions to be held to the end; if you don't allow the audience to deal immediately with something that's confused them, you run the risk of creating a fracture in comprehension they may never recover from.**

I have given thousands of presentations, and I can't remember a single one where I asked for questions at the end. Early in your presentation, as you go over the ground rules, stress that you genuinely welcome questions as you go. Giving the room permission at the outset will help them feel free to ask when the time comes. You won't get many questions in a big ballroom, but it never hurts to offer.

So, inbound questions are your friend, but you need to handle them correctly. The cardinal sin here is rushing to an answer before you've fully considered the question (and sometimes even before the questioner has finished). Don't do this; if you rush to an answer, it likely won't be very good, and you may even have misunderstood the true question. Make it a practice to pause and reflect a moment. Even if you've heard it a hundred times and you absolutely know the answer, still pause, because it honors the questioner. Try to keep the following A.R.T. approach in mind.

A = Affirm

Thank the questioner and affirm them for asking. Aside from the fact that it's polite, it will also prime the other potential questioners in the room. ("Thanks for that. Good question.") Some writers warn against the "good question" affirmation, as though this somehow alienates the person whose question you didn't affirm, but this is unduly sensitive. It's fine to affirm the question, and either way, thanks is always in order.

R = Restate

I've lost count of the number of times I've seen speakers answer a different question to the one that's actually been asked. It's usually a simple misunderstanding, and it's not a huge deal. But when the questioner looks puzzled, the speaker now has a completely unnecessary ball of yarn to double back and untangle. The rule is, if you're in any doubt, check that you've understood by restating the question: "Let me just check that I understand that . . ." This honors the questioner, avoids you looking stupid, and serves to clue in those folks who didn't hear the question in the first place.

T = Think

This is the hard one, because I'm not simply saying, "Don't rush to answer." You actually do need to think! And especially about a more complex question. "Let me think about that for a second . . ." is a perfectly acceptable response, and pausing thoughtfully while you ponder your answer isn't weak: it's actually a sign of tremendous self-confidence. Stopping and thinking also honors the questioner, but most importantly, it makes it far more likely you will get to the best answer the first time.

Because questions often draw presenters into less familiar terrain, don't be in the least afraid to say, "I don't know," and throw it back out to the room. We've all seen the presenter who somehow feels that as the expert, they're required to know everything, and as a result, they blurt out some truly idiotic answers. This is infinitely more damaging to them than a simple, "I don't know." Given that you don't know everything about everything, when you do answer, make it clear where your answer is definitive and where it's your informed opinion.

Finally, while inbound questions may feel random, they aren't, which means you're more in control of Q&A than you might realize. With a little forethought, you can often anticipate many of the questions you might get, especially for a presentation you've made before. It's a valuable exercise to think through and even rehearse your possible answers.

THE ANTAGONISTIC INDIVIDUAL
AND THE SHOT FROM THE BUSHES

The toughest inbound question to deal with comes from that lone individual who's decided to take a professional or personal dislike to you. This is the person I described earlier who shows up in those anonymous evaluations, but they may also reveal themselves in an unusually antagonistic question. Recently, the CEO of a company asked us to come in to help them with their sales messaging, against the wishes of the head of sales, who (I later learned) felt that this was an implicit criticism of the messaging he had helped build. It didn't take long for this to show up. Early in the workshop, he made several comments attacking our approach that fell somewhere between passive-aggressive and openly belligerent.

In these moments, which most speakers have faced, you have to tread an exquisitely fine line. Your antagonist's comment is a baited trap, designed to provoke a fight, so the first job of your response is to be exaggeratedly polite and gracious, which places you—importantly—on the moral high ground. The room will be perfectly aware of what's going on, and the overtly gracious response not only sends a tremendous signal about your professionalism, but also tells them that you aren't about to let a fight break out. This is an enormous relief to the group, who will be extremely uncomfortable about what's brewing. Getting into a verbal brawl with this questioner is something you can only lose, even if you win.

But the other side of the fine line is not to cave. When you do answer, it's important to hold your ground when you're sure the ground is firm under you. It's unwise to defend a position where you aren't completely sure it is correct, but where you are confident of your point of view, take a stand. The rule is, on matters of opinion, hold your position loosely—but be willing to go to the mat, albeit ever so politely, on what you know to be true.

MANAGING THE DISCUSSION

Whether inbound or outbound, legitimate questions usually trigger the rest of the audience to get involved, and a true discussion breaks out. It's a wonderful moment when the discussion moves from "front to back" to "side to side," and the group takes on the conversation within itself without your active involvement. However, at this moment, your continued leadership of the room is vital because this is where things can unravel rapidly. You now pivot into the role of leading through facilitation, which involves two important skills.

Manage the Clock

Discussion can be a rich time of learning, but be careful: that time will fly by, and it's easy to lose precious minutes you're going to need later. However satisfying the conversation, you will not enjoy leading a deeply unsatisfying sprint through the last fifteen minutes of material. The best tool here is to set the parameters for how the discussion will end. When you sense that time is becoming an issue, indicate those final people whose comments you'll allow before re-turning to the planned agenda: "Okay, last two comments, Mike and Susan," or simply indicate that you're taking your last comment. The higher-level and more nuanced skill is to segue back to your teaching. Once a topic has been discussed as much as you want, look for an opening that allows you to draw the group back to the core presentation content: "That's a great point, and actually, that's exactly where we're going next, if you look at the bottom of page three . . ." Even if the connection is tenuous, that's okay.

The bottom line is, when the time comes, have the courage to step back in and gently but firmly close the discussion down. "Folks, that was great: we could debate this one all day, but if you don't mind, let's get back to the main story. We've got a lot more to talk about." This is one of those moments where the audience, admittedly sometimes grudgingly, grants you the implicit authority to keep the event on track.

Manage the People

If the discussion doesn't involve the whole group, and you want it to, it's your role to invite others in through deft facilitation—and it isn't difficult. You might say, "Okay, there are two interesting points of view here. I'd love to hear from some of the other folks in the room." Open it up, but don't force people to speak. If you're presenting to adults, treat them that way. It's your job to give them the opportunity to contribute, but if they don't want to take it, that's just fine. As the conversation flows, keep it centered on high-value areas that are relevant to most of the group. Continue to make sure that anyone who wants to speak can do so, especially where you have a few dominant voices. And then shut it down when it has run its course.

THE TWO NUCLEAR MOMENTS OF DISCUSSION MANAGEMENT

There are both moments where you need to intervene and where intervention is going to be a little tense. But as you manage the people debating in front of you, there are two high-stakes moments where you need an iron grip on the wheel. Don't be afraid in these situations; the room isn't simply granting you authority to act, they're absolutely begging you to do so.

The first is where one individual is completely dominating the conversation and wildly irritating the rest of the room in the process. It's easy to spot, and it's your job to shut them down. The polite way is, once again, to open it up to the room, but this time, do so in a more pointed way, as in, "This is great. I'd love to hear from some of the folks on that side of the room." That's polite, but only barely. If you need it, the true nuclear option is: "Bob, that's really interesting, thank you. But I'd like to hear from some other folks on this." This is stunningly effective, especially if you turn away from Bob as you say it. This is a legitimate leadership behavior, but it's not exactly subtle, which is why it usually keeps Bob under control for the rest of the session. He probably isn't going to buy you a drink that evening, but the group will adore you for it. One exception to the "don't let Bob dominate" rule is when Bob is the CEO, a head of state, or a Nobel laureate. In that case, it's, "Bob, no problem. Go right ahead, take all the time you want."

The second situation is where two people are heatedly beating a topic to death, while the rest of the room is completely bored and checked out. You'll receive clear signals when this point has been reached: restlessness, secondary discussions, people checking email or walking out. Some will even be staring at you with a "Why aren't you doing something about this?" look on their faces. At this moment, your credibility is palpably on the line, so you need to be strong enough to deal with it. The nice thing about the solution is that it works without being too personally bruising to the offenders. You simply want to say, "Will and Grace, you're obviously really passionate about this one. I love that, but I sense it's not as big an issue for the rest of the room. Why don't we talk about this at the next break . . . but for now, let's get back to where we were." Problem solved, respect earned.

Great communicators don't simply *present* to a group. They *work with* a group. When you hone this set of skills, you can take the most unpredictable element of a presentation and make it largely controllable, and with the exception of those on whom you have to drop a small nuclear bomb, you improve the experience for all concerned.

SECTION THREE
Who You Are on the Day

Having discussed everything that goes into the preparation for and the execution of the mechanics of the big day, this final section lifts us to a higher altitude. Beyond *What You Do* lies the loftier topic of *Who You Are*—or put another way, your presentation style, persona, or presence.

CHAPTER 14

Reflections on Style, Persona, and "Being Yourself"

THE POWER OF PERSONA

As I've mentioned, my all-time favorite speaker is Holocaust survivor Eva Kor. Right up until her recent passing at age eighty-five, she continued to traverse the globe on a mission to educate people on matters of courage, tolerance, and forgiveness—the life lessons she drew from her experience walking through the hell of Auschwitz as a sweet but ferociously strong twelve-year-old girl. I vividly recall the first time I heard her speak. As brilliantly crafted as her presentation was, there was also something intangibly wonderful about Eva as a person, and I felt myself deeply drawn to her at a level that was somehow apart from her material. Obviously, some of this connection stemmed from my natural empathy with her suffering, but it's a mistake to ascribe this warmth only to her personal struggle; I've heard many other Holocaust survivors speak, and while I've always found their stories moving and heartbreaking, I haven't always felt that same connection with them personally.

In total contrast, Don Leavens is one of the world's leading economists, and I heard him speak on the subject of global macroeconomic trends back in 2013. It was certainly interesting, but the topic (as Don would agree!) was about as devoid of "human interest" as it gets. And yet, as he worked through his highly technical material, I felt a similar connection with him as I'd felt toward Eva—which is not something I normally feel for economists. I'm sure you've experienced something similar: instinctively, you simply like some presenters, even though you might not be able to pin down the exact reasons why. This presents an intriguing question: if this feeling of personal connection doesn't stem from a speaker's subject matter, then where does it come from? Clearly, there are some intangible forces in operation here that, like the poles of a magnet, have the power to either gently attract us to or gently repel us from certain speakers. These are forces we need to understand.

A good place to start is with Aristotle. His writings on rhetoric propose that a speaker can use three basic kinds of appeals to persuade an audience. **Logos** is the appeal to logical reasoning; **pathos** is the appeal to emotion; and **ethos** is the appeal of the speaker's persona or character. Logos and pathos are the pieces we tend to understand well because they're bound up in the processes of communication design we've already considered—we use fact and data to appeal to the rational (logos) side of an audience, and we use story and imagery to appeal to their emotional (pathos) side. But Aristotle is saying that there's a third pillar of persuasion, which has less to do with the content of an argument and more to do with the character of the person making it.

As we try to unravel this, there's an ancient saying that sheds some light on how it works. **"Speak, that I may see thee"** is a phrase whose author is tough to pin down (it's been variously attributed to Socrates, Petrarch, Erasmus, and Ben Jonson), but it points to a deep underlying truth:

> **Whenever we speak, we reveal something of our inner selves to our hearers, and what we reveal affects how those hearers receive both us and our message.**

Now, the idea of revealing your inner self to the budget committee may feel pretty uncomfortable (both to you and the budget committee), but it's going to happen to some extent, whether you want it to or not. As much as the Western rational mind may dislike the idea, every presentation—even one on the rather sterile topic of macroeconomic trends—is accompanied by some view into the human being who's up there making it, along with all their accompanying strengths and virtues, flaws and frailties. And because what the audience sees in the person is going to have a potentially significant influence on how that presentation is received, the big question is whether a communicator can shape this revealed persona in such a way as to ensure that what's on display is attractive to the audience rather than repulsive. You can obviously change what you do as a speaker, but can you actually change who you are? Can you cultivate a style or persona that's more likely to lead to success?

The answer is yes. More than you might think.

A DEEPER UNDERSTANDING OF "BE YOURSELF"

Of course, at a fundamental level you can't change who you are, nor should you ever try. I actually did once hear someone attempt to fake a British accent in order to sound smarter (and before you ask, no, it didn't work out too well). Hence, the baseline advice to "be yourself" we looked at earlier is absolutely sound and trustworthy—but it isn't quite the whole story. There's more nuance to the idea of "be your-self" than first appears, and here's the key question: Is there only one real and legitimate "yourself"? The answer is no.

My preferred, natural style is to be irreverent and humorous, and whether I'm delivering a toast to the team after a great year or presenting on a serious business topic, this is my default persona. It is undeniably who I am . . . most of the time.

A couple of years ago, I lost a close friend, Mike Klein, to cancer, and I was honored to be asked to speak at his funeral. Mike was that rare guy we all wish we were more like, and his life had touched hundreds of people in unfailingly positive ways, so there was much good to be said. But nevertheless, it was a tragically early passing, and he left a wife and three precious teenage daughters behind. As you can imagine, it was a totally different "me" who spoke that day, and almost the polar opposite of my typical style. There actually *was* a little humor, but for the most part the tone was sober, reflective, mournful, hopeful, and most definitely tearful. But it was still me. I wasn't faking anything. I didn't select some artificial persona for the occasion; it was quietly and naturally formed, as it always is, through the tone of my remarks flowing naturally from the setting and the sadness. Persona is essentially defined as "the aspect of someone's character that is presented to or perceived by others." But we all have different personas we adopt at different times, instinctively and un-consciously, based on the occasion—and in almost all cases, each one is legitimately "us."

What this all means is that your presentation style is not com-pletely fixed. It varies more than you might realize, and if that's the case (setting aside the special case of the funeral eulogy), at the level of the everyday business presentation, what are those aspects of per-sona that, when cultivated, are more likely to help presenters connect with their audiences? As I've studied this question of how speakers draw us toward them in some personal way, I think it can be boiled down to two critical dimensions: 1) Your presentation "presence," that is, the person you portray yourself to be, and in particular, the way you handle yourself and your audience; and 2) The way you use language. And while you will have certain defaults in both categories, in both of these areas you have considerable latitude to change what you're doing, with potentially beneficial effects. The chapters that follow unpack these two personal dimensions.

A Critical Moment for Leaders

This question of presentation persona is important for all communicators, but it's especially vital for those who hold leadership roles. The following chart indicates how people answer the question, "If a leader makes a poor presentation, to what extent does this affect your perception of their overall leadership ability?" Note that the question isn't asking about the leader's communication ability, but their actual ability to lead. The data is rather striking.

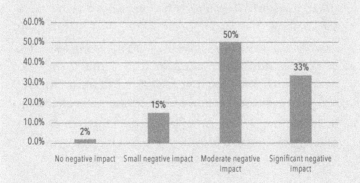

As you can see, 83 percent of respondents say that poor communication has either a moderate or significant negative effect on their perception of leadership skill. The conclusion is clear: **when leaders communicate, they face a unique challenge. They're being carefully scrutinized, and it isn't only their argument that's at stake. Their leadership itself is being evaluated. For this reason, the strength of their persona becomes more important, and leaders need to cultivate a certain leadership presence that is woven into the fabric of their personal communication.**

Many leaders find this idea intimidating, especially those who've risen to seniority based more on their operational or technical strength than on the power of their personas.

I have a friend who oversees executive development at one of the world's largest companies. Her role is to steward thousands of leaders through their journey toward the company's most senior positions, and she recently told me that the most common question she's asked is, **"How can I have the leadership presence I need without having to put on an act?"** It's a great question. If you're someone who doesn't have that natural "big stage" personality, can you still have executive presence while remaining fully yourself? Yes, of course. You don't need to worry, and there's no need to fake anything, because as we're about to see, a powerful presence flows from attributes like authenticity and the skillful use of language. Presence doesn't mean performance. It's within the reach of everyone.

CHAPTER 15

A Winning Style:
The Three Pillars of Presence

Hyperlinks

As we dig into the topic of a presenter's style or persona, you'll see why some of the earlier chapters were so important. Topics like energy, humor, and taking appropriate authority over your speaking event each play a role in developing a winning style. I'll refer back to those earlier chapters, but I'll also restate the important concepts here to ensure that this section is complete and self-contained for future reference.

A CHALLENGE OF MEASUREMENT

Seeking to understand how presentation style connects to presentation effectiveness inevitably leads us into more subjective terrain. Both style and effectiveness are hard to measure objectively, making it even more difficult to correlate them in any meaningful way—which likely explains why there hasn't been a great deal of actionable research in this area. Additionally, style isn't actually one thing; it's an umbrella term that sits over at least a dozen narrower attributes, like passion, energy, and authenticity, and that further complicates matters. For example: if a speaker is both passionate and authentic, and is also effective, how do we interpret that? Did the passion drive the effectiveness, or was it the authenticity, or was it both? Or was it something else entirely? You see the problem. It's a hard task to line up style and effectiveness.

Across the past couple of years, our team has attempted to solve this, or at least add some substance to the debate. Our team members constantly attend all kinds of live presentations, whether at big conferences where we're speaking, or in smaller settings where client presentations are being made. Plus, we have the same access to YouTube as everyone else, enabling the observation of countless video presentations from every field and walk of life. So we designed a research approach to explore the relationship between various attributes of style and speaker effectiveness. Across a fairly large sample of presentations we had observed, we did four things:

> First, we eliminated any presentation where the content was poorly organized (tons of slides, confusing, unclear, etc.), because major content problems have such a big impact on effectiveness that they completely mask any consideration of style. In other words, we only studied presentations where the content was at least decent, so we could begin to isolate how the speaker's style had added to or detracted from their cause. We were left with a sample of about one hundred.

> Second, we formed an evaluation of the speakers' **"Stylistic Effectiveness"** based on a simple high–medium–low

ranking. Stylistic Effectiveness was based on whether we felt moved to support their position, but more importantly whether we felt drawn to them in a personal way, reflecting a sense of warmth, confidence, and trust. Put another way, did we leave this presentation positively or negatively disposed toward the speaker who had delivered the message?

➤ Third, we set aside the "medium effectiveness" speakers, and took only the effective and ineffective speakers. We then assessed them on what they were doing across sixteen style attributes. Again, we graded the presenters on a low–medium–high scale for each attribute. For example, under "Humor," they might have been very humorous, somewhat humorous, or not humorous at all. You get the picture.

➤ Finally, we looked at the relationships between the style scores and overall Stylistic Effectiveness, seeking to determine whether any particular style variables notably correlated with better performance. In other words, imagine that being well dressed kept showing up in speakers who were stylistically effective, but never showed up in speakers who were stylistically ineffective. You would then have good reason to believe that the style element "Dress" actually *does* contribute to a speaker's stylistic effectiveness. In contrast, imagine that good use of humor showed up equally in both effective and ineffective speakers. You would then have reason to believe that "Humor," while it's probably a good thing to have, isn't actually a driver of better performance.

One Big Caveat

Let me stress that this was not a scientific research study in any academic sense. Attributes like authority, humor, and energy are, by definition, highly subjective, as is the measurement of a presenter's Stylistic Effectiveness. Hence, please view the following results as reasonable conclusions rather than scientific results. "Results" suggests the kind of empirical data that this study did not set out to generate, and for the same reason, I'm not presenting any numbers, because those would also create the illusion of quantification. Do I think the conclusions are correct? I do, and I also think they're important. But have we proven any statistical correlations here? Absolutely not, because correlations are about quantification, and "Humor" is simply not quantifiable.

STUDYING STYLE

The following list contains sixteen style variables we looked at. To counter some of the subjectivity (what you deem as well-dressed and what I deem as well-dressed are probably quite different), we tried to have two sets of eyes on each speaker we were evaluating. Additionally, everyone doing this analysis was a highly seasoned communication consultant. The tested attributes were:

1. Eye contact
2. Body language
3. Speaking volume

4. Perceived self-confidence

5. Authenticity (revealing their humanity, the person behind the mask)

6. Evidence of nerves

7. Energy/Passion

8. Interactivity (involved the room in the conversation)

9. Humor

10. Modulation (variation in delivery)

11. Authority (poise, being in control of the room)

12. Dress

13. Movement

14. Directiveness (making recommendations/conclusions vs. presenting material)

15. "Right first time" language (smooth vs. fumbling for words)

16. Speaking speed

THE RESULTS: STYLE UNMASKED

Before digging into our findings on style, remember the importance of getting the content right. Bloated and confusing presentations were almost never effective, which is why we had to remove them from the study. You *must* get your message architecture right. However, when the content was solid and we were better able to isolate the impact of style, the findings were fascinating. Not surprisingly, there were no style elements that actually make you ineffective, but when it comes to helping you draw an audience toward you, some style elements don't seem to matter at all, some matter somewhat, and three appear to be absolutely critical.

What Didn't Matter

Six of the style elements we studied simply did not correlate with effectiveness. That is, speakers could have extensive eye contact and be effective, or have no eye contact at all and yet still be effective. Please note, we absolutely aren't saying these are bad things to have. We're saying that these things don't seem to meaningfully contribute to a winning style. The attributes where we couldn't find any correlation were:

➤ Eye contact

➤ Dress

➤ Body language

➤ Voice volume (except at extremes: very quiet was a problem, as was yelling)

➤ Perceived self-confidence

➤ Evidence of nerves

Quite an interesting list. What first jumps out is that several attributes that receive emphasis in traditional training (particularly eye contact, body language, and dress) don't appear, from this analysis, to have much to do with true effectiveness. This supports the view I've already asserted several times, and it shouldn't surprise us: we know that when people leave a presentation, they're rarely even aware of, let alone discuss, the quality of the speaker's eye contact or how they were dressed. Again, that doesn't mean these are bad things to cultivate (I'm a big believer in dressing professionally at all times), but they don't seem to drive genuine effectiveness.

The other noteworthy finding was around the unimportance of nerves and perceived self-confidence (which are similar attributes) as they relate to stylistic effectiveness. This is enormously comforting for those who struggle in that area, but again, it's not entirely surprising. Everyone understands how stressful it can be to present in public, and I think that instinctively, many people feel genuine empathy for the nervous speaker who's struggling. To be contrarian, perhaps it could be argued that visible nerves might boost effectiveness because they reveal the humanity or authenticity of the speaker—which as we're going to learn, is a factor of singular importance.

Before we move on, one more important conclusion. There's a slight caveat to the idea that these attributes are "what didn't matter." Hopefully, it's obvious that we're talking about what happens **within the normal limits of behavior.** If you go to extremes, it's quite certain that all of these *do* matter, and at some point any one of them can seriously harm you. To speak a little quietly is okay, but if you speak so quietly you can't be heard, it's going to have a negative impact. Likewise, dress may not matter within normal tolerances, but if I turned up to a professional speaking engagement clad only in leopard-skin shorts and a raccoon-skin hat, I don't need a research survey to tell me that's going to be a problem.

What Mattered Somewhat

The second grouping was of seven attributes that did appear to correlate with a more effective style, although only moderately so. In other words, these are things that show up quite frequently in speakers who are effective, and they could also sometimes be found in ineffective speakers, meaning that these do seem to help, but they aren't the "be all and end all" in presentation effectiveness. These attributes were:

➤ Energy/Passion
➤ Movement

➤ Interactivity

➤ Humor

➤ Speaking speed

➤ Modulation

➤ "Right first time" language

Instinctively, this probably makes sense. Wouldn't you say these are attributes you like in a presenter and are generally drawn to? One interesting underlying theme is reflected in four of the seven factors. The fact that energy/passion, movement, interactivity, and humor all made this list points to the fact that the greatest value is created when you impart **energy** to the room. Humor is known to raise the energy level of a group, and likewise with interactivity—the right activity or exercise can often bring a crowd to life, especially in that mid-afternoon time slot. And of course, the speaker's own energy and movement affirm the same idea. The second theme is seen in the remaining attributes: speaking speed, modulation, and "right first time" language. These are all aspects of the way you're actually speaking. It's genuinely important to deliver your material in a crisp, clear, and precise way.

The main conclusion from these moderate correlations is this: these attributes will genuinely help you to have a winning style, although they're still not critical. You can be a lower-energy speaker and not especially funny and still be highly effective, but a little dose of both will almost certainly make you better. (For cross-reference, recall we've previously tackled the specific topics of humor and speaking speed in Chapter 8, energy and movement in Chapter 10, and modulation in Chapter 12. Getting your language "right first time" was dealt with under the banner of rehearsal in Chapter 5.)

What Mattered a Lot . . . "The Pillars of Presence"

Now we get to the most interesting factors. Out of the sixteen, three attributes appear to be significantly correlated with a high level of effectiveness and a strong speaking style. In other words, these attributes were consistently present in more effective speakers, but rarely present in ineffective speakers. I genuinely believe that when it comes to style, if you peel away all the noise, these are the three things you expressly want to get right. At the outset, I want you to notice that these three Pillars of Presence (unlike more external attributes like how you dress and how you move) each connect directly to your personal character, the very thing Aristotle said was the foundation of ethos. They are:

➤ **Authority**: Being in control of the room.

➤ **Directiveness**: Being willing to say what you think, and recommend what you believe is right.

➤ **Self-Disclosure**: Being a real and genuine person; authenticity.

These are the attributes you most want to work on, but what's interesting about each of them is that **more isn't automatically better.** There's some danger in going over the top with any of them, and a moderate level is what you're actually shooting for. Think of these as "Goldilocks" attributes, where you want to be not too hot, not too cold, but just right. This will become clear as we explore them.

PILLAR OF PRESENCE #1: THE VOICE OF AUTHORITY

Authority Defined

It's not surprising that we find authority on the list of the Big Three. This is the degree to which the speaker embraces their role as leader of the room, taking the authority that the audience grants them to control anything that needs to be controlled. You'll recall that aspects of this attribute have already surfaced in earlier discussions, particularly in the context of dealing decisively with problems in the venue and managing difficult individuals and out-of-control conversations.

There's a wonderful story surrounding Winston Churchill (sadly unconfirmed) that perfectly illustrates the significance of this idea. Apparently, a BBC broadcaster was once sitting next to him as he gave a speech which, as usual, had his audience spellbound. The broadcaster noticed, however, that what appeared to be a set of notes in Churchill's hand was actually a laundry list. Shocked, he later asked Churchill if he had truly been waving around his dry-cleaning order as though it were notes, to which Winston replied, "Yes. It gave confidence to my audience." Whether it's true or not, this story presents us with a wonderful lesson. What was Churchill getting at here? Clearly, he wasn't lacking in confidence, and if he had his speech perfectly memorized, why would he bother to hold fake notes at all? It takes us back to a topic we introduced when discussing how important it is to get the presentation opening just right. We all understand that presenters get nervous, but we often fail to grasp that audiences also worry that this is a bad use of their time, or that the speaker isn't going to do a good job, or that things might not be under control. With his reply, Churchill revealed his profound understanding of this particular audience dynamic—in this case, the concern that their speaker might not be properly prepared (pretty ironic, given Churchill's fanatical preparation habits).

The higher point here is that **the audience's desire for the speaker to be in charge is very real.** This fact was vividly illustrated by a personal example I shared in *The Compelling Communicator*, and is worth retelling here. Many years ago, I was teaching a two-day workshop in New York where, sadly, one of our attendees had a mental breakdown overnight. On the morning of the second day, he took an early walk in the rain, and in his confused mental state, rather than go up to his room and change, he simply removed his wet clothes before sitting down, stark naked, as we opened our session. The audience quickly became aware of his nakedness, and as funny as it seems now, at the time it wasn't funny in the least. This was not normal behavior, and most people were genuinely frightened. So what did they do? After looking at him, they turned as one and looked at me. That was the moment when this truth about authority was permanently seared into my brain. It didn't matter that I hadn't taken this man's clothes; I was the speaker, and it was very clear that it was now my job to fix this. Embracing my new role, I announced an "early break while we get this gentleman the help he clearly needs." We called security and had him gently removed. All was well, but the "presence" lesson is very clear. Whether it's laundry lists or naked men, audiences look to the speaker to calm their fears.

Why the Middle Matters

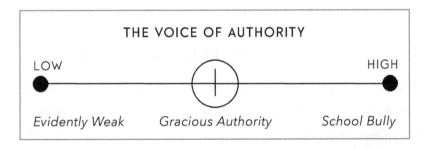

Looking at the graphic above, it's clear why you want to sit in the middle. If you live on the left, you're both projecting weakness and actually *being* weak in those key moments when authority matters. If two people are talking and ruining the experience for everyone else, the group will blame you if you fail to deal with it. One particular challenge here is that many speakers want to win the approval of the group they're presenting to, and like weak parents who don't want to be unpopular with their children, this causes them to shy away from exercising authority in any way. This is a trap. Rather than winning the room over by being nice, this failure to take charge actually communicates weakness and insecurity. From this, an important rule emerges:

> **If you seek the audience's approval, you will lose the audience's respect.**

In contrast, if you drift too far to the right, it creates an entirely different problem. Possessing the mic does not grant you the authority to boss people around in a heavy-handed way, and an excessively overbearing exercise of power creates an unbridgeable chasm with your audience. "You two—stop talking," might work in a nineteenth-century schoolroom, but it's not the authority we're talking about here. The group will let you lead, but it won't let you bully.

Getting Practical: The Right Level of Authority

What does "right" look like with this attribute? It's a firm tone, but one that is also gentle and polite, best described as **"gracious authority."** In other words, you want to exercise your authority gently, displaying a humble, gracious leadership over the room. And because you are being most closely scrutinized at the beginning, as we discussed in Chapter 7, make sure this leadership is clearly on display in those critical opening moments. From a practical standpoint, as the presentation unfolds, remember that there are three areas over which you need to exercise this authority.

> ➤ **Manage the Time.** Know your timings, make sure people know those timings, and start and end on time. Gently call people back from breaks, and rein in discussions that are getting off track.

> ➤ **Manage the Distractions:** Don't be afraid to work with the venue. Plates don't need to be cleared, and leaf-blowing doesn't need to happen right now. Naked men can be gently removed.

> ➤ **Manage the People:** Explain the "rules of engagement" and gently enforce those rules. Restrain those who are dominating, and draw in those who want to participate but are having trouble breaking in. Declare conversations closed when broader priorities dictate.

This isn't a complete list, but rather examples of good authority practices. And remember, this is what the audience wants. Busy people don't want a break to run twenty minutes long simply because Jerry and Rachael haven't seen each other in a while.

PILLAR OF PRESENCE #2: DIRECTIVENESS

Directiveness Defined

Directiveness is defined as the degree to which the communicator is prescriptive or descriptive in the guidance and direction they give the audience, particularly concerning conclusions and recommendations. A more directive speaker will clearly make recommendations and offer thoughts to the audience regarding the action he/she thinks they should take based on the material presented, whereas a less directive speaker is almost the "humble scribe" presenting data or findings, but making no recommendations.

The reason why this makes the list of the Big Three style attributes most critical for effectiveness ties directly back to the limitations of the human brain. When people are taking in new information, it's generally asking too much to expect them to do deep interpretive analysis and draw conclusions unaided out of that material. The right level of directiveness sidesteps that mistake. It's all about giving people some help by telling them what your material means and what you think they should do as a result.

Why the Middle Matters

Looking to the left, a speaker with very low-directiveness presents facts, data, and information, but leaves the audience completely to their own devices when it comes to drawing the right conclusions and deciding on possible courses of action. This tends to be frustrating, because people don't want to have to figure out what it all means for themselves; they want to know what *you* think or recommend. This is why research presentations are so often unsatisfying; they frequently focus entirely on the data, but never actually get to implications, conclusions, or meaning, ultimately leaving the audience with more questions than answers. When speakers fail to draw conclusions or make recommendations, there are two possible outcomes, and they're both bad. The audience will either draw no conclusions at all, which means they've gained nothing from the material, or they'll draw the wrong conclusion.

Many years ago, I was observing a Chicago company making a presentation to executives from other local companies on how they excel at customer service. At one point, they were discussing how much they care for their own staff and how that care then motivates their staff to better care for their customers. After the classroom session, they took us to a break room with great seating, great food, flat-screen TVs playing weather and traffic updates, and a range of genuinely useful free vending machines as evidence of their "caring" culture. At the end of the day there was a round-table session, and one attendee, a senior executive, was asked what his main takeaway was. He answered, "We really should do flat-screen TVs. Those are cool." He had completely and utterly missed the point. The big idea wasn't TVs in the break room. The idea was, "You need to care more for your people. When you do that, they'll start caring more for your customers." He totally missed it, but it wasn't his fault. When the presenter failed to draw the conclusion out, he had simply drawn his own. That's the problem of low directiveness.

In contrast, excessively high-directiveness speakers make the opposite mistake by being too forceful in telling their audience what they need to do.

> **When a speaker is too pushy, audiences will reject them—not because their ideas are wrong, but because of the forcefulness itself.**

It's a quirk of human nature, but we've probably all resisted good advice when it's been delivered in the wrong way, because no one likes to be given orders, even when those orders make sense. Pushy speakers leave no room for their hearers to make their own decisions, and by backing the audience into a corner, they often get rejected on purely emotional grounds.

Getting Practical: The Right Level of Directiveness

"Humble directiveness" is the goal. In other words, be willing to tell people what you think they should do. As long as you aren't overly forceful, you won't be viewed as arrogant. Most of the time, well-reasoned recommendations are welcomed by a time-oppressed audience whose brains are already full of other things. And because people often struggle to make decisions, a gentle directiveness is also helpful in getting them comfortable with a decision they need to make. Most importantly, remember that they always have the option to disagree with your recommendation and choose a different path—and if they choose to exercise that right, you need to be completely okay with that. That's the "humble" part of humble directiveness: if they disagree or reject your idea, be willing to let it go. In summary, tell them what you think, and let them make their own decision. But *do* tell them what you think, as in:

> ➤ Know the main conclusions of your presentation, and deliver them in a way that's clear to the audience.

> ➤ Suggest what might reasonably be the right course of action based on the conclusions you've presented. Suggest, don't demand.

> ➤ Be prepared for a reasonable cross-examination of your recommendations. That's to be expected.

> ➤ Stand your ground. When you believe something, don't cave. Politely defend your point of view if challenged. Have the courage of your convictions.

➤ After you've made an appropriate argument, be completely comfortable if the group opts to reject your recommendations. You can recommend, but you can't require.

➤ Setting does matter here. Sales presentations, for example, often require a greater degree of prescriptiveness than is always comfortable (for either party), and more than you see in other business settings. Plentiful evidence exists that over-performing salespeople are willing to create and endure the tension of the more prescriptive approach.

Postscript: Be "Selectively Directive." Be careful not to be too prescriptive where it's not fully merited. If you're presenting as a subject matter expert, your opinion carries real weight; and because people may act on it, you have a duty to your audience to advise them with integrity. As such, making strong recommendations without good reason is reckless. Whenever I'm asked some question that takes me into the realm of speculation, I try to remember (though I'm sure I often get it wrong) to make it clear that my answer is based more on my opinion than on any real evidence, and that the audience should hold it far more lightly as a result. **The lesson: Even the more directive speaker isn't directive in everything.**

PILLAR OF PRESENCE #3: SELF-DISCLOSURE

Self-Disclosure Defined

Self-disclosure is the most interesting, and probably the most important, of the Big Three. It's the degree to which a speaker reveals aspects of their *own personal humanity* as they present. At one extreme, they might reveal almost nothing of themselves, this being a low self-disclosure or "detached" demeanor. At the other extreme, they reveal a great deal of themselves, this being high self-disclosure, or an "unguarded" demeanor. I wrote earlier that something of your humanity is always on display when you present, but the question in view here is **how much** the audience gets to see of the human being standing behind the presenting mask. The wrong level of self-disclosure (either too little or too much) can be devastating for a presenter; but at the right level, it has the power to connect people in a profound way.

Human beings are highly social animals. The extent varies by individual, but in general we want to know others and are ourselves willing to be known. That's what makes this attribute so important; it connects you to your audience. Another great word to describe self-disclosure would be **candor**, defined as "the quality of being open and honest in expression," or **authenticity**. Each of these terms conveys essentially the same idea.

Why the Middle Matters

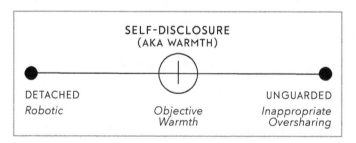

As you can probably anticipate, there are huge problems at either extreme, and you've likely witnessed both. A very low self-disclosure speaker reveals nothing whatsoever of themselves, leading to descriptions like "impersonal," "cold," "robotic," or "detached." They will seem personally disconnected both from the material they're presenting, but more importantly, from the audience too. The problem with low-disclosure speakers isn't that they're difficult to like (although they are), it's that they're difficult to trust because there doesn't seem to be a human being there to know and connect with. Characters like Mr. Spock (of *Star Trek*) and Sheldon Cooper (of *The Big Bang Theory*) may be interesting to watch, but that's precisely because they're detached from those around them, and there's great dramatic or comedic mileage to be had in exploring that detachment.

Real life isn't quite as much fun. Without making any political comment, a recent example of a "colder" speaker from US public life would be Hillary Clinton. Regardless of her other merits, it has been commonly noted that her speaking style, and especially her formal speeches, lack any element of self-disclosure, and that very little of her true self ever appears to be on display. Consequently, people have found her difficult to trust, and many commentators have observed that this style issue, and the downstream trust problem it has created, has seriously hindered her political success.

The high-disclosure style is also a problem, but for entirely different reasons. The term "oversharing" has recently come into common use, and that's an apt descriptor of this type of person. The high self-disclosure speaker has no mask or filter; they reveal everything, putting their inner thoughts, feelings, and emotions on full display. They'll share deeply personal information, often accompanied by a raw display of emotion and tears. Sadly, this has been the hallmark of some of the most loathsome religious charlatans of recent times, who've used this "style" quite effectively to manipulate others for their personal financial gain. In professional settings, this persona is less common, but it does show up—and when it does, it's highly inappropriate. Not only does it make people extremely uncomfortable, but with the emotions seemingly running the show, it signals a complete loss of objectivity.

If the low-disclosure speaker is difficult to trust, the high-disclosure speaker's lack of objectivity makes them difficult to believe. I know of one senior corporate leader who had a tendency to tear up almost every time he presented. If this had been an occasional thing, it would have been no problem, especially where the setting merited it. However, in his case, it became so frequent that his team felt manipulated and uncomfortable, and a complaint was eventually filed with his HR department.

There's no inherent problem with expressing emotion at the right time and place. If you're delivering the retirement address for a dearly beloved mentor, emotions might be running high, and it's clearly acceptable to cross the "normalcy" line in those moments. But in most situations, such excess is uncomfortable, unwelcome, and unprofessional.

Getting Practical: The Right Level of Self-Disclosure

As you move away from these problematic extremes toward the center, something wonderful happens. The middle of the spectrum, which I call "objective warmth," is an exceptional presenting persona because it captures the best of both positions, while suffering the problems of neither. It blends the logical, objective detachment that draws an audience to the argument, with the authenticity that draws an audience to the person who's making it. And because both of those things are valued by an audience, the combination is powerful. It's a tremendous experience for an audience to have an important topic presented in an objective and intellectually robust fashion, but at the same time, to have it done so by an authentic person who brings it to life in an honest and transparent way. Many of history's greatest leaders have demonstrated a high degree of objective warmth, with their communication revealing an unexpected degree of their inner selves, yet without straying into emotional manipulation.

Former President Bill Clinton was an exceptional communicator who commonly put his feelings on display, which drew many people to him. (An interesting contrast with his wife). Likewise, Winston Churchill was unusually open and authentic, especially considering the reserved British culture of the 1940s, but buried in his writings we actually find a glimpse into his mind on this specific aspect of public speaking. In his 1897 essay "The Scaffolding of Rhetoric," he writes: "If we examine this strange being [the orator] by the light of history we shall discover that he is in character sympathetic, sentimental and earnest . . . Before he can inspire them with any emotion he must be swayed by it himself . . . **Before he can move their tears, his own must flow.**"

I mentioned earlier that rather than being a liability for the speaker, nerves may in fact be viewed as an asset. As crazy as that may have sounded, now you can see why. Whatever else they do, visible nerves put our humanity on clear display, and in doing so, they provide a window into the real person beneath the surface. Given the importance of authenticity, that may be a very positive thing indeed.

The Magic of Hamlet

It's no coincidence that this attribute of self-disclosure is regarded as a key aspect of some of Shakespeare's most compelling and enduring characters, with Hamlet being the most famous example. To avenge his father's murder, Hamlet must kill the king who murdered him, an act he knows will cost him his own life. As he walks this dark road toward his inevitable destruction, we're deeply drawn to Hamlet's humanity because in a series of soliloquies he shares the agony, fear, and self-doubt of his position. "To be or not to be . . ." (a reference to being alive or dead) is the haunting speech where Hamlet debates with himself whether suicide might not actually be the easier choice, compared to the horrors of the path he has been forced to follow. The genius of Shakespeare is that we don't simply see what Hamlet does in the play: we enter into how he feels.

Providing guidance here is a little more complex, because your level of self-disclosure will be influenced by context and topic. As I mentioned, some presentations, like that retirement address, lend themselves to a degree of self-disclosure that a budget review clearly doesn't. That said, here are a few general rules:

> Be willing to reveal your own personal thoughts and feelings on a topic, as appropriate to the setting. And in all ways, be honest. If you're going to share a personal thought, make sure it's authentic.

> Be willing to share a personal story or anecdote as an example or illustration of an important point, but make certain that any personal story you use has a clear teaching purpose. If it seems as though the story was told purely for its own sake, it can be seen as gratuitous and manipulative. Earlier, I told the story of a funeral eulogy I delivered. It taught the point that personal style varies based on setting. The teaching purpose makes room for the personal story.

➤ In general, unless you know a group well, avoid personal sharing too early in a presentation. It's better to have some credit built up on the objectivity side of the balance sheet before you open up the more personal side. You have a lot more latitude when you've formed a relationship with the group.

➤ Be extremely cautious about oversharing. People are typically uncomfortable with deeply personal details, especially those surrounding personal tragedy. If in doubt, test your planned story with an objective person whose judgment you trust.

➤ **Critical, but easy to miss: validate self-disclosure in others.** If people are willing to share their fears and frustrations, hopes and regrets, don't leave them hanging— sincerely thank them and affirm their contribution to the rest of the group. That kind of group leadership can completely change the tone of a conversation.

A Word from Don Leavens on Personal Connection

It's funny. I haven't spoken to Don Leavens in several years, but I wrote to him asking for permission to use his name. He graciously replied that I could, but the rest of his email was telling. See below for a leading economist's take on making a connection with the audience:

I think you are onto something. My performance is usually better when I socialize with the audience the night before at a reception or dinner. When I speak cold with no connection, I am less animated and confident. I must consciously work to reach the audience, despite presenting essentially the same information. I am sure you have found the same thing in your many engagements.

You spotted the key lines, I'm sure: "When I speak cold with no connection, I am less animated and confident. I must consciously work to reach the audience." Don connects with people in a wonderful way. Few presenters (and hardly any economists!) understand this central truth.

CLOSING THOUGHTS ON STYLE AND PRESENCE

We've all had that wonderful experience where we've felt powerfully drawn toward some speaker like Eva Kor or Don Leavens, knowing that the deep connection was coming from somewhere rather mysterious—something apart from their presented content. As I hope I've demonstrated, such connections come from this intangible thing called persona, and we've seen that it's both possible and appropriate to seek to develop a persona that's more likely to drive success, while still remaining true to ourselves. That improved style won't redeem an intellectually deficient, horribly constructed argument, but it *will* make a good argument better. Put another way: success happens when great style meets great substance, never when great style attempts to rescue bad substance. As you seek to upgrade your own speaking style, here are three closing thoughts.

1. *Your Current Style Probably Isn't Hurting You*

All speakers have a default level for the style attributes we've looked at, which are generally on display most of the times they present. You may be more or less funny, more or less energetic, or better or worse dressed, and that's fine. None of the attributes we looked at correlated with being ineffective, so unless you're doing something genuinely extreme, such as being absurdly aggressive or so low-energy that your audience needs to check your pulse, your current style probably isn't hurting you.

2. *Working On Various Elements of Style Will Boost Your Effectiveness*

As you ponder your default style, while it may not be hurting you, there may be some areas where a little work would likely yield an improvement in your communication performance. Certain attributes are important enough to be worth tweaking, as we saw in the "Mattered Somewhat" list:

- ➤ Energy/Passion
- ➤ Movement
- ➤ Interactivity
- ➤ Humor
- ➤ Speaking speed
- ➤ Modulation
- ➤ "Right first time" language

Do you need to raise your energy level? Inject more humor? Design more interactivity? If so, guidance on all of these can be found in earlier chapters.

3. *Pay Extra Attention to the Big Three Pillars of Presence*

If your goal is to develop a really effective speaking style, the biggest impact will come from developing a healthy level of the Big Three. You may have one or all of these mastered already. But where you see a gap, this would be a good place to invest some focused attention. As you can see from the following diagram, if you can navigate toward the middle of each attribute, that aggregate bullseye will likely have a substantial impact on your effectiveness. As a helpful start, take a moment now, grab a pen, and plot where you think you currently are on each of the three axes. It will tell you which way you need to be moving. The bullseye itself lies at the intersection of three simple ideas.

> ➤ **Pursue gracious authority.** Be in control of the event. Take the authority that the audience gives you. Know what to control and how to control it, but do it graciously.

> ➤ **Pursue humble directiveness.** Be willing to take a position. Tell your audience what your material means and what they should do with it. Defend the views you hold strongly. And if they don't go your way, humility says that's okay.

> ➤ **Pursue objective warmth.** You're human. Let your audience see that. Don't go so far as to make them uncomfortable, but people like seeing the real person. Be objective and logical, but be willing to take off the mask.

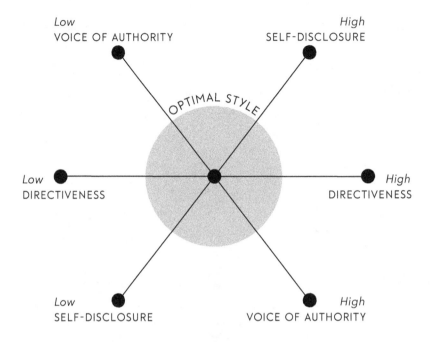

The Three Pillars of Great Presence. The most effective persona lies in the shaded central zone, the midpoint of all three axes. As a practical exercise, you can plot where you currently lie on each to determine the developmental changes you might want to make.

EVA KOR: THE PERFECT PRESENTATION PRESENCE?

As I pause to reflect on exactly why I felt so drawn to Eva Kor, if I look at the question now through this new framework, it all becomes incredibly clear. She brought a real measure of directiveness. I can hear her words now, loving but firm: "Don't judge people based on what they wear or how they look. That's exactly what the Nazis did to me. You can only judge people on their actions, nothing else." Eva didn't pull her punches; she told you what it all meant, leaving you only to decide what to do with your own prejudices. But above all, she brought a perfect objective warmth to her conversation, and that's why I loved her so much. In one moment, she described the routine of Auschwitz with a frankness and objectivity that would do justice to the finest Reuters reporter. Yet in the next moment, as she described the classmates in her village school turning on her, pivoting within a few weeks from close friendship to calling her a "dirty Jew" as Nazi doctrines began to take hold, you still heard the bewilderment and sadness of a frightened little girl. If there is truly a presence to aim for, Eva's was it.

CHAPTER 16

Language, Part I:
Harnessing the Power of
"Muscular Language"

~∞~

THE DOUBLE LIFE OF LANGUAGE

I think everyone implicitly understands that there's something strange and special about language. At one level, it's the most mundane of things: we talk continuously, uttering a daily average of around sixteen thousand words, or about one hundred minutes of continuous speech.[4] Thanks to this near-constant use, we naturally tend to view language simply as the utilitarian tool we use to convert our silent thoughts into a form that others can understand. My brain tells me I'd like the salt, so I say to my son, "Hey, Fergus, pass the salt, please." That's language. It's simple.

Except it's not, because everyone also knows that the coin has a reverse side that's altogether deeper and more transcendent. Far beyond the simple communication of thought, language has an almost

---

[4] Interestingly, there used to be a stereotype that women speak significantly more words than men each day. Recent studies show that's not really accurate. The numbers vary by study, but the consensus is that there's no statistical difference between men's and women's use of words. On average, women speak 16,215 words per day, and men speak 15,669 words per day. See https://ubrp.arizona.edu/study-finds-no-difference-in-the-amount-men-and-women-talk/.

mystical ability to touch, motivate, move, rouse, or inspire us in ways that can be hard to explain rationally. Almost all of us can remember moments in our past when some crucial words, whether from a grand speech or the quiet counsel of a friend, changed the direction of our lives. And beyond the individual, we're also keenly aware that at certain pivotal moments, language has changed the entire course of human history. In these final chapters, my aim is to awaken you to the idea that language is not only a weapon of tremendous power, but also, more importantly, one you can wield to great effect even in your everyday communications. Most of us aren't destined to change world history, but I can guarantee that in your personal future, you will deliver some important speech or presentation in which you'll need to mobilize language toward some higher purpose. The key is to remember that the very same tool that mundanely clarifies the desired level of starch in your dry-cleaning can also compel a listener to a life-changing course of action.

Language is an intimidating topic. It's been continuously studied since at least the fifth century BC, when Greek and Roman scholars first explored the concepts of rhetoric. I can't add even a single brushstroke to this immense canvas, but what I hope I can do is to boil this huge terrain down to a small number of important ideas that will be genuinely useful for a twenty-first-century reader who wants to use language more effectively, but without taking a doctoral course in rhetorical theory.

In this chapter, I'll explore exactly how language exerts its power over us, and then I'll demonstrate how to harness that power practically in your general use of language. In the final chapter, we'll dig into the topic of rhetoric and, in similar fashion, try to tease out what subset of its immense breadth is actually useful to today's presenter. Rhetoric is like a vast and ancient toolbox about which we will ask: Which of those tools can make a difference in the modern world?

Is Change Possible?

You may already be wondering if you can modify your language in any meaningful way to make it work more effectively for you. The answer is yes, because you already do exactly that. No one in the world speaks like you. It's startling to realize that of the hundreds of millions of native English speakers, no two use the English language in exactly the same way. **We are linguistic snowflakes**—everyone's use of language is completely unique and personal, based on a complex mix of upbringing, education, geography, gender, social group, age, media choices, etc. We already use language in the way that works best for us, leaning on the words, phrases, and grammatical structures we like and find effective, and staying away from those we don't. Doing that more intentionally is no great task.

The Broad Power of Language

Let's begin by considering how language works at those higher altitudes. The outstanding movie *Darkest Hour* is an account of Winston Churchill's early days as British prime minister following the outbreak of the Second World War. A central theme of the film is his legendary ability to inspire others through language, and in one scene, he says something extraordinary to an informal gathering of ministers in the halls of Westminster. The phrase is real; Churchill definitely *did* say it, but it wasn't to an impromptu gathering, which is significant. He actually said it in a formal, prepared speech, which means this wasn't some off-the-cuff remark, but rather a carefully crafted phrase. What he said was:

"If this long island history of ours is to end—at last—let it end only when each one of us lies choking in his own blood upon the ground."

This is a titanic phrase. Please indulge me by reading it again, slowly. (And if you would **really** indulge me, say it out loud, because only then do you get its full effect.) Think about how this phrase would make you *feel*, knowing that the battle for the very life of your country was looming. Would you feel more inclined to the fight, or less? Obviously, wartime rhetoric lives by its own set of rules, but even so, this is unusually vivid and deeply rousing. So why did Churchill, who was so intentional with his language, deliberately choose such dramatic verbal imagery? Because he knew that this was exactly what was needed at that pivotal moment in history. When this speech was delivered on May 28, 1940, Poland, Holland, Czechoslovakia, Belgium, and France had all fallen, and Britain, now alone, faced the near-certain prospect of invasion and defeat. Most of the political leaders of the time saw no hope and wanted to surrender, but Churchill did not; he was convinced that Britain must fight on, to the bitter end if necessary, and the film does a wonderful job documenting this historic battle of ideologies. Churchill understood that to win the argument, he needed to mobilize both Parliament and the exhausted British people toward a heroic resistance, which would certainly have been needed had Hitler actually invaded. And language like this, with its power to rouse, was the way he did it.

This phrase, along with the better known "We will fight them on the beaches" speech, delivered seven days later, vividly demonstrates the power of language not simply to prevail in an argument, but to truly change the course of history. Britain rallied. They fought on, and ultimately, in partnership with their transatlantic and Russian allies, they *did* prevail. People often describe Churchill as "defiant"; here he uses language as the vehicle to export that defiance to an entire nation.

The very last line of the film is telling. Churchill wins the support of Parliament with his "We shall fight them on the beaches" speech, and someone asks Lord Halifax, "What just happened?" to which Halifax replies, "He mobilized the English language and sent it into battle." By the way, that line was also real, but American readers will love the fact that it wasn't Halifax who said it; it was American journalist Edward R. Murrow.

From a surprisingly early age, Churchill had a profound understanding of the power of language to underpin the great movements of history. In his essay, "The Scaffolding of Rhetoric," published at age twenty-three, he says, "Of all the talents bestowed upon men, none is so precious as the gift of oratory. He who enjoys it wields a power more durable than that of a great king. He is an independent force in the world." It's fascinating to consider that when he wrote those words, he had no way of knowing that forty years later, his own rhetoric would help save the free world.

If you feel you can't relate to Churchill (and who can?), it's worth remembering that he was far from a natural speaker. He fought a lifelong struggle with a lisp and a stammer, and he suffered from both paralyzing nerves and frequent crises of self-confidence. In other words, he was a lot like most of us. Where he was different was that he pushed himself; by great effort and focus, he cultivated his linguistic skill in pursuit of his career and leadership goals. That same path is open to all of us.

And Then There Was Hitler

I'd love to leave this introduction entirely with the memory of Churchill, because in addition to his communication skill, he was also clearly on the side of "right." Sadly, there are important lessons in the darker side of the story as well.

Adolf Hitler was an equally masterful orator who also clearly understood the importance of language in rallying others to his cause.

In his book, *Mein Kampf* ("My Struggle"), published in 1925, there's a chilling observation that would foreshadow a terrible future: "I know that men are won over less by the written than by the spoken word, and that every great movement on this earth owes its growth to great orators and not to great writers." And his actions certainly followed this belief: in his twelve years at the helm of the Third Reich, he delivered over five thousand speeches, a staggering number for a politician of that time. His words were also highly effective, successfully persuading a hesitant people to unite behind his deranged agenda. The German population of the 1930s was in no way inherently evil or bloodthirsty. They were certainly bruised and angered by the outcome of the First World War, but they absolutely weren't looking for another war. Consequently, it can be argued that Hitler's achievement was a greater example of the power of oratory than even that of Churchill.

But somewhere in our souls, we don't like this line of reasoning because its implications are too dark and frightening. It's easy to love language for its role in supporting the cause of peace and justice. It's harder to love language when we see it enlist an entire nation into a crusade of brutality, destruction, and genocide.

A Collision of Rhetorical Giants

Given how rare great oratory is, it's oddly curious that two absolute masters of the spoken word would be pitted directly against each other at this poignant moment in history. While the real battles were unquestionably fought by men and women in bloody fields all over the world, there's no doubt that the language of these towering leaders played an immense role in the forming and shaping of the two sides, and in the ultimate outcome of the conflict. But while they wielded similar rhetorical weapons, their motivations could not have been further apart. Churchill loved his people. As he once said, "They were the lions, I had the roar." In contrast, Hitler once wrote that repetition in speeches was important because the people were stupid. Hitler's use of rhetoric arose from a darker place: a deep, underlying disrespect for the people he would lead, and ultimately betray.

Beyond the Second World War, history is filled with examples where language was employed to such great effect that the words themselves have become etched into the national consciousness. The pinnacle from US history is President Lincoln's Gettysburg address, delivered in November 1863, and which, at a shocking 272 words, lasted less than three minutes. (Apparently, the photographer was still setting up when Lincoln sat down, which is why we don't have any pictures.) As an example of language effectively mobilized, it is simply unmatched, as this short extract demonstrates: "But, in a larger sense, we cannot dedicate, we cannot consecrate, we cannot hallow this ground. The brave men, living and dead, who struggled here, have consecrated it, far above our poor power to add or detract." While the Gettysburg Address stands out, almost all of Lincoln's speeches exhibit a similar level of linguistic skill.

Alongside political speeches, certain social speeches have risen to the same level, and Dr. Martin Luther King's 1963 "I Have a Dream" speech is among the most enduring. While it contains possibly the most famous line in American oratory, if you go back and read the transcript, the entire seventeen minutes contains some of the most beautiful and powerful language you will ever encounter. And even the seemingly mundane business world can be touched with the same power. Steve Jobs was rightly recognized as a contemporary rhetorical genius, and one of the rare few from outside the political arena. I always appreciated his speaking, but it surprised me to learn that this wasn't just raw ability. He deliberately used several classical rhetorical devices in many of his legendary product launch presentations, some of which we'll discuss in the next chapter.

The mistake we make with eloquence is to think that it is somehow confined to great moments of history. Certainly, these stand apart, and rightly so because they have defined the course of nations. But in truth, great eloquence is everywhere. It may not be celebrated, but it's there on display in all walks of everyday life—whether in a stunning best-man speech, a heated argument between friends in a pub, or a sensitive farewell retirement address. And it absolutely plays a role in the typical business presentation. There's a legitimate place for eloquence, even in the humble world of the Tuesday morning staff briefing.

THE IMPACT OF LANGUAGE UPON THE AUDIENCE

To understand how to upgrade your language in a practical way, it's important to dig beneath the generic idea that "language has power," and explore the specific ways in which language acts upon an audience. While I'm oversimplifying, the operational power of language lies in three things:

➤ People enjoy great language;

➤ People judge speakers based on language;

➤ But most importantly, people act in response to great language.

People Enjoy Great Language

David Crystal is a British professor of linguistics. In his outstanding book on eloquence, *The Gift of the Gab,* he makes the point that language has the power to delight its hearers, because people take pleasure in the skillful manipulation of words in much the same way they take pleasure in the skillful manipulation of paint or stone that creates great physical art. This intuitively makes sense: while language has no physical form, we've already seen that it has the same power to move people as might Michelangelo's *David* or Picasso's *Guernica.* Poetry is a high form of art, yet composed only of words; and to me, countless music lyrics (especially those of Roger Waters of Pink Floyd) represent true artistic achievement. Crystal goes on to say that eloquence is above all an appeal to "our aesthetic sensibility"; in other words, our inherent love for beauty. We don't tend to think of spoken language as an art form, probably because it lacks a physical form, but its ability to move us is no less compelling.

Why does all this matter? Because this isn't merely some philosophical reflection; from a practical standpoint, it can only help if a presenter's use of language brings a certain pleasure to their audience, and more importantly, language that elevates the audience's experience is going to be more memorable, even when it's used in an everyday setting. Recently, at a quarterly business review, I wanted to convey to my team just how much I felt they had accomplished in a time of very heavy workload. It was a simple idea and an ordinary meeting, and there was nothing particularly special about the occasion, but I chose to make the point by means of a line from a famous poem:

"Every morn brought forth a noble chance, and every chance brought forth a noble knight."

The idea I was trying to communicate was that I felt that every day recently had presented a big challenge (the noble chance), and every single time, on each of those days, someone on our team had stepped up to that challenge (brought forth a noble knight).[5] Was this a little bit over the top? Of course, as evidenced by a few good-natured "What the heck are you talking about?" comments. And that was just fine. Moments like that are intentionally more fun than serious. But here's the point:

> I could have simply thanked them for their hard work, but expressed this way, the idea landed far more powerfully.

The point was both understood and appreciated at the time and, crucially, many months later it was one of the few moments from our retreat people remembered.

Don't be afraid to move in this direction; people love language that's used a little bit more imaginatively. Of course, the corollary is also true—when language is bland, pedestrian, and unimaginative, it might convey information adequately, but it does nothing to engage aesthetic sensibility and is immediately forgettable. You don't want to be that presenter.

People Judge Speakers Based on Language

One particularly interesting aspect of language is that, however justified or unjustified, audiences are apt to make sweeping judgments concerning speakers based solely on the language they use. In particular, vocabulary is often equated to intelligence, probably through

---

[5] By the way, Churchill used this exact line to convey his immense gratitude to the pilots of the Battle of Britain (that's where I found it), although he did not write it. He actually adapted it from a poem by Tennyson titled "Le Morte D'Arthur," changing the wording slightly to make it fit. Only Churchill could pull that off.

the inferred link of education. There isn't much research on this topic, but I was able to turn up one fascinating older study from the *Duke Law Journal*, looking at the legal system in the US, which set out to evaluate the way witnesses' use of language influenced the jurors who heard them. In this 1974 study, more than 150 hours of courtroom testimony were taped and analyzed by Duke researchers. Based on the specific language patterns they had used, the witnesses were sorted into two categories—those who used "powerless speech" and those who used "powerful speech." The findings were shocking: the study found that when witnesses used powerless speech as they gave their testimony, it significantly affected whether they were perceived by the jury as:

➤ Convincing   ➤ Intelligent

➤ Believable   ➤ Trustworthy

➤ Competent

> **What's most noteworthy here is that these perceptions had nothing to do with the quality of the testimony itself. The judgment stemmed ONLY from the language that the witnesses had used to express that testimony.**

It's understandable that jurors might form an opinion on a witness's intelligence based on their language, but the idea that trustworthiness and believability are also being assessed is shocking, and a clue that much more may be at stake in our language than we realize. Given that trustworthiness and believability are important characteristics for any speaker to cultivate, it's worth looking at the language that seemed to undermine them.

"Powerless speech" was characterized by the frequent use of modifying words and expressions that convey a lack of forcefulness in speaking. The five reported attributes of "powerless speech" were:

> **Hedge phrases,** like "I think," "you know," "kinda," and "sorta."

> **Hesitation forms,** words that hold no meaning but create pauses, like "uh," "um," and "well."

> **Overly polite forms,** words like "sir" and "please."

> **Question intonation,** or making a declarative statement with rising intonation, which conveys uncertainty. This is now often referred to as "uptalk," where the speaker ends every phrase on a rising note.

> **Weak Intensifiers,** words to exaggerate emphasis such as "very" and "definitely."

It's telling that these speech elements were identified as more common among those of little social power. In contrast, powerful speech was a more straightforward and direct manner of testifying, with many fewer of these weak modifying expressions in view. It was the greater use of powerless speech that led to the view that these witnesses were less believable and less trustworthy. Indeed, jurors perceived the witnesses who used powerless speech as less competent overall than their more "powerful" counterparts.[6]

As old as it is, I think this study contains two vital lessons for today. First, while the use of specific language has changed over the years, there's no doubt that similar weak forms of speech still exist (including "like" and "you know"), which presenters would do well

---

[6] If you'd like to read it, the study reference is: https://scholarship.law.duke.edu/cgi/viewcontent.cgi?article=2686&context=dlj

to avoid. In fact, most of this study's powerless speech forms are still an issue today: here in 2019, political bias aside, President Trump is routinely criticized for his frequent use of the word "very" in his speaking and tweets. "Very" is still viewed as a generally weak intensifier in both spoken and written English. Second, and more broadly, this study points to a surely permanent truth.

> **Every time you open your mouth, and particularly in the public spotlight of a presentation, important aspects of your character are being judged based on the type of language you use, and not on the content of what you say.**

The good news is that generally, this isn't a problem: regular, commonplace language is what people are expecting, and audiences aren't drawing any conclusions from this at all. You have to start throwing out some serious grammatical blunders for it to become an issue, although if you use the powerless word "like" six times in every sentence, you may be getting close. More importantly, if you're able to use a slightly more elevated vocabulary, employing stronger, more powerful, and more imaginative language, this is likely to have a positive effect on your audience—creating valuable perceptions of intelligence, trustworthiness, and credibility.

The Strange Case of the Africa Scam

Perhaps the strangest evidence that people judge communicators by their language is a bizarre reversal of the usual principle. There's one situation I'm aware of where writers deliberately use shockingly flawed language *precisely* because they want to be judged and rejected by more sophisticated readers. I'm talking about the famed Africa scam, a recent example of which from my own inbox follows:

> "This is to officially inform you that we have written to you before without getting a respond from you and we believe that our previous mail did not get to you therefore we write you again.The United Nations Compensation Commission payment exercise has deposited your payment of (US$ 2.5,million US dollars with BANK OF AFRICA,This is regarding the draws the Secretary General Antoni Gutters organized on his visit to Africa to help individuals/Internet Scam victims and charity organization which your Email address was listed among those who are to benefit from the compensation exercise."

And so it goes on. I'm sure you've received your share of these crazy emails, where the fabulously incorrect language is so comical that you wouldn't give the fake offer so much as a second look. But if you've ever thought that these scammers are stupid to write so poorly, because a better-worded offer would surely sucker more people, you'd be wrong. They're not stupid at all; they understand how language is evaluated, and the obvious mistakes are a deliberate tactic designed to weed out more educated readers who instantly see through the scam. **That rejection is exactly what they want, because that's not who they're after. Sophisticated people won't send them money. They're**

fishing for the gullible. The people they are targeting are primarily the elderly, who are less likely to see through the grammatical errors and are therefore more prone to be drawn in, and, sadly, those are precisely the people they regularly do ensnare. As morally repulsive as this is, it's fascinating proof that people do infer things about communicators from the language they use, which in this case can be used in reverse to deliberately eliminate the more sophisticated reader, thereby giving criminals a clean shot at the naïve.

People Act on Great Language

Most important for the communicator is the fact that humans are motivated and inspired to take action based on great language. History is filled with examples of people being drawn by great speakers to enlist in a cause. You will recall Churchill's line: "If this long island story of ours is to end—at last—let it end only when each of us lies choking in his own blood upon the ground." Had I been one of those original listeners, I can absolutely imagine responding by wanting to take my place on the battlefield. I hope I would have been brave enough. Similarly, great movements of social action have often been underpinned by great oratory. Lincoln's speeches pleading for the end of slavery, and the great Civil Rights speakers of the 1960s calling people to stand against injustice and inequality, come most clearly to mind.

And again, this doesn't only take place on the national stage. I've met countless individuals who have taken some major step in their lives based on a speaker they've heard, and one of the most powerful places where this is seen is the tradition (held in much higher regard in the US than elsewhere) of the graduation or commencement address. As a parent of four adult children, I've heard several of these speeches, and on more than one occasion have been personally moved by the call of the speaker. In 2005, Steve Jobs delivered a legendary commencement speech at Stanford entitled "Stay Hungry, Stay Foolish," and to this day people report having their lives completely changed by this one speech. It's still studied from a rhetorical perspective.

Tragically, language has a similar power to motivate people toward evil action, as we saw with the effectiveness of Hitler's anti-Jewish rhetoric. And sadly, even today, the connection between hateful speech and violence lives on. As the *New York Times* reported[7], it seems likely that when Facebook failed to prevent hate speech aimed at the Rohingya people in Myanmar, it was a partial driver of the genocide that was unleashed upon them. Similar concerns are now being raised about anti-Semitism proliferating via social media in the US. In October 29, 2018, Zach Schapira of Reuters wrote, "Generation after generation, demagogues have poisoned minds, but society still underestimates the ability of words to arouse action." And that's the central idea: whether the setting is global or individual, **words arouse action.**

HARNESSING THE POWER OF LANGUAGE

People delight in language, they judge speakers based on language, and they act in response to language. That being the case, how do you, in an everyday setting, actually craft language that will have these effects? It's simpler than it appears.

---

[7] https://www.nytimes.com/2018/10/15/technology/myanmar-facebook-genocide.html

The Answer Is "Muscular Language"

For the everyday presenter, the goal isn't the high and lofty language of "choking in his own blood upon the ground." Rather, the aim is to simply find the best possible words and phrases for any given situation. As Churchill also wrote in his "The Scaffolding of Rhetoric" essay:

> **"There is no more important element in the technique of rhetoric than the continual employment of the best possible word."**

The general aim here is that you should be looking to employ "muscular language," which is best explained by the graphic below. As you see on the X-axis, words can be generally understood or not generally understood, and on the Y-axis, words can be in common use, or not in common use. Every word therefore falls into one of the four (actually three) categories.

THE MUSCULARITY MATRIX

	GOAL	UNACCEPTABLE
Not Commonly Used	MUSCULAR SPEECH *Impactful and Memorable* Example: "Minuscule"	INCOMPREHENSIBLE SPEECH *No One Will Get It* Example: "Mellifluous"
	ACCEPTABLE	DOESN'T EXIST
Commonly Used	EVERYDAY SPEECH *Fine, but Forgettable* Example: "Small"	(If a word is commonly used, by definition everyone understands it.)
	Generally Understood	Not Generally Understood

(Y-axis label: Levels of Usage)

Level of Comprehension

There's nothing wrong with everyday speech in the lower left. If your words are understandable and in common use, it's going to work—it's just not going to be working very hard. Muscular language, however, differs from everyday speech by being that little bit more imaginative and interesting, and the way you get that is by using words that are in slightly less common use. That's the upper left quadrant, and the presenter's general aim. While an everyday word like "small" will work, more muscular words like "minuscule," "meager," or "modest" will work more powerfully on your behalf. You just need to avoid going over the top. If you stray into the upper right—often by trying to impress—you cross the comprehension boundary line, which you cannot do. If you're incomprehensible, not only is that an obvious problem in itself, but you'll also come across as irritating and pompous. Muscular language should be slightly, though not dramatically, different from ordinary, everyday speech, yet without sending people scurrying for the dictionary. And it's not for every sentence. You aren't looking for something erudite in each breath, but you *are* looking for a fairly constant peppering of interesting language into otherwise workmanlike speech, and you generally want to use it for your more important ideas.

> **Muscular Language is the presenter's goal, especially for their more important points and ideas. It is that language that is in less common use (and therefore somewhat more erudite), which makes it interesting and memorable, but which is, at the same time, fully understood.**

If you think it sounds paradoxical to be both unusual and comprehensible, it's not. There's an almost limitless supply of words that aren't in particularly common use, but that are perfectly well under-stood by most people. You probably don't use the words "minuscule," "atrocious," or "breathtaking" that often, because everyday language naturally defaults to simplicity. But you know what they mean. When used in the right context, your audience will both understand and enjoy them, and you'll sound a good deal smarter. Don't be afraid to use more of the richness of our language: just be careful to avoid anything that your gut tells you is not generally understood. And if in doubt, test it on someone. As a rule, if you understand the word, the chances are most other people will, especially if you use it in proper context, because that's where words derive much of their meaning. Mellifluous is a great word, for example, but you probably shouldn't use it. I'm not being condescending. I actually have no idea what it means.

An everyday example will bring the concept of muscular language to life. Imagine you've discovered a wide gap between your company's actual and projected revenues, and it's not a good gap. When presenting, you could easily describe this as "a very wide gap." This wouldn't be wrong in any sense, and it would perfectly express the idea. But it's still an anemic phrase. Thanks to thirty seconds and an online thesaurus, we find that better alternatives would be:

- A troublingly wide gap
- A historically wide gap
- An alarmingly wide gap
- A frighteningly wide gap
- A disturbingly wide gap
- A shockingly wide gap
- An unexpectedly wide gap

Or, if you want to add the power of a metaphor, you might go with, "A canyon-like gap." (Or if you want to have a little fun, go with "A French-to-English gap.") And if you want to mess with the noun as well, because "gap" is a little pedestrian, it gets even more powerful: "There is an **alarming chasm** between where we are and where we wanted to be." As simple as this everyday example is, four extremely important lessons emerge.

> ➤ **First:** Do you see how easy this was? It's literally a minute's work with a thesaurus. It takes very little effort to improve your language, but there's a very high return on that effort. Sorry: there's an **enormously** high return on that effort.

> ➤ **Second:** Notice that all these alternatives are absolutely guaranteed to be understood. This is the most important point. There's a lot of maneuvering room here—you can be vastly more interesting in your use of language, but still never come close to creating a problem of comprehension.

> ➤ **Third:** I hope you can hear how each option is richer and more impactful than the basic "very." Each creates a better, more memorable phrase, without being pompous or arrogant. Remember, people like the skillful manipulation of language. Do you need a certain confidence to use language that's a bit more elevated? A little, perhaps, but give yourself permission. Once you've tried it, any concerns will subside. You'll enjoy using it, and your audience will enjoy hearing it.

> ➤ **Fourth:** Notice also how each alternative contains a far more nuanced meaning. "Troublingly wide" suggests a meaningfully different idea ("We need to worry about this") than does "unexpectedly wide" ("We never saw this coming") or "historically wide" ("We've never seen this

before"). These are meanings you simply don't get with the vanilla "very," and those are the meanings you want to go for. Put another way, you aren't simply looking for a better word, but a word that also contains the exact sentiment you want to convey. I can't stress enough how important this aspect of muscular language is, because it isn't only about looking smarter, it's also about your argument getting clearer and more precise. One great virtue of the English language is its enormous breadth. You almost always have alternatives that are muscular, but that also carry more precise meaning, allowing you to express a richer, more nuanced thought, without necessarily using more words.

A slightly more extensive vocabulary will have a notable impact on your communication effectiveness. Interestingly, it's estimated that Churchill had a vocabulary around twice the size of his contemporaries': somewhere around 65,000 words compared to his peers' 25,000, which was surely a contributing factor in his success. And as you think about deploying a more imaginative vocabulary, let me address one final concern: don't worry. As long as you don't cross the comprehension line, you aren't going to make people feel dumb or intimidated. In fact, the reverse is true. Aside from actually enjoying the richer and more nuanced language, at some level, your audience loves to learn. When your presentation contains a slight element of linguistic education, that's a positive.

Here are a few examples to get started and to show you how easy this is. As you see these typical words and their superior alternatives, think about how any of these would improve a presented sentence.

Samples of Muscular Language

Weak Words	Stronger Equivalents
get	acquire, obtain, secure, accumulate
put	place, attach, establish, assign
help	aid, assist, support
show	display, exhibit, present, indicate
begin	open, launch, initiate
decide	determine, settle, choose, resolve
boring	dull, tiring, unimaginative
explain	elaborate, clarify, interpret
great	noteworthy, distinguished, remarkable
interesting	fascinating, engaging, provocative
make	create, construct, design
say	inform, notify, advise

GETTING PRACTICAL:
HOW TO DEVELOP MUSCULAR LANGUAGE

If it seems daunting to develop your use of language by broadening your vocabulary, it truly isn't. It may require a bit of intentional effort, but the tools themselves are quite simple.

LANGUAGE, PART I | 237

Use a Thesaurus

Everyone wants the easy way out. This is it, and there's nothing wrong with it. A thesaurus allows you to get the exact result you're looking for with practically no effort, and there are dozens of websites that will locate synonyms for a word you've already identified. Whenever I'm writing or working on a presentation, I'll commonly take a bland word I'm struggling with and search for synonyms of it. Without fail, I'll find several I can plug in. (I've already done this a dozen times in this chapter alone). Typically, pondering a list of synonyms is an interesting exercise because you'll first identify several that might work, then instinctively you'll begin to screen them, first for whether they're usable or not (because they're too obscure), and second for whether they convey exactly the right meaning.

Read More (of the Right People)

This one takes some effort, but it's worth it—although, for most people, reading good writers isn't work at all; we've simply forgotten to make time to do it. If you really want to develop a broader vocabulary, nothing comes close to the practice of immersing yourself in great writing. Older writing is wonderful, but past a certain point, the language may have changed so much that the vocabulary no longer applies. So to me, modern but elegant writers are the answer. Above all, I recommend Alain de Botton. His books are not only wonderful guidebooks to life, but they also contain some of the richest and most elegant language you're likely to encounter, yet used in a modern way. For breadth of language, you can't go wrong with Ernest Hemingway, John Steinbeck, and Herman Melville (his book *Moby Dick* uses about seventeen thousand unique words). And of course, for pure unsurpassed beauty of language, the not-yet out-of-date J.R.R. Tolkien and *The Lord of the Rings*.

Read the Dictionary

I worry about recommending this one, because the only precedent you may have for it is White Goodman, the obnoxious owner of Globo Gym in the movie *Dodgeball*, who reads the dictionary because "I like to work up a mental sweat, too." Unfortunately, while he's a jerk, the practice is quite sound.

Notice What You Hear

I said earlier that eloquence is everywhere. It's hard to get through a day without being exposed to some speaker on YouTube, a podcast, or a news broadcast. Now, given the general decline of language in recent years, most of these are going to be painfully bad, but from time to time you hear something amazing.

Write It Down

However you source it, whether it's intentionally reading, You-Tubing, or simply noticing, have a place where you write this new language down. I keep one to-do list that isn't actually a to-do list; it contains interesting phrases or words I've picked up, and it's surprising how often these find their way into my future speech. Perhaps I'm a geek in this area (a geek with a large vocabulary), but in my view this kind of learning is intentional and doesn't happen by accident. To my list I recently added the phrase "the law of unintended consequences," and I've begun using it in several places, describing any negative side effects of some other phenomenon. Where did I get it? I was actually watching ESPN's *First Take*, and Max Kellerman said it in relation to some issue in college sports regulations. I wasn't particularly interested in that, but the phrase does have some useful applications in my world.

Absolutely Avoid Overused Language and Clichés

Many speakers hurt themselves by using phrases that are so tired they've lost all meaning, rather like a song you've heard too many times. Phrases come and go, and while describing a particularly nasty confluence of events as "the perfect storm" might have been okay for a short period, at this point in history it's become so hackneyed that it only weakens your narrative. At best, clichés wash over people with little effect; at worst, they suggest the speaker is lazy or unimaginative. At that point they become more negative than neutral in their effect, because I think people take subtle note that the speaker couldn't come up with anything better—at least, I do. The rule is, if you've heard it a lot, don't use it. You always have an abundance of wonderful alternatives; you simply need to take a moment to look for them. Consider my current most despised phrase in the business lexicon (which I hope you will never, ever use again): taking something "to the next level." This phrase is so grossly overused that I feel like I hear it daily in some new context. And yet, with just a few minutes' thought and the Googling of a couple of synonyms, we find a rich array of better alternatives: "We are taking our business to . . .

➢ a higher elevation

➢ a new altitude

➢ a higher altitude

➢ a new dimension

➢ a higher dimension

➢ the next season

➢ our next era of achievement

➤ a new plateau

➤ lofty new heights (peaks)

➤ a higher plane

➤ a new season of accomplishment / fruitfulness / abundance / prosperity

These alternatives are all richer and more interesting, while still being perfectly understandable. And again, each conveys something slightly different, which allows you to be much more precise. "The next level" is a meaningless term, but "a new era of achievement" conveys a precise idea. When you set out to be more interesting, the byproduct is that you're also going to be far more clear.

Rehearse and "Groove"

When you've found the exact word you want, get it into your speaker notes and remember to rehearse, because that's how you get comfortable with new language. What's interesting is that once you've started using that word, it will tend to stick in your brain, and in this way your overall practical vocabulary (words you actually use, not just words you know) expands. Suddenly and without noticing, you will find yourself saying "tremendously" instead of "very" quite naturally. And there it is—you've taken your vocabulary to the next level (pun intended).

Subtly Define Where Needed

When you're using language you think might not be entirely clear to everyone in your audience, but where you still want to use it, a valuable practice is to subtly define it as you say it. "Synthesis" is a good example. Not everyone fully understands it, but it's an essential word we need to use when we're teaching people about how the left and right hemispheres of the brain function. Hence, when we first use it, the phrasing will be something like, "So the left brain does analysis, breaking things apart, whereas the right brain does synthesis, taking the pieces and putting them back together." No one will be insulted by that, because what I'm doing is so subtle they don't even notice, but it allows me to use a word they didn't originally understand. This invaluable practice gives you the ability to employ language that's rich, even straying beyond comprehension, but without running the risk of losing anyone. In fact, most people like the exposure to the broader vocabulary when it's explained. Remember, people like to learn.

Use Powerful Phrasing . . . And the Magic of Ten Syllables

Beyond individual words, phrasing is important, and especially so for key ideas that you want to emphasize. Both brain science and history demonstrate that phrases of about ten syllables have a structure that the brain loves and finds sticky. For this reason, a lot of poetry, and the majority of Shakespeare, is written in this ten-syllable form. It has a horrible name, "iambic pentameter," which simply means ten syllables with stresses on the alternate syllable, as in de-DUM de-DUM de-DUM de-DUM de-DUM—or "Once more unto the breach, dear friends, once more." I don't want to get us too far down the rat hole of iambic pentameter, but this type of phrasing has been said to be the exact way English speech wants to happen, and too many syllables, more or less, doesn't work quite as well. Shakespeare didn't invent it; it was well known before he ever put quill to parchment, but boy, he knew how to make it work. Ponder the closing lines of Romeo and Juliet, when they're all lying dead on the floor and the herald emerges to close things out:

> A glooming peace this morning with it brings;
> The sun, for sorrow, will not show his head:
> Go hence, to have more thought of these sad things;
> Some will be pardoned and some punish-ed:
> For never was a story of more woe
> Than this is Juliet and her Romeo.

This is incredibly powerful, with an added element of poetry. But even when the writing isn't poetic, it's just as powerful. When you start looking for this form, you see it showing up in lots of places where the author or speaker wants to make a seriously important point. If you're a lover of *Lord of the Rings*, you may have noticed that Tolkien reserves iambic pentameter for some of his best lines:

> "Not lightly do the leaves of Lorien fall."
> "And smote his ruin upon the mountainside."
> "The blade that cut the ring from Sauron's hand."

Setting classic literature aside, many contemporary speakers make deliberate use of this form, because it's easy to utilize and just as powerful today. When we teach our class, one of the most important single lines in the day is: "Ideas are the traffic of the mind." I deliver that phrase exactly and deliberately, and I note that almost everyone writes it down. In similar fashion, we were recently working with a client in the electrical utility industry who was seeking a rate increase to fund some large investments in wind and solar power. That entire set of messages to politicians, regulators, and the general public was based on one big idea: "The grid we have is not the grid we need." Pure Shakespeare. I wouldn't contort myself to force an important line into the ten-syllable format, but if I were trying to get a key idea across, I'd certainly spend a few moments seeing whether it could be well captured this way.

This discussion of the phrasing of big ideas opens up the topic of rhetoric, which we'll explore in detail in the next chapter, but for now the lesson is this: for any key idea, reduce it to a great phrase of about ten syllables, and if you can get it to exactly ten in iambic pentameter, you've got it exactly right. You'll feel good and your audience will notice.

Your dad would have been very proud today.

We will not let this moment pass us by.

I love the way this team does not back down.

It's a good skill to have in your back pocket, and when you use one well, and see it resonate . . . you will enjoy the moment when it comes. (See what I did there?)

Pre-Test

Whenever you're developing a presentation of any significance, it's usually worth pre-testing it on people who aren't going to be in the real audience. Friends, colleagues, and spouses are fine; in addition to helping you refine your core argument, they're a great test of your language. I recommend pushing the boat out a bit further with your language when you're testing it, because you can always dial it back later if someone thinks you've gone too far. But it's surprising how often more imaginative language gets high marks from your test audience. Not only is this a good way to check whether you've pitched your language at the right level, but it also boosts your confidence that it's going to be well received.

FINAL THOUGHT: LANGUAGE WITH SUBSTANCE, NOT LANGUAGE OVER SUBSTANCE

While I hope this chapter has encouraged you to broaden your linguistic horizons, when it comes to communication, you must never let language replace substance. Just as we saw with great presentation "style," even the most elegant language won't overcome a deficiency in content—it's the ideas that matter most, and without the ideas the rhetoric will be hollow and shallow. Which is precisely why **the great moments in rhetoric are ALSO, by definition, great moments in ideas.** When Lincoln spoke the words, "that government of the people, by the people, for the people, shall not perish from the Earth" it was captivating language, but it was also a towering idea. Likewise, "I have a dream" isn't just a catchphrase. Its underlying idea is colossal: a vision of a future where centuries of prejudice and persecution have ended. So, in practice, be careful not to let the language draw attention to itself. As beautiful as the language can and should be, let the ideas be the central focus, and have the language draw attention to those. Remember our thesis: "A word aptly spoken is like apples of gold in settings of silver."

Language matters. It's going to make a
difference, so stretch yourself:
Don't be afraid to be interesting.

CHAPTER 17

Language, Part II: Rediscovering Rhetoric

AN INTRODUCTION TO RHETORIC

No discussion of the use of language in presentations would be complete without an examination of rhetoric, which at its simplest can be defined as "the art of persuasion," or "skill in the effective use of speech." The principles and tenets of rhetoric were first documented by the ancient Greeks as early as the fifth century BC, and the topic continues to be studied to the present day. It's easy to understand why the interest persists: for reasons that are hard to explain, the human brain has a particular love for certain types, or *patterns*, of language, and communicators have always been fascinated by the idea of harnessing the power of these hidden patterns to their advantage. Consider the following two phrases, which communicate precisely the same idea:

> **"There's probably never been a time in any war, where a whole people was as grateful to just a small number of their soldiers as we are today."**

— or —

> **"Never in the field of human conflict was so much owed by so many to so few."**

Which of these two versions works better? Even if you can't articulate why, I'm certain you felt that the second was more powerful, and if you did, you were right; that's why Churchill chose it as his way to honor the pilots of the Battle of Britain. It prevails because it works on the brain in a different way, and I'll explain later exactly how it got under your skull.

Rhetoric is simply the study of the various devices that make phrases like this not only special but more effective. It attempts both to catalog all these patterns, and to teach us how they may be used to strengthen the verbal quality of an argument. In one *New York Times* article, Mark Forsythe describes rhetoric as: "little tricks that don't change the meaning of a sentence but make it more memorable."

I like that.

THE PROBLEM WITH RHETORIC

Given that rhetoric has the potential to make our communication substantially more effective, you'd think everyone would dig into it with gusto. But they don't; most people shy away from it. So, what's the problem with rhetoric? Actually, there are three.

Problem One: It's Irrelevant and Impenetrable, a.k.a., "What the Hell Is Zeugma?"

If you don't know anything else about rhetoric, you probably know that it all started thousands of years ago with strange dudes like Socrates and Aristotle wandering around Greece in flowing white robes, giving speeches while holding one hand in the air. As a result, it can be legitimately hard for today's iPhone-toting executive to see how something so ancient and weird could possibly connect to the modern world in a meaningful way. And beyond being ridiculously old, it certainly doesn't help that the Greeks got to name things, because many of those names survive, some of which are absurdly unhelpful. There's no doubt that you can battle through this, but for most of us, the time it would take to figure out "Epizeuxis" or "Zeugma" seems like time we could better spend on other things.

But that's a tragedy (might I say a *Greek* tragedy? Yuk yuk yuk) because when you understand what rhetoric is and how it can help, you find that not only is it absolutely relevant to today's communication, but even better, most of the devices are simple to understand and use, once you get past the crazy names. "Anadiplosis" might sound like that weird girl your brother dated in college, but it's actually a great tool that's effective, fun, and childishly easy to apply. **Once demystified, rhetoric is both simple to use and of enormous value to a modern presenter, however far from ancient Greece today's world of finance, legal, or operations might appear to be.**

A topless old guy with his arm in the air.
How exactly does that help me today?

Problem Two: So Many Devices. Which Ones Matter?

By some counts, there are over 140 rhetorical devices. Most books describe them all, but even when they don't, any book on rhetoric worth its cover price will list out and describe at least sixty. While that might make the book academically rigorous (and give it enough pages to be sellable), that's incredibly unhelpful for the average person, because trying to get your head around even sixty tools is still overwhelming. Furthermore, it's quite clear that these tools are not all equally valuable. While some are both powerful and easy to apply, others are so complex that even the greatest communicators have struggled to use them effectively. All of which raises the question that most students of rhetoric eventually ask: "If all these devices aren't created equal, which ones really matter and are worth learning to use?" That question deserves an answer.

Problem Three: It's "of the Academics, by the Academics, for the Academics"

The final problem is that the topic of rhetoric has historically been owned by academia, and as a result, I don't think it's been made nearly relevant enough for modern business people and the settings in which they work. It would be perfectly possible for someone to study rhetoric today, but thanks to the academic slant, while they might understand "antimetabole" at a theoretical level and see how the device was used by Tennyson or Milton, they still wouldn't know how to use it to strengthen their next quarterly business review.

As a result of these three problems, most presenters today simply ignore rhetoric and the many potential benefits it might bestow upon them. All over the world, thousands of executives are preparing for upcoming board presentations, and I guarantee that 99 percent of them (at least) won't give even a moment's thought to how a good isocolon might help them achieve a more successful outcome. But that's the wrong way to think; in virtually any setting, it is supremely valuable to be able to take a drab, uninteresting sentence and convert it into something of stunning memorability and stickiness.

DEMYSTIFYING RHETORIC: A THREE-PRONGED APPROACH

The good news is, all of these problems can be solved. While the topic of rhetoric is actually quite broad, encompassing things like vocal delivery and memorization, what I want to focus on are the figures of speech themselves: the ways you can actually craft language to improve your argument. Specifically, I want to demystify the subject in three ways: Reduction, Explanation, and Application.

Reduction

I'm going to boil the 140 known devices down to the handful I believe are the most powerful and relevant for a modern-day presenter. As I've studied communication and observed some of the world's greatest communicators, I see the same few tools showing up over and over again in their work. This is the "Letterman Top 10" we're going to dig into. At some point in the future, I may get punched in the face by some self-obsessed rhetoric professor for daring to suggest that you can live a happy life without embracing "catachresis," but it's a risk I'm willing to take.

Evidence suggests that rhetoric follows the classic 80–20 pattern: i.e., that a small number of rhetorical concepts are all you need to substantially boost your effectiveness. Interestingly, among academics there's quite a lot of disagreement about rhetorical terms. Some of the devices I'll describe are also known by other names, and some aren't always classified as true rhetorical devices at all. I don't really care. It's on the list because it works.

It's Personal

One health warning: while I've taken a thorough look at a wide range of rhetorical devices in search of the most powerful, this is still a subjective, personal list, based on what I've seen that works for others and for me. But if you've found something else you like and that works for you, go right ahead and use it.

Explanation

Having narrowed the field, I'll provide plain English definitions and explanations of the chosen tools—especially those with impenetrable Greek names—to make sure it's easy to understand what they mean. At first glance, "epistrophe" would freak most people out, but "finishing a series of phrases with the same words each time" is within the grasp of a five-year-old . . . and that's all epistrophe is.

Application

In addition to providing historical examples, I want to make this review highly practical by showing you how to look for places where each device might be used in a presentation today, and by illustrating what that device will look (actually, sound) like when it shows up in an everyday setting. Most people will struggle to see how Julius Caesar relates to their world, but it all suddenly gets easier when you learn that the device that gave us "I came, I saw, I conquered" is the exact same one that gives us "We win with our product, we win with our service, and we win with our people."

Finally, as you dig into these, there's one thing I particularly want you to notice. There is frequently a certain rhythmic quality to rhetoric, and that's important. If you've ever wondered exactly *why* rhetoric works, that's the heart of the answer: the brain loves rhythms and patterns, and it attaches quickly to them, which is often what makes rhetorical structures so sticky. Consider the opening of Charles Dickens's *A Tale of Two Cities*:

> It was the best of times, it was the worst of times,
> it was the age of wisdom, it was the age of foolishness,
> it was the epoch of belief, it was the epoch of incredulity,
> it was the season of Light, it was the season of Darkness,
> it was the spring of hope, it was the winter of despair.

Do you hear the rhythm of the phrasing "It was the . . ." as it repeats twice in each clause? The author uses that lilting rhythm to draw us in as he walks through an interesting series of contrasting ideas. It's exactly the same effect that Barack Obama (a serious user of rhetoric) achieved in his 2008 Presidential election victory speech with his repeating use of "Yes we can." That phrase was repeated at the end of seven distinct clauses, and once the crowd had spotted the pattern, they joined the chant with gusto, adding great force to the rhythm of the repetition. That sense of pattern is something the brain loves and is a big part of rhetoric's power.

RHETORIC'S HALL OF FAME: THE TOP TEN TOOLS

How to Use the List

First, get generally familiar with the ten tools. They all have the potential to make your speech more impactful, so you want a basic understanding of each. Then, for any presentation you're working on, actively look for opportunities to use them, picking different ones based on setting, need, and opportunity. To help you with this, Appendix II provides a summary table listing each tool, along with an example (and is also downloadable at www.oratium.com/resources). If you can weave a little rhetoric in with little effort, then do so—and heaven knows, some of them are supremely easy to use. However, don't burn a morning trying to create the perfect isocolon. If it isn't coming to you, just move on. Unless you're writing your Nobel Prize acceptance speech, you probably have better things to do with that time.

Note that you don't want to use too much rhetoric in any single presentation. If you overuse rhetorical devices—whether by using one too often, or too many in total—you'll ruin everything because it'll sound weird and contrived, as though you're trying too hard. Your goal isn't to beautify every single sentence. Most of your language and phrasing will be workmanlike, which is actually why, when you do drop in a particularly poignant phrase, it really pops.

Because history tends to immortalize only the famous phrases, like "Ask not what your country can do for you—ask what you can do for your country," we tend to think that when great speakers open their mouths, nothing but pearls fly out. That's nonsense. If you read the full text of any great speech, the high rhetorical moments will certainly stand out, but the majority of it will simply have been solid (though hopefully muscular) language. So it should be with you.

> You aren't looking to make every phrase a gem;
> you're looking to craft a few gems at key moments.

And if you ever hear yourself rehearse and think your words have gotten heightened to the point of sounding pompous or absurd, then they probably have. Just dial it back and you'll be fine.

Tool #1: Antithesis

IN PLAIN ENGLISH: Setting two ideas against each other.

Antithesis is everywhere; it's easy to find, easy to use, and is a wonderfully powerful tool for any communicator. It creates ideas that are particularly sticky, and as you begin to tune your radar to antithesis, you start to see it sitting proudly at the center of some of history's most famous and memorable ideas, across an incredibly broad terrain, whether it's:

> ➤ *Philosophical* (Shakespeare/Hamlet): "To be or not to be? That is the question."

> ➤ *Political* (John F. Kennedy): "Ask not what your country can do for you—ask what you can do for your country."

> ➤ *Revolutionary* (Emiliano Zapata): "It is better to die on your feet than live on your knees."

> ➤ *Commercial* (M&Ms [called Chocolate Treets in the UK]): "They melt in your mouth, not in your hand."

> ➤ *Literary* (Charles Dickens, *A Tale of Two Cities*): "It was the best of times, it was the worst of times" (and the entire opening).

> ➤ *Reflective* (Winston Churchill): "I am always ready to learn, although I do not always like being taught."

> ➤ *Biblical* (*Ecclesiastes*): "Better a live dog than a dead lion."

➤ *Proverbial* (Alexander Pope): "To err is human; to forgive, divine."

➤ *Musical* (Billy Joel, "Only the Good Die Young"): "I'd rather laugh with the sinners than cry with the saints."

➤ *Cultural* (Neil Armstrong): "That's one small step for man, one giant leap for mankind."

➤ *Sporting* (Joe Louis): "You can run, but you can't hide."

➤ *Educational* (Antoine de Saint-Exupéry): "The designer has achieved perfection not when there is nothing more to add, but when there is nothing left to take away."

➤ *Instructive* (Patches O'Houlihan from the movie *Dodgeball*): "If you can dodge a wrench, you can dodge a ball."

➤ *Realistic* (The Who, "Won't Get Fooled Again"): "Meet the new boss / Same as the old boss."

➤ *Disturbing* (Jame Gumb, *The Silence of the Lambs*): "It rubs the lotion on its skin or else it gets the hose again."

➤ *Funny* (Shakespeare, Macbeth on alcohol and sex): "It provokes the desire but takes away the performance."

ANTITHESES MAKE YOU THINK. I'm sure you knew most or all of these, and that's what's so significant. Whether it's Shakespeare, Kennedy, or Patches, a good antithesis has an uncanny ability to stick in our memories.

But here's the question: why is this? The answer lies in the brain. Readers of my first book might remember the discussion of the respective roles of the left and right hemispheres of the brain, and the fact that the left brain "sees" pieces and parts, while the right brain "sees'" patterns and meaning. This is the reason why antithesis is so powerful: because it's dealt with in the right brain. Wrestling with the meaning of the antithesis and, in particular, untangling and reconciling the contrasting ideas is a challenge that only the right brain can take on and which it finds irresistible—and when you activate the right brain, information sticks. You see this in all of the prior examples, but to pick one: aren't you drawn to grapple with the seeming contradiction that lies within "I am always ready to learn, although I do not always like being taught"? How can both be true? But they are! You can't just fly past an antithesis like this. It makes you stop and think. "Do *I* like to learn? And if I do, why do I resist being taught? How odd." That's the magnetic power of antithesis.

In the traditional wedding ceremony, we are presented with a series of three thought-provoking contrasts:

> For better, for worse,
> In sickness and in health,
> For richer, for poorer.

Lovely as they are, once again, these contrasts compel us to reflect. What couple hasn't discussed: "Would you still love me if we lost everything?" or "Would I love you the same way if you were in a wheelchair?"

When Hemingway offers a classic antithesis like "Write drunk, edit sober," it's funny, but your right brain immediately goes to work pondering how drunkenness fosters creativity (up to a point, presumably), while sobriety fosters precision. By the way, I've proved his theory correct through years of careful research.

A truly extraordinary example comes from essayist and poet Heinrich Heine. Born in 1797, Heine is considered one of the most significant of the German romantic poets. He was also a Jew. In 1821, he wrote a play containing a line that chillingly anticipated what would come to pass over a hundred years later:

"Wherever they burn books,
in the end they will also burn people."[8]

Tragically, his prediction was fulfilled: The Nazis burned books in 1933, including Heine's books, and they were burning Jews less than ten years later. Aside from its extraordinary prophetic nature, it's another good example of the way antithesis forces you to think. "What kind of people burn books?"; "Does burning books signal more is to come?"; "If you're willing to burn your opponents' books, what else might you be capable of?" Antithesis draws people in: it's a potent way to get them to engage with a key idea.

PRACTICAL APPLICATION. Antithesis is the communicator's dream. It makes your ideas sticky, but it's also one of the easiest devices to find and use. Often you need to look no further than simply the alternatives your audience is facing:

> ➤ "If we come together as a team, we can get through this crisis. If we don't, it will tear us apart."

> ➤ "We can press on and succeed, or we can shrink back and fail."

> ➤ "It's not the safest investment, but it will yield the greatest return."

Similarly, it's generally easy to find one in the attributes of people:

> ➤ "Alan was the first to help but the last to criticize."

Finally, in any presentation, there's almost always a powerful

---

[8] In its purest form, antithesis is the presentation of direct opposites. However, here antithesis refers to two ideas that are in contrast, rather than opposition.

antithesis hiding in plain sight—simply the difference between the audience taking and not taking the action you want them to take:

➤ "If we approve this headcount increase, we can complete the project on time. If we don't, there will be a significant overrun."

➤ "If we fund this shelter every night this winter, forty kids will sleep in warmth, comfort, and safety. If we don't, they'll spend those nights cold, lonely, and in danger."

Tool #2: Antimetabole
(an tee met AB oh lee)

IN PLAIN ENGLISH: Creating an antithetical idea by reversing the same words.

Antimetabole is a variant of antithesis and is one of my absolute favorites. It's our first horribly off-putting name, but don't let that deter you: it's a powerful idea and easy to use. If you're a speaker, you want to know how to come up with a good antimetabole once in a while. It works by taking a thought and creating a contrasting thought by inverting the exact same words. Put another way, it's antithesis with an extra bit of fun thrown in. You might not know the term "antimetabole," but you absolutely know the construct, because they're everywhere, and they're highly sticky when done well. Here are some simple examples you'll recognize:

➤ "All for one and one for all."

➤ "When the going gets tough, the tough get going."

➤ "It's nice to be important but it's more important to be nice."

➤ "It is better to have and not need, than to need and not have." (Franz Kafka)

➤ "Let us never negotiate out of fear, but let us never fear to negotiate." (John F. Kennedy)

Perhaps the most well-known antimetabole is the one that created one of history's stickiest ideas: President Kennedy's, "Ask not what your country can do for you—ask what you can do for your country."

We've just discussed how the brain loves chewing on a good antithesis, but when those antithetical ideas use the same words, the brain loves the additional element of the clever symmetry that's involved. That's what makes it so powerful; the symmetry and antithesis work on the brain in two different ways. One of my favorites comes from Churchill: "I've taken more out of alcohol than alcohol has taken out of me." That's Churchill at his mischievous best, but this phrasing was no accident; as a lifelong student of rhetoric, he understood the appeal of that structure very well. In this example, the repeated words "taken" and "alcohol" mean the same thing both times, as they do in most examples. However, when you can use the same word but have it mean two slightly different things, then it gets particularly impactful because your audience's brains now have to figure out the subtle distinctions embedded in the language.

For example: "It's not the size of the dog in the fight, it's the size of the fight in the dog." If you look at this phrase carefully, you'll see that the words work slightly differently: "dog" means the same thing both times, but "fight" doesn't. In the first clause, it means a literal fight—a scrap. But in the second clause, it means "fighting spirit" or just "spirit." It's a small distinction, but this kind of nuance in the underlying meaning is intoxicating for the right brain.

My all-time favorite antimetabole came from a man called Jim Elliot. He was a Christian missionary, and in 1956, at the age of twenty-eight, he tragically died in the field, killed at the hands of those he had gone to serve. The amazing thing about his story is the very last thing he had written in his diary before sailing from the US. Take a minute to figure out what he's saying, and then let the weight of the idea wash over you: "He is no fool, who loses what he cannot keep, to gain what he cannot lose."

Aside from being both haunting and comforting in its prophetic content (this diary entry was treasured by Jim's widow, the legendary Elisabeth Elliot), it's an incredible example of the way antimetabole bends the mind. There's a profound idea—and question—hidden in the dualism between what you choose to "lose" vs. "keep." What is temporal? What is eternal? Which should you choose?[9]

PRACTICAL APPLICATION. You want to be good at creating the occasional antimetabole, and the way to do that is to toy around with the words until it emerges. This is definitely one of the trickier ones, because there isn't an obvious one sitting under every rock you turn over, but when you find one, it's often a knockout. My all-time favorite boss had a famous phrase about agreeing on targets with leadership. He'd say, "I'd rather have one hard conversation followed by twelve easy ones than one easy conversation followed by twelve hard ones." His point was simple: fight to set a reasonable target, and then beat it every month rather than take a difficult target and miss it every month. He was my boss in 1983, so that idea has stuck with me for almost forty years. That's the power of antimetabole, but the

---

9 I hesitate to mention this, but if the words aren't exactly the same, as in the Jim Elliot example ("keep" and "gain" have the same meaning, but are not exactly the same words), it's not technically an antimetabole, it's called a chiasmus. Rhetoric scholars have gone to war over this difference. Honestly, who cares?

example also gives us a clue regarding how to find one. That phrase works by simply switching the two adjectives around ("easy" and "hard"), which is often a great way to create a good antimetabole (e.g., "Do you want to be a big fish in a small pond, or a small fish in a big pond?"). But the best practical advice is to look for a place where you have a noun and verb that can be reworked, as Churchill did with, "I've taken more out of alcohol than alcohol has taken out of me." For example:

➤ "I've learned more from my children than my children have learned from me."

➤ "Barry, you gave more to this organization than this organization gave to you."

➤ "I am stuck on Band-Aid brand 'cause Band-Aid's stuck on me." (A memorable Band-Aid commercial)

➤ "We can beat this goal, or let this goal beat us."

Tool #3: Triples or Tricolons
(TRY ko lons)

IN PLAIN ENGLISH: Presenting an idea in three parts, or using a set of three to describe something.

In rhetoric, a tricolon is a rhetorical device that comprises three parallel clauses, phrases, or words that typically come in a single phrase without any interruption. (Tricolon comes from the Greek *tria*, meaning "three" and *kôlon*, meaning "clause.") The clauses tend to be short, although technically they don't have to be. A sentence with a tricolon is described as tricolonic, which doesn't sound nearly as much fun. Let's just call it a "triple."

This one is big. (I would have made it Tool #1, but it kind of has to be Tool #3, right?) When you take a look at the way triples show up in everyday life, it's striking how many things are organized in these parallel sets of three. "Ready, aim, fire"; "Eat, drink, and be merry"; "the good, the bad, and the ugly"; "lock, stock, and barrel"; "stop, drop, and roll"; "hook, line, and sinker"; "wine, women, and song"; "up, up, and away." I could go on indefinitely because triples are so common.

As with so much of how language works, there's no real explanation for why our brains love things organized in threes, but they truly do; and if you want to see how significant this Rule of Three actually is, try naming sets of four. It's odd; fours are rare, but threes are everywhere. As we were going through these examples, I wonder if you were expecting to see Winston Churchill's "blood, sweat, and tears." If you were, it's a fantastic example of our love for triples, because Churchill never actually said that. What he said was, "I have nothing to offer you but blood, toil, tears, and sweat," but history doesn't like the four. We prefer to remember the triple that never was.

Why is this structure so powerful? There are actually three reasons. (How apt.) First, a big part of the impact comes from the idea of "completeness." Scholars tell us that the triple structure is the smallest possible organizing framework in which you can still have a complete story. You can see this in several of the examples above, such as: "stop, drop, and roll" or "ready, aim, fire." Julius Caesar's "I came, I saw, I conquered" ("*Veni, vidi, vici*" in Latin, also making it wonderfully concise and alliterative in that language) actually contains a full story with a beginning, a middle, and an ultimate resolution. Second, triples tend to be brief, often containing few words (three or six in those examples), which makes them both easy to comprehend and easy to store in our brain's limited working memory. Third, it's also a device where you see the rhythm that the brain loves so much. The ideas, "I came, I saw, I conquered" or "the good, the bad, and the ugly" both contain a subtle rhythmic element that we find satisfying in an intangible way. Oddly and mysteriously, the rhythm isn't nearly so satisfying when the idea has four parts. So the humble tricolon is powerful, thanks to brevity, rhythm, and story. (See?)

And if you want one final proof, what if the entire wisdom of the world's diet industry could be boiled to one idea, captured in one elegant tricolon of only seven words? In Michael Pollan's outstanding little book *Food Rules,* he drops this bombshell: "Eat food, not too much, mostly plants." That's a breathtaking tricolon.

Given their power, it's not surprising that triples show up in some very famous speeches. In the Gettysburg Address, Lincoln deliberately used a triple for the towering conclusion: "that government of the people, by the people, for the people shall not perish from the Earth." He clearly wanted that closing triple rather badly, because he stretched quite a bit to get it. Have you ever noticed that "of the people" and "by the people" are essentially the same idea? But take out a clause and make it a "double," and it just doesn't work. Try it.

Earlier, I introduced the subject of rhetoric with lines from Churchill's legendary Battle of Britain speech: "Never in the field of human conflict was so much owed by so many to so few." Now you can see why it beat out all lesser alternatives. That's about as good a triple as you can make: brief, rhythmic, and yet a shockingly complete idea. Hard to believe for only seventeen words.

PRACTICAL APPLICATION. As you seek to apply triples, this is another tool that's invariably simple; just look for natural "threes" in your own argument, as in: "This solution is elegant, simple, and fast." It's not hard to find three big things that matter, but if you get stuck, use Lincoln's "cheat" and fabricate a third. If your new product actually provides simplicity and reliability, it's not that much of a stretch for the final phrase to be, "This control system will redefine the industry in terms of simplicity, reliability, and transparency." We've done this several times in our sales messaging consulting, and the final messages were always the better for the more powerful and poetic phrasing. If Lincoln got away with it, you certainly can.

Note that a true tricolon is more than just a simple list of three things; be on the lookout for an intellectual connection that creates the completeness of a set. For example, "life, liberty, and the pursuit of happiness" are three core values upon which the USA is founded, but they're related ideas; taken together, they describe the critical dimensions of freedom. Not so with "eggs, potatoes, toilet paper." Good contemporary examples would be more like:

> ➤ "We care for each other, we cover for each other, and where necessary, we challenge each other."

> ➤ "This shelter will offer warmth, comfort, and safety for all who use it."

> ➤ "This project will be exceptionally quick, highly effective, and extremely inexpensive."

When you deploy a tricolon, you present your idea in a simple, powerful, and satisfying way, with a natural rhythm that adds a subtle poetic echo your audience will immediately attach to. This brings us to three fabulous devices that all harness the specific power of pattern and rhythm.

Tool #4: Isocolon
(AYE suh koh luhn)

IN PLAIN ENGLISH: Stringing together a series of phrases, all of which contain the same grammatical structure.

An isocolon presents two or more thoughts, but does so by deliberately using the same grammatical structure for each thought. It's another device that's straightforward to use, and it's powerful because the repetition creates a rhythm that's pleasing and sticky to the listener. A good example of an isocolon is one of the triples we looked at in the previous section. "I came, I saw, I conquered" contains three ideas, but it also repeats the grammatical structure; "I + verb," which gives it a clear rhythm. (It actually scans even better in the original Latin as "*Veni, vidi, vici.*") By the way, this example illustrates an important point in rhetoric: frequently, a single phrase can contain multiple rhetorical devices at the same time. "*Veni, vidi, vici*" manages to simultaneously be a triple (a three-part story), an isocolon (a repeating grammatical structure), and an alliteration (clauses begin with same letters). I don't know if that makes it three times more powerful, but I'm sure it helps.

At its simplest, we see isocolon in phrases of only two clauses:

➢ Feed a cold, starve a fever.

➢ Risk little, win little.

➢ Nothing ventured, nothing gained.

➢ Float like a butterfly, sting like a bee.

➢ Finders, keepers; losers, weepers.

➢ Hurt people hurt people (an interesting phrase I picked up from a counselor friend of mine).

There's a little line in C. S. Lewis's classic *The Lion, the Witch and the Wardrobe* that seems unremarkable, and yet so many people remember it: "Always winter, never Christmas." It's a wonderful example of a good isocolon. The repeating structure makes it memorable, but also note how powerful the idea is that it creates. That is: "By keeping Narnia permanently frozen, the queen subjects her people to all of winter's misery without ever letting them enjoy its one redeeming feature." All that from four words. By the way: as you can clearly see in several of the examples above (including Lewis's), thanks to the parallel grammatical structure, an isocolon is often destined to contain an antithesis—as in Muhammad Ali's famous "Float like a butterfly, sting like a bee." This adds the additional dimension of a contrast, which in turn increases the impact of the phrase. But the main point to see with isocolon is the presence of the repeating patterns that the brain locks on to, and it's much more obvious when it's applied to more than two clauses, as seen in a well-known nursery rhyme first published in 1842 (though the author remains unknown).

Solomon Grundy,
Born on a Monday,
Christened on a Tuesday,
Married on a Wednesday,
Took ill on a Thursday,
Grew worse on a Friday,
Died on a Saturday,
Buried on a Sunday.
That was the end of Solomon Grundy.

The repeating "on a" creates a rhythm and pattern that builds and grows. It's funny, halfway into the poem, you can actually feel that your brain has spotted the pattern and is looking for the next "on a." I don't remember much from my childhood, but this old rhyme has stuck for over fifty years, which is the whole point.

Churchill uses a wonderful isocolon as the introduction to his history of the Second World War. As you read it, note that there's a completeness to each clause, and yet the combination of the four parallel ideas creates a more powerful, more complete, and more poetic whole:

In war, resolution.
In defeat, defiance.
In victory, magnanimity.
In peace, goodwill.

And one of my favorites: in *Lord of the Rings*, when Pippin swears a loyalty oath to the barking mad Denethor, Denethor responds chillingly: "And I shall not forget it. Nor fail to reward that which is given. Fealty **with** love, valor **with** honor, disloyalty **with** vengeance." It's a scary moment and a fabulous isocolon, but given that a few minutes later Denethor sets himself on fire and jumps off the roof, it doesn't work out too bad for Pippin in the end.

PRACTICAL APPLICATION. Isocolons are super easy to create by taking a series of points you want to make and looking for a common grammatical structure you can apply. Put simply, take a list of points and convert it into an isocolon with a common adjective or verb. The ability to take a basic set of ideas and embed them into a stronger, more poetic, and more memorable structure is what makes isocolon a go-to tool for today's presenter.

> ➤ "We sell better than them, we execute better than them, we manage better than them, and we innovate better than them."

➤ "Happy staff, happy customers, happy CFO, happy shareholders."

➤ "Let's fight together, and let's win together"—or better, perhaps—"Let's fight together, let's win together, and let's celebrate together." (nicely incorporating a triple)

➤ "Keep the faith, stay the course, win the prize."

Tool #5: Anaphora
(uh NA for uh)

IN PLAIN ENGLISH: Beginning a series of clauses with the same word or words.

Anaphora is another tool whose appeal stems from the repeating pattern it creates, but in this case, the impact comes from the opening words being repeated, as in; "I love your eyes, I love your hair, I love your skin, I love everything about you."

From the commercial slogan "More saving, more doing" (Home Depot) to the legendary Gettysburg address: "**We cannot** dedicate, **we cannot** consecrate, **we cannot** hallow this ground," we can tell that this is a powerful device from the places it shows up. When Churchill, Lincoln, and Teddy Roosevelt all use it, especially in speeches they felt were of great importance, I think that's telling. The specific trick of anaphora is that it layers one idea on top of another, using the repeated opening phrase to set each new brick in the wall. This creates a cumulative effect that builds as the argument progresses.

If we look at Roosevelt's legendary "Man in the Arena" speech from 1910, we see an extreme example of this: no less than eight uses of "who" as he seeks to paint a vivid picture of the heroic individual. "(The person) . . . **who** strives valiantly; **who** errs, **who** comes short again and again, because there is no effort without error and short-coming; but **who** does actually strive to do the deeds; **who** knows great enthusiasms; **who** spends himself in a worthy cause; **who** at the best knows in the end the triumph of high achievement, and **who** at the worst, if he fails, at least fails while daring greatly . . ." It's aspirational content, and again, if you listen to a recording of the speech, or read it out loud (as it was intended), you particularly feel each new "who" landing like a fresh hammer-blow on top of the last.

Anaphora must be taught at American President school, because Abraham Lincoln actually uses it twice, back to back ("with" and "to") in his second inaugural address: "**with** malice toward none, **with** charity for all, **with** firmness in the right as God gives us to see the right, let us strive on **to** finish the work we are in, **to** bind up the nation's wounds, **to** care for him who shall have borne the battle and for his widow and his orphan, **to** do all which may achieve and cherish a just and lasting peace among ourselves and with all nations." And of course, one of the most well known: Churchill very deliberately firing the big gun of anaphora in that most critical speech where he needed to persuade a fearful nation to fight on. This is similarly stirring:

> We shall fight in France,
> we shall fight on the seas and oceans,
> we shall fight with growing confidence and growing
> strength in the air,
> we shall defend our island, whatever the cost may be.
> We shall fight on the beaches,
> we shall fight on the landing grounds,
> we shall fight in the fields and in the streets,
> we shall fight in the hills;
> we shall never surrender.

Not surprisingly, Hitler also employed this weighty device. As a skilled rhetorician, he would frequently make use of anaphora in his speeches, most famously: "*Ein Volk! Ein Reich! Ein Führer!*" ("One people! One empire! One leader!"), one of the Nazis' most-repeated political slogans. Scholars contend that what makes anaphora so compelling and effective is the way the repeating phrase at the beginning of each clause sets up the audience's anticipation for the new idea to come. Think about Churchill's original audience: once their brains had locked in on the pattern, they would have been actively listening for the next place he would name, the next place "we shall fight."

I'm certain you already noticed that anaphora sounds an awful lot like isocolon (a repeating grammatical structure), and if you did see that, you'd be right. By definition, an anaphora is always also an isocolon, because it's a repeating grammatical structure, with the distinction simply being that it's the opening words that repeat. Hence I don't need to explain it any further. Think "front-end isocolon" and you've got it. Also, several of the isocolons I gave you in the previous section were, in fact, also examples of anaphora.

PRACTICAL APPLICATION. Once again, anaphora has the virtue of being easy to use in a modern-day presentation. As with isocolon, one practical trick is to take a list of items you wish to discuss and build from there by creating that repeating front end. It certainly seems plausible that this is how Churchill may have created the "We shall fight on the beaches" speech.

Some time ago, I built a presentation about data visualization that was fully scripted because many different people were going to deliver it. Within it was the account of how the *Challenger* space shuttle crash could have been averted, had the data on O-ring damage been presented differently. That story ended with this line:

"Here's the point: if the right people had seen the right data in the right format, this story would surely have ended differently."

It's a classic modern anaphora, and if you asked anyone after the presentation what the big idea was, without fail, they would have answered that this was it. Other possible examples:

➤ "We have the best products, we have the best people, and we have the best strategy."

➤ "Fight hard, fight smart, fight fair."

➤ "These kids deserve our support, these kids deserve our love, and these kids deserve our care." (An anaphora I found in my notes from a recent fundraising banquet speech—but a phrase I had not even intentionally crafted.)

➤ "Stay hungry, stay foolish." (The title and theme of Steve Jobs's legendary 2005 commencement speech at Stanford. A lovely anaphora.)

International Rhetoric

At some point, you might be wondering whether these various rhetorical devices work in other languages, and the answer is, absolutely yes. Remember that their original "discovery" was by the ancient Greeks. "I came, I saw, I conquered" was originally in Latin, Hitler's examples were all German, and there's an anaphora in French that you probably know and sometimes use: "*Plus ça change, plus c'est la même chose.*" ("The more things change, the more they remain the same.") Remember: the brain loves patterns, and with some important distinctions I won't go into here, French brains and British brains aren't that different.

Tool #6: Epistrophe
(eh PI struh fee)

IN PLAIN ENGLISH: Ending a series of phrases or clauses with the same word or words.

If you've been tracking thus far, this is a piece of cake. Isn't this just anaphora in reverse? Yes. If isocolon is about repeating the sentence structure, and anaphora is the variant where the repeating words are at the beginning . . . well, guess what? Epistrophe is where the repeating words come at the end, as in: "See no evil, hear no evil, speak no evil," or Lincoln's legendary conclusion of the Gettysburg address: "that government of the people, by the people, for the people shall not perish . . . ." We saw this earlier as a triple; we now see it's also an epistrophe. My favorite can be found in the classic Bill Murray movie *Stripes*. The members of the dysfunctional new platoon are getting to know each other,when the psychotic Francis finally speaks:

Psycho: The name's Francis Soyer, but everybody calls me Psycho.
Any of you guys call me Francis, and I'll kill you.
And I don't like nobody touching my stuff. So just keep your meat-hooks off. If I catch any of you guys in my stuff, I'll kill you.

Also, I don't like nobody touching me. Any of you weirdos touch me, and I'll kill you.

Eliciting the legendary response from Sergeant Hulka: "Lighten up, Francis."

I'm certain that for many of you, reading this epistrophe brings back the scene, with the guys sitting in the barracks in their green fatigues, however long ago you saw the movie. And the fact that I haven't seen it in over twenty years, but could still recall those lines when I was looking for an example, is a testimony to how memorable epistrophe can be (although Google obviously helped me get them exactly right).

Earlier, I mentioned Barack Obama's 2008 inauguration speech, and the potent clause, "Yes we can!", which repeated seven times at the conclusion of seven big ideas. That was an outstanding example of epistrophe, and almost every recent writer on rhetoric agrees that this was one of the most effective speeches of this century.[10]

There's an interesting point here. It's logical to think that whether the different phrases begin with the same words (anaphora) or end with the same words (epistrophe), the effect of the repetition would be roughly the same, but it's not. Far from it: the effect on the hearer's brain is quite different. As I said earlier, with anaphora ("We shall fight . . .") the sense is one of anticipation: "What will the next one be?" but with epistrophe, it's quite different. The sense is more one of "all roads lead to Rome": that there is only one conclusion, and the epistrophe always leads there. Hence, it's not anticipation, but inevitability. I can lay out a series of challenges, but no matter what they are, the answer is always, inevitably, "Yes we can."

---

[10] By the way, this epistrophe was no accident. Textual analysis of many of President Obama's speeches, and especially the "Yes we can" speech, reveals the sophisticated use of many advanced rhetorical devices. For a wonderful discussion of this speech, see David Crystal's book *The Gift of the Gab.*

PRACTICAL APPLICATION. Epistrophe completes our set of three devices that make use of the brain's love of repeating patterns, and once again, it's easy to use. All the practical tips from the previous two devices carry over to here. Take the series of ideas you're trying to develop, and this time, find a powerful closing thought to append to each. For example:

➤ "Manual processes; that's yesterday's thinking. Untrained people; that's yesterday's thinking. High-risk investments; that's yesterday's thinking."

➤ "A fighter? That's Jenn. A mentor? That's Jenn. A friend? That's Jenn."

➤ "If you pack too much in, you lose. If it's too confusing and hard to follow, you lose. If you make it too much about yourself and not enough about the customer, you lose." (This is close to a verbatim line from our workshop. When we talk about the wrong way to present, we often summarize the three big problems with this phrase.)

In Conclusion: The Magic Trick

Look at the three examples above. Without the epistrophe, they're each no more than a simple list of items. And if you wish, look back at the examples of isocolon and anaphora where you're going to find the same thing. Imagine Churchill had said, "We shall fight them on, a) the beaches, b) the landing grounds, c) the fields, d) the streets, e) the hills" and so on. Presented that way, it's a miserably uninteresting list, but I want to stress how valuable that is. All three of our core "Rhythmic Repetition" tools (isocolon, anaphora, and epistrophe) have the potential to allow a speaker to do something remarkable: to take a simple list of items, which is one of the least-liked and most boring of all organizing structures that audiences are forced to endure . . . and magically transform the exact same content into a form that isn't simply more powerful but that, as we've seen, might actually end up being the single most enduring idea of the entire narrative. At least it worked out that way for Lincoln, Roosevelt, Obama, Churchill, and Psycho. From now on, if you have a list, you know what to do with it.

Tool #7. Anadiplosis
(an uh dip LOH sis)

IN PLAIN ENGLISH: Opening a phrase with the word you used to end the previous phrase.

As annoying as the Greek term is, this is a great tool to have up your sleeve. You'll tend to use it less often, and it's a little harder to craft, but a good one can be stunningly powerful. Anadiplosis works by starting a phrase with the word that ended the previous phrase, which creates a "cascade effect" that dials into the brain's love of pattern and rhythm. One great example is hanging on my office wall:

Sow a thought, reap an action;
sow an action, reap a habit;

sow a habit, reap a character;

sow a character, reap a destiny.[11]

I've always liked the principle embedded in this sequence—that the way we think creates important downstream consequences in our lives—but it's the rhetorical construction that truly makes it come alive. You can feel the rhythm; it's poetic, even though there's no rhyme. But even more powerful is the "building" effect that's created as each piece of the idea flows directly out of the one that preceded it. **In fact, this example helps us to fully demystify anadiplosis. Think of it as describing a chain of events.**

The following poem is a good example. It dates from thirteenth-century Germany, and the very fact that you probably know this seven-hundred-year-old poem from an unknown author proves that anadiplosis is a pretty sticky device.

For want of a nail the shoe was lost.

For want of a shoe the horse was lost.

For want of a horse the rider was lost.

For want of a rider the message was lost.

For want of a message the battle was lost.

For want of a battle the kingdom was lost.

And all for the want of a horseshoe nail.

What's noteworthy about this construct, which you can see clearly in both of these examples, is that each thought tends to be a complete idea in itself, as in, "Your daily actions drive the habits you

---

[11] This one is really tough to pin down. It's directly attributable to Stephen Covey's *The 7 Habits of Highly Effective People*, but Covey actually borrowed the construct from the Indian leader Gandhi: "Our thoughts become our words, our words become our actions, our actions become our character, our character becomes our destiny." But to further complicate things, it's also been attributed to an old Chinese proverb, Ralph Waldo Emerson, William Makepeace Thackeray, George Dana Boardman, Marcus Fabius Quintilianus . . . and several others.

form," which makes that thought interesting and worthy of the audience's attention on its own. But then the full progression sitting above these creates an additional larger story, as in, "We were missing one single nail and it ultimately cost us the entire kingdom." Put another way, anadiplosis works on you in two ways: it contains several smaller ideas that are interesting in themselves, but also creates one overarching big idea. If ancient poetry isn't your thing, Yoda saves the day with his own famous example:

> "Fear leads to anger.
>> Anger leads to hate.
>>> Hate leads to suffering."

And finally, a line from the excellent movie *Gladiator*, which also became the movie's tagline. I think it's significant that they chose this one rhetorical phrase to represent the entire film:

> "The general who became a slave;
>> the slave who became a gladiator;
>>> the gladiator who defied an emperor."

PRACTICAL APPLICATION. As you can see in all these cases, anadiplosis is about a progression of thought, which means that it commonly shows up in the kind of well-structured, well-sequenced narrative you should be aiming to build. But the real trick to finding one is to look for a chain of events in your argument; when you find one, you may be close to a great anadiplosis. You see this in each of the following examples, any of which you might find in a modern presentation.

> ➢ "I'm so grateful to the Chicago team. Their new idea led to a new product, that new product led to a new business, that new business led to three hundred new jobs."

➤ "Yes, onboarding matters. Poor onboarding leads to unhappy staff; unhappy staff leads to unhappy customers; unhappy customers leads to bad social media coverage; bad social media coverage leads to lower sales."

➤ "If these kids don't have homes, they can't get work; if they can't get work, they can't escape poverty; if they can't escape poverty, our town has failed."

➤ Anadiplosis creates a powerful "chaptered" story; a chaptered story creates better audience engagement; and better audience engagement creates better presentation outcomes.

Tool #8: Monosyllables

IN PLAIN ENGLISH: Using one-syllable words.

In the previous chapter, we talked about the mysterious way the ten-syllable sentence structure simply "clicks" with the brain. That structure works no matter how long the individual words are within the phrase, but something very interesting happens when you use only words of one syllable; the **"punch" of the idea is significantly amplified.** This is why, across history, many writers have reserved this tool for some of their most important lines. Technically, "monosyllables" doesn't feature on most lists of rhetorical devices, but as I said, I'm more interested in the tools that actually work. Let's look at a few examples of the "power punch" of monosyllables, starting with Shakespeare. It was a favorite trick of his, and if he had a big line to deliver, this is how he often did it, as we see here in *Henry V.*

Once more unto the breach, dear friends, once more;
Or close the wall up with our English dead.

A little context: King Henry is imploring his soldiers to defend the breach in the wall that the French have blasted—fighting, if necessary, to the death. It's a brutally forceful idea, and one of the most powerful lines in the play (indeed, actors often portray Henry as pretty crazed at this moment). Look how Shakespeare constructs it to get the effect he wants: eighteen words, and all but two are monosyllables. A gentler example comes from his legendary love poem, Sonnet 18, which begins: "Shall I compare thee to a summer's day? Thou art more lovely and more temperate." It's a poem that describes how deep his affection is for his lover, and it ends on a magnificent conclusion that, in plain English is: "This poem is going to survive until the end of the world; and because of that, you, my love, will also live forever." It's a huge idea—a bit arrogant perhaps, although he was actually proved right. But again, the lines are so important that he goes for pure monosyllables (note: "this" refers to "this poem").

> So long as men can breathe, or eyes can see;
> So long lives this, and this gives life to thee.

The reason why lines like this are so powerful is that the monosyllables hit the ears with a staccato punch, like the blows of a hammer, and that's what the brain notices and reacts to. If you're interested, the underlying reason is fascinating. A *polysyllabic* word will typically have some syllables that are stressed and some that are unstressed, but, by definition, a *monosyllabic* word is entirely stressed or entirely unstressed. This gives a writer/speaker a particularly interesting opportunity, which is to use only monosyllables to create an idea that is entirely stressed. (It's almost impossible to do that with a polysyllabic phrase because of the unstressed syllables.) You see this clearly in another line from *Henry V.* Before another battle, Henry is incensed that his generals are saying they need more men. When he tells them that they have enough to get the job done, his exasperation shines through: "God's will I pray thee wish not one man more." You can feel the force, even the anger, of that line because every syllable is stressed.

Finally, Edgar Allan Poe does the same thing in the closing line of his poem "The Raven." It reads: "Take thy beak from out my heart, and take thy form from out my door!" It's the only monosyllabic line in the whole poem.

PRACTICAL APPLICATION. This one is beyond simple. There's no training required; when it comes to a particularly big line or idea, think about building it either completely or mostly in monosyllables. You'll recall how we helped an electric utility base an entire investment case on one idea: "The grid we have is not the grid we need." It was an excellent example of the ten-syllable structure—but as you now see, it was made even more effective by also being pure monosyllables. By the way, the case got approved.

Other modern examples might be:

➤ "We will not let this chance just pass us by."

➤ "There is no way we do not win this fight."

➤ "The best way forward is not to look back."

Tool #9: Congeries
(CON guh rees)

IN PLAIN ENGLISH: A list, with elements piled on top of each other for effect.

I put congeries after monosyllables because in a subtle way, they're a pair: congeries creates an effect that's similar to the "staccato punch" we saw in those monosyllabic lines. The word "congeries" derives from the Latin for "pile" or "heap," which provides an important clue regarding how it works. It's another unnecessarily unclear term, because a congeries (yes, congeries is singular) is simply a list. By the way, to make things more irritating, the plural of congeries is also . . . congeries. It may surprise you to see this device in rhetoric's Top Ten because I've argued passionately that a list is generally a horrible way to organize information. The lack of context makes the individual elements too easily forgettable; plus, people generally don't like them or find them engaging. Simply put, lists are a lazy and ineffective way to structure information.

So why does congeries make the cut? Because it's a list with a difference, and the difference is significant. Congeries stems from the Latin root "heap" because it's all about "heaping" the words on top of each other to create an overall impression. **With congeries you aren't building a list for completeness, and certainly not for memorability; you're building it for effect.** Imagine if, in a speech, Winston Churchill had said, "We need more tanks, planes, ships and artillery," that's a list. Those actually *are* four things you need. But when he described the impending conflict with Germany by saying, "I have nothing to offer but blood, toil, tears, and sweat," that's not a list. He is not saying "there are four things here that I'm offering"; he's saying, via the cumulative effect, "This is war. Buckle up. It's going to be unbelievably hard."

Think of it this way: with congeries, you're laying out a set of individual words (often powerful words) that wash over an audience like waves on a shore. And it's the cumulative effect of the full set that creates the impact, not the meaning of any individual word. This device is better demonstrated than described.

I recently made a presentation at a fundraiser, and there was a moment in it that perfectly called for a congeries. After showing some pictures of homeless kids, I simply said:

"Cold. Hungry. Lost. Abandoned. Unloved."

It wasn't overly dramatic, although I delivered the series with a certain gravitas and with notable pauses between the words. But it also wasn't a list in the normal sense of the word; the last thing I wanted was for the audience to remember the individual elements like a list of cake ingredients. **What I wanted was for them to attach to the bigger idea of the deep pain of these children, and with congeries, the naked isolation of each word serves to create that powerful cumulative effect.** Perhaps a good metaphor is this: I was painting a word picture where each word was an individual brushstroke, but where it was only the complete picture that mattered.

Part of the power of a congeries derives from the stark nature of the grammar; there are no verbs, conjunctions, or adjectives to stitch it together into a cozy and familiar sentence. Take note that I didn't add the grammatically correct "and" between abandoned and unloved, precisely because I didn't want this to be seen as a list. In fact, adding the word "and" would have corroded the effect, because it would have sent a signal to the audience saying, "Oh, this is a set of five things he wants me to remember." Say it out loud and you'll see.

We see an excellent example in *The Lord of the Rings* when Gimli the dwarf describes the orcs by saying, "Gnawing, biting, breaking, hacking, burning." It's all about the aggregate idea that "these are loathsome creatures," not the individual words.

Lastly, a congeries isn't always serious, and I'm pleased to finally have the opportunity to inject a Monty Python example. In one skit where John Cleese plays a career guidance counselor, he says: "Our experts describe you as an appallingly dull fellow, unimaginative, timid, lacking in initiative, spineless, easily dominated, no sense of humor, tedious company, and irrepressibly drab and awful. And whereas in most professions these would be considerable drawbacks, in chartered accountancy they're a positive boon." A classic congeries.

PRACTICAL APPLICATION. This is a good device, but one you will employ less frequently than most; it can't be overused because it's so "obvious." The way to spot a possible congeries opportunity is to look for situations where you want to paint an overall picture about something, especially something important. When that happens, simply brainstorm and bring together a set of adjectives or nouns that create the overall impression you're going for. Some examples of contemporary use are below. By the way: the more words you use, the clearer it becomes that it's a congeries and that you aren't asking the audience to remember any individual item. You see that clearly in the final example.

> ➤ "Quality, reliability, simplicity, durability."
> ➤ "Funny, charming, bold, quick-witted, smart: that's Angus."
> ➤ "What a team: resourceful, creative, flexible, agile, hardworking, unconventional, whimsical. This is the best team I've ever managed."

Look at that last example again. It's extremely unusual in a presentation to be using individual words that genuinely don't matter that much, and that you don't actually need the audience to remember. That seems to break all the rules of presenting, but you clearly see the reason and the desired effect in this rhetorical situation. "This is an amazing team"; that's the big idea. That's the house I want you to see. I don't care about you seeing the individual bricks.

Tool #10: Alliteration

IN PLAIN ENGLISH: Beginning a few words in a phrase with the same letter.

This is certainly the best-known of the Top Ten. Alliteration gives us "Intel Inside" and "Deliciously Different." The brain likes the repeating letters because even a little pattern beats total randomness. Thus, the phrase "Bold as brass" is better than "Bold as a king," and the book title *Pilgrim's Progress* is better than *Pilgrim's Journey*, despite the fact that "journey" would have been more accurate. In the movie *Ocean's Eleven*, when they're talking about taking out the power in Las Vegas, Basher asks, "Do you want broke, blind, or bedlam?" That phrase is fun and memorable, whereas a non-alliterated version of the phrase wouldn't have worked at all. Even when you're expressing the simplest idea, alliteration will create a little more elegance.

In the previous section, you read, "This device is better demonstrated than described." If it had read, "This tool is better illustrated than described," it would have worked, but it wouldn't have been nearly as elegant. Finally, because the brain attaches to them, alliterated phrases aren't only pleasing, they also tend to be sticky. US college basketball has built a brand out of its alliterations: "The Sweet Sixteen," "The Elite Eight," and "The Final Four" (and I guarantee that if they could make one work, there'd be an alliteration for the final game itself, but the "Tremendous Two" or the "Pre-Eminent Pair" is never going to stick). And when Boeing's "Model 299" first rolled out of the hangar, the plane was a lot more impressive than its name, until a watching journalist commented that it looked like a "flying fortress," and the rest is history.

PRACTICAL APPLICATION. Alliteration is remarkably easy to pull off, and it's a simple way to enrich an otherwise mundane phrase.

Start with the word you know you want to use, such as "robust," and then look for an alliterated partner. I generally find that if you start with the noun, the alliterative adjective is easier to find, e.g., "remarkably robust." It won't necessarily create the biggest impact, but the phrase will be a bit more muscular and memorable courtesy of that little extra effort, as in:

> ➤ "I'm pleased to say, this quarter was remarkably robust."

> ➤ "These two charts are strikingly similar in what they tell us."

> ➤ "Perfect plan, tremendous team, record results."

> ➤ "This solution is effective, it's efficient, and it's elegant" (Quick quiz: in addition to alliteration, which other two devices does this phrase employ?)

One Rhetorical Device NOT to Use: Litotes

IN PLAIN ENGLISH: Saying what you want to say by putting a negative on its opposite.

HOW YOU PRONOUNCE IT: Who cares? Don't use it.

In communications it's vital to say precisely what you mean. So—what if there was a rhetorical device in common use that made you do exactly the opposite; that is, instead of saying what you mean, you merely say one single thing that you don't mean, leaving every other possibility on the table? Put that way, it sounds like madness, except that device *does* exist, and we all use it every day.

Welcome to "litotes"—saying what you mean by putting a negative on its opposite. That sounds complicated, but you'll instantly recognize it when you see it: "She's not wrong," "He's not the best designer on the team," or "This is not the worst pudding I've ever tasted." Those are both litotes (and by the way, just to be more annoying, litotes is singular and the plural is also litotes). Thus, "good" becomes "not bad," and "I suck at putting my dirty clothes in the laundry" becomes "Honey, I will concede, I'm not world-class at putting my dirty clothes in the laundry."

I suspect people use litotes because at one level, they do sound a bit more erudite and sophisticated, as in, "Well, I must say, I am not opposed to this proposal," but as impressive as it may sound, the problem is that once you get away from simple ones, you start to become horribly confusing. A simple litotes, like "She was not happy" is fine (plus, people understand this actually means "angry"). But the moment it gets more complex, it creates a thought that's awfully difficult for the hearer to untangle: "Well done, Emma, that was a not unimaginative solution!" or "Come on in, I'm not completely undressed." All the litotes is actually doing in these cases is unnecessarily clouding the meaning of what you're saying. When a TV golf announcer recently said, "Everyone agrees, Rory McIlroy isn't the strongest putter on the tour," it is literally impossible to interpret that statement. The litotes eliminates Rory as "the strongest," but leaves the door open for all possible alternatives to be the true meaning. So, what kind of putter is he? Nearly the strongest? Abysmal? Average? Who knows?

Litotes are so good at obscuring the real meaning that they've occasionally been used for that exact purpose, and there's a wildly extreme example from history.

On August 15, 1945, when Emperor Hirohito announced Japan's surrender following the Allies' use of nuclear weapons at Hiroshima and Nagasaki, within the surrender speech he used the phrase: "The war situation has developed **not necessarily to Japan's advantage.**" This phrase just might be the most staggeringly misleading in history, and it certainly was to its hearers. Obviously, in no way am I making light of one of humanity's most tragic moments, but the miscommunication here is astounding. To describe having two atomic bombs dropped on your country as "not necessarily to Japan's advantage" seems absurd, until you learn that the miscommunication was almost certainly intentional. Hirohito understood the ability of a litotes to obscure the real meaning of a statement, and historians now agree that this was, in fact, a deliberate attempt at a "face-saving" misdirection. And that's my point. **If litotes can create phrases that are so baffling that they've actually been used by speakers to deliberately hide the meaning of what they're saying, then it's probably a device you need to avoid.**

Litotes inevitably leads to the question, "What do you really mean?", and that's not the question a communicator wants to hear. When you say: "The customers weren't entirely satisfied with the most recent shipment," what does that mean? Were they partially satisfied or filled with rage? Who knows? It's completely unclear from that phrasing. In short, don't do litotes. Instead, be direct. "The customer was extremely unhappy with our last shipment." If that's what you mean, that's what you should say. This will create a significant improvement in your speaking.

PRACTICAL APPLICATION. None. Don't do it.

SUMMARY

That's our tour through rhetoric. I hope you agree that it's not that hard after all! When you boil it down to the most powerful devices, demystify the impenetrable language, and illustrate with modern examples, you end up with a manageable set of practical tools you can go away and use, and one weird one to stay away from. Most of the people I know don't hate rhetoric; they're simply indifferent because they don't think it matters. They couldn't be more wrong. Whether you're in sales, finance, or any other modern-day function, it may be far from ancient Greece, but if you're willing to apply a little effort, using these tools will have a tremendous impact on your effectiveness. For future reference, the summary table in Appendix II (and online at www.oratium.com/resources) gives you an easy way to remember and access these priceless devices.

EPILOGUE

Thank you for making it this far. We've covered a lot of ground: how to prepare for the day, what you do when the day comes, and who to be while you're up there. The topic itself drove the breadth of the terrain, but if that feels overwhelming in aggregate, then to help you as you seek to apply what you've learned, the checklists that follow will be invaluable. All the important, practical guidance you've read is captured in these handy summaries.

And remember the eternal truth of presentations, talks, or speeches everywhere: If you did it all, leaving everything out there on the field, then you can and should feel great. This book will substantially increase the likelihood of your success, but there are no absolute guarantees. Some things will always lie outside of your control, but as long as you did everything you could to succeed, that's good enough. Let the cards fall where they may.

Please let me know how it goes. I'd love to hear from you.

timpollard@oratium.com

APPENDIX I

Checklists

BEFORE THE EVENT: GENERAL PREPARATION

1. Learn any helpful audience background information, and adjust the tone of your presentation accordingly (Are they tired? Burdened by deadlines? etc.).

2. Even if you discard it later, script your opening, closing, and big ideas (and for the rest of your presentation, create good notes).

3. Fully rehearse your presentation at least three to four times, and do so under the same conditions as the real presentation (out loud, standing up, etc.).

4. In rehearsal, spend more time on the critical moments of your presentation: the opening, closing, insights, transitions, and humor. (Use your script, then discard it when you know it.)

5. For high-stakes presentations: audio-record your rehearsal and listen, then correct.

6. Write your timestamps in your notes (so you know where you need to be at all points in time).

7. Design and employ imaginative and muscular language as often as possible.

8. Eliminate overused language and clichés, and find alternative ways to express overused phrases.

9. For your important points, find and use an appropriate rhetorical device to enhance the point.

10. Ensure you have extra copies of the handout with you.

11. **English as a Second Language (ESL) Audience Issues:** Determine the percentage of ESL attendees who will be at your presentation. Modify it if more than 20 percent are ESL, and a) be prepared to slow down to 70–80 percent of your normal speed; b) simplify your language; and c) ensure that references are clear and culturally unbound. (Avoid idioms like "At the plate," and "On deck.")

BEFORE THE EVENT: OPTIMIZING THE VENUE

1. Arrive at least an hour early.

2. Identify any distractions in or near the room (noises like vacuuming, etc.), and do all you can to remove or adjust them.

3. Keep the room cool. Locate the temperature controls and make sure they are set to a comfortable temperature.

4. Check your screen lighting and visibility from all angles and seats of the room, and adjust if necessary. Ideally, present from the longest wall in the room, but make sure that natural light is not behind you.

5. If you have access to natural light, use it.

6. Make sure seating isn't cramped, and ensure that all the chairs are front-facing.

7. Pre-test ALL technology, and carry all current adapters for your laptop and any other electronic devices you have.

8. Back up your presentation in the event that your laptop fails, and have the backup available to you.

9. Be prepared to present without technology by using your handout.

DELIVERY FUNDAMENTALS: THE OPENING

1. Walk off your nerves in the few minutes prior to presenting.

2. Quietly rehearse your opening multiple times shortly before taking the stage.

3. Where appropriate, issue a "two-minute" warning to the audience before you begin.

4. Distribute the handout *before* your presentation.

5. Where appropriate, have someone else introduce you, and have the introduction focus on the audience's problem. Don't use a bio.

6. If you're nervous, keep your hands engaged with something during the opening (in your pocket, holding notes, resting on the podium, etc.).

7. Open with a gracious authority in your tone.

8. Set the rules for phones, email, and breaks at the beginning of the session. Reassure people that they will have ample time to deal with email and communications.

DELIVERY FUNDAMENTALS: MECHANICS

1. Make sure you're as rested as possible. Protect your energy level by getting sufficient sleep, doing light exercise ahead of the presentation, and avoiding eating large meals.

2. Before you get up to speak, visualize yourself being lively, witty, and sparkling.

3. Speak conversationally. Just be yourself.

4. Be conscious of your speaking speed. In general, don't speak too quickly, and in the case of important points, slow down to emphasize them.

5. For eye contact, look at your audience like you would look at someone in a regular conversation.

6. For body language, be normal and be expressive.

7. Don't turn your back on the audience. If referencing the screen, turn sideways.

8. Match your physicality to the content and tone of the message. If you're making a more serious point, be still and quiet. For a more upbeat point, be lively and energetic.

9. Point people clearly to where you are in the handout at all times.

10. Be aware of the audience's reactions to your remarks. If you are sensing any disagreement or skepticism, address it with a question. Don't ignore it.

11. Plan enough discussion time and don't go over.

12. Answer questions in the moment rather than asking that they be held to the end.

13. Fully listen to questions before responding.

14. If you don't know the answer to a question, say so.

THE THREE PILLARS OF PRESENCE

Authority

1. Use an authoritative tone, but be polite and gracious throughout.

2. Manage the time. Know your schedule and adhere to it. Gently call people back from breaks.

3. Manage the distractions (plates don't need to be cleared this minute, leaf-blowing doesn't need to happen now).

4. Manage the people. Explain the rules of engagement for a productive session. Prevent participants from dominating the conversation, and draw in quieter participants.

Directiveness

1. Know the main conclusions of your presentation and deliver them clearly to the audience.

2. Stand your ground. Politely defend the points you believe in.

3. Don't be overly forceful in your defense. The audience has the right to disagree with you.

Self-Disclosure

1. Avoid being too closed off (robotic) or too open (raw).

2. Be human and honest. Share personal perspectives (as appropriate) after rapport has been built.

3. Validate audience contributions that are of a personal nature (sharing a hope, fear, or concern).

APPENDIX II

Summary of Rhetorical Devices

Rhetorical Device	Description	Example
Antithesis	Setting two ideas against each other	"Ask not what your country can do for you – ask what you can do for your country." –John F. Kennedy
Antimetabole	Creating an antithetical idea by reversing the same words	"When the going gets tough, the tough get going." –Billy Ocean
Triples or Tricolons	Presenting an idea in three parts, or using a set of three to describe something	"This shelter will offer warmth, comfort, and safety for all who use it."
Isocolon	Stringing together a series of phrases, all of which contain the same grammatical structure	"Nothing ventured, nothing gained."
Anaphora	Beginning a series of clauses with the same word or words	"Fight hard, fight smart, fight fair."

Rhetorical Device	Description	Example
Epistrophe	Ending a series of phrases or clauses with the same word or words	"A fighter? That's Jenn. A mentor? That's Jenn. A friend? That's Jenn."
Anadiplosis	Opening a phrase with the word you used to end the previous phrase	"Fear leads to anger. Anger leads to hate. Hate leads to suffering." –Yoda
Monosyllables	Using single syllable words to amplify the "punch" of an idea	"There is no way we do not win this fight."
Congeries	A list with elements piled on top of each other for effect	"Quality, reliability, simplicity, durability."
Alliteration	Beginning a few words in a phrase with the same letter	"Perfect plan, tremendous team, record results."

APPENDIX III

Prompting Yourself: Script or Bullets?

In Chapter 5, we established that it is unwise to try to deliver a presentation entirely from memory and that it's almost entirely advisable to have prompts for your remarks.

You have three options for self-prompting. Ironically, the first is the most frequently used, but it's also so awful that it's the one I hope, pray, and plead that you will never use again.

Option #1—The Unacceptable Option:
Take Your Cue by Glancing at the Bullets on Your Slides

Hopefully, this option is already ruled out, because the whole notion of text slides on screen is the tired model I'm trying to get you to break away from. If you're using a screen, it should be for the higher purpose of projecting authentic visuals that teach or illustrate your big ideas. When you put text points on a slide, not only are you using visuals incorrectly, but you're creating disconnection. Your audience is typically going to read ahead, finish the slide before you do, and disengage until you get to the next one. Even if this approach helps prompt you through your material, it's a horrible communication model in all other ways.

Options #2 and #3—The Bigger Debate:
Full Script or Abbreviated Notes?

If "script on screen" is ruled out, you're left with a choice between two legitimate options: full script or abbreviated notes/note cards. Here it gets interesting because conventional wisdom will generally tell you not to fully script on the grounds that a) it will make you seem wooden and unnatural, b) it will disconnect you from your audience, and c) you will freeze when you inevitably lose your place. These are real issues, which is why most people tend toward notes: it seems like whatever benefits scripting provides, it isn't worth the risks.

However, to jump from the difficulties of script to the conclusion that you should never use it is a mistake, because, as is so often the case, conventional wisdom is wrong. The argument is more nuanced than simply "notes are good, script is bad." As it turns out, there are clear advantages and disadvantages to each approach, depending on the setting—and furthermore, all the challenges of scripting can be easily overcome. Consider the table on the following page, which sets out the relative merits and disadvantages of the two approaches.

As you study the upper left of the table, the advantages of summarized notes are clear, which is why most people use them. They're quick and easy, you can connect with the audience by simply being "you," and you don't lose your place as readily. Likewise, the disadvantages of a script in the lower right push us in the same direction. A script is hard to create, hard to use, and can disconnect you from your audience. But take a moment to consider the other side of the argument. If you ponder the disadvantages of using notes in the lower left, you can see some serious problems.

A Balanced Analysis

	Notes/Bullets	Full Script
A D V A N T A G E S	• Quick and easy to create • Forces you to be spontaneous • Can easily be tied to visuals • Mobility • Can include some mission-critical language • Keeps you well connected with the audience • Hard to lose your place	• Precision in language, without relying on the mind in the moment • Allows total replicability of rehearsal • Holds perfectly to designed sequence • Perfectly protects planned timing • Makes inhibition easy • A presentation to be made multiple times can be repeated or transferred with no loss of quality
D I S A D V A N T A G E S	• No guarantee you can replicate rehearsal • BIG potential to muff key points when it matters • Forces you to create great language on the fly • Unpredictable timing – can vary widely, depending on where your head is • Huge potential for embellishment – strong tendency to repeat	• Hard to do right • Time consuming, especially given multiple edit rounds • Somewhat of a learned art • Requires writing of spoken English • Needs serious rehearsal to avoid being wooden • Easy to lose your place – that's trouble

THE PROBLEM WITH NOTES

With notes, there's no guarantee you can flawlessly replicate your best rehearsal. Many times, we nail a presentation in rehearsal, but the notes method forces us to recreate that same great language on the fly, and that's risky. It simply might not be there. As we discussed in rehearsal, for your lesser points, exact linguistic precision may not matter; but in those critical moments, you definitely don't want inferior or unclear phrasing. This will especially show up at the opening, when the pressures of the moment can take that cool and elegant introduction you had planned and turn it into something faltering and clunky.

The other big issue is time management and embellishment. Using notes will definitely give you a sense of freedom, which is one of the main reasons people choose it over scripting, but it's easy to abuse that freedom with unplanned trips to the briar patch of embellishment. That perfectly timed 29 minutes you hit in rehearsal can become a perfectly irritating 39 minutes on the big day, precisely because of the dubious "freedom" afforded by those note cards.

As liberating as notes are, and as much as they allow you to be yourself on the day, this may not always be what you want. The rambling "yourself," whose points don't come out clearly enough, and who runs twenty minutes long thanks to various unplanned detours, isn't going to win any awards for great communication.

THE BENEFITS OF SCRIPTING

In contrast, look at the benefits of scripting in the table's upper right, which are the exact converse of what you've just read. The precision you lose with notes you gain back with scripting. We'll talk about being "wooden" in a moment, but great speakers have always known that if there's one truly great way to say something, scripting is the way to make sure you say it. And by extension, scripting allows you to recreate your rehearsal perfectly. When I'm rehearsing new material, I'll toy around with multiple possible turns of phrase, and when I eventually find one I love, I call that the "ooh baby" moment, which is my code for a really lovely phrase. That then gets captured in the script and is thus secured; I don't have to trust my mind to re-find it on game day. The other great benefit is that scripting restrains all forms of embellishment, thereby holding you to time, protecting your flow, and preventing a career-ending Freudian "Nazi" remark. For this reason, many companies today require scripting for presentations with any possible legal consequences.

So, based on this analysis of notes and scripts, what's the conclusion? One big idea:

Both are valuable, so use them in combination.

We tend to think of script versus notes as a binary choice: you can use either one or the other. That is entirely untrue; in fact, the right answer is the reverse. **In most presentations, you should use a blend of both.** The precision of scripting suggests it should be used for the more critical moments you absolutely want to get right, and as we've already learned, that would be your opening, closing, transitions, and big ideas. But for the rest of the presentation, where you have a little more freedom, it's fine to use notes, as long as you're disciplined enough to stay roughly on track while using them. And if you're a serial embellisher, as many people are, you should lean more on a script to keep you within the guardrails. Either way, this advice raises a new question: do you now have to learn how to deliver material from a script?

"SCRIPT" VERSUS "SCRIPTING"

The answer to that question is no, because of the way things eventually work out. When you've developed some scripting, even if only for those critical moments thanks to the process of rehearsal, that critical language will begin to imprint itself on your brain. You will often reach that wonderful moment when you know you've truly "learned" your material, at which point the script, like a booster rocket, has served its purpose and can be jettisoned. You can now go back to abbreviated notes, even for your critical content, safe in the knowledge that the script is now safely locked inside your head. But there's a critical distinction: **by working through the exercise of scripting first, the resulting notes are no longer simply prompting a general idea, but rather prompting the recall of some specific and powerful language. In other words, when they emerge from the exercise of scripting, your notes are working in a completely different way.** And if you truly have that one killer phrase that's non-negotiable? Write it down longhand in your otherwise abbreviated notes. It's too precious to risk.

Where to Write Your Notes

While note cards are fine, the best place to physically write your notes is on your copy of the audience handout or "leave-behind," if you're using one, because it's the most natural place for them. The handout already contains all your main points and ideas, and you'll be referencing it constantly, so the notes you put there will simply be the supplementary points you're going to make beyond the printed content, along with some key phrasing you want to get right. "Teaching from the handout" makes several things easier for the presenter, as well as creating a natural and vital connection to the audience. I unpacked this particular skill in Chapter 8.

THE FINE ART OF SCRIPTING

All this leaves us with one final question: If you do choose to go with a script, perhaps where the setting requires no deviation from planned remarks, how do you do it? Can you use a script without it being wooden and stilted? Absolutely, and it's much easier than you think. It's merely a matter of how you write it.

Writing Spoken English

The reason scripting can sound wooden and odd is that most people are only ever trained to write written English, and written English doesn't sound natural when you try to speak it. Written and spoken English aren't quite two different languages, but they *are* governed by completely different rules. Curiously, spoken English works perfectly well when written on the page: if you read the text of any great speech, it's pleasant and easy to comprehend. But the reverse isn't true; written English uses much longer sentences and more complex grammar to develop more elaborate ideas, and that's difficult to take in aurally. This is why many people, myself included, don't enjoy audiobooks. In a presentation setting, when a speaker is working from a written-English script (the worst case being an engineer reading a technical paper at a conference), it's almost physically painful. Fortunately, the problem is easy to solve, as every playwright and screenwriter in history knows. Spoken English differs from the written language in three ways.

1. **IT'S HIGHLY COLLOQUIAL AND MUCH LESS BOUND BY STRICT RULES OF GRAMMAR.** When a script contains the lines, "So, if you look at this chart—upper left in blue— that pie chart—see what's going on there . . ." that casual language works perfectly well in an aural setting. Please say

it out loud; it's great scripting. But I'll resist pointing out the grammatical errors. You would never write anything close to that in any formal setting.

2. **IT'S BUILT FROM SHORT, CHOPPY SENTENCES.**
   Spoken English has to accommodate that pesky "breathing" thing, which is totally irrelevant to written English. Long, complex, multi-part sentences are the hallmarks of written language, but when spoken aloud, not only are those sentence structures impossibly hard for an audience to follow, because they require them to hold too many competing thoughts in their minds, but also, and comically, they can almost turn a speaker blue as they pray for a moment to come up for oxygen. And to prove that, try reading that last sentence aloud, from "Long, complex . . ." See how multi-clause sentences work on paper, but not so much verbally? Now breathe.

3. **IT USES SHORTER WORDS AND SIMPLER LANGUAGE.**
   Remember that the reader of the written word has the luxury of rereading a paragraph as often as they wish until they've absorbed the idea. The listener has no such luxury. They have to get it the first time—and instantly—because the speaker is already moving on. Hence, spoken English will typically use somewhat simpler language than the written equivalent to accommodate the higher cognitive strain you're putting on your audience.

WRITING SPOKEN ENGLISH

If spoken and written English are different, but most people are only experienced in writing written English, how do you solve for that? Actually, it's not hard, though it takes some practice. Writing spoken English begins with a governing principle: you have to write it EXACTLY the way you would say it, and the way to do that is as simple as it is obvious.

Rule #1. Speak, Then Write.

You speak it out loud, as often as you need to, and when you're happy with it, you write it down. This is the key to not sounding "wooden" because, by definition, you're creating true spoken language. Don't try to write it on your computer, because only professional screenwriters can do that. You need to speak it first. Don't worry if it looks ugly and colloquial on the page. It should. Remember our earlier example: "So, if you look at this chart—upper left in blue . . ." It's ugly on the page, but if that's how you're going to say it, that's how you should write it. It worked for Shakespeare. It will work for you.

Rule #2. Allow for Edit Rounds.

It's a curious fact of scripting that the first round of "speak, then write" will feel great, but when you stand up and say it again, it suddenly sounds wrong, which you immediately notice. This isn't a problem—it's a wonderful journey to refinement. As you say it again, write down the new, better version that comes to you. A few edit rounds later, you'll have it.

Rule #3. To Avoid Losing Your Place,
Write in Short Blocks of Text.

When the script is right, we've solved for all problems except for one. We haven't solved for the paralyzing problem of losing your place. This is an easy fix: don't write in long blocks of text. Create paragraphs of no more than three to four lines, which is consistent with the more abbreviated patterns of spoken language anyway. As you glance down, your brain takes in the full clause, which you then deliver (probably looking back up), and as you conclude and glance back down, the next one is waiting for you. You can't lose yourself in a short paragraph, but take your eyes off a long paragraph at your peril.

DELIVERING FROM A SCRIPT

When you've built a script using "speak, then write," coupled with short paragraphs, you'll sound natural as you deliver it. Rather than head-down reading, you can now stay fully engaged with the audience as you bounce your eyes off those short paragraphs on the page. In a former life, I delivered all-day presentations entirely from script, and countless times, when people came up to me at the end and realized that the entire day had been fully scripted, they genuinely couldn't believe it.

LAST THOUGHTS ON PROMPTING YOURSELF,
WHETHER SCRIPT OR BULLETS

First: As you give the presentation, if this is a talk you may give again, capture great discussion/anecdotes/questions for future use.

Don't be afraid to pause and take notes. Presentations evolve, so it's crucial to integrate improvements. When you take a moment to do so, audiences actually like that.

Second: Always keep a backup set of notes. The rule is to have two physical copies, not in the same place, but at least keep a flash drive or some second virtual copy. One day you WILL leave your notes on the plane.

ACKNOWLEDGMENTS

Almost everything good that happens in life is the product of a great team, and if this book is any good, it's surely because of the wonderful team who helped create it: Jerry Wall and Bryce Leverich for editorial support; Heidi Feneis for her painstaking research; Grace Quartermaine for her great work on graphic design; our expert book consultant Stacey Aaronson; and our fastidious editor, Floyd Largent.

As ever, all our thinking is pushed and sharpened by our most progressive clients. The ever-challenging (!) Mike Edmonds, Andrew Jones, Chris McCarthy, and Brianna Civella of S&C Electric; Jodie Schroeder, Hugh Wellington, Vicki Staffeldt, and the feisty Patty Roberts of Rockwell Automation; the turbulent Paul Jameson and the disciplined Cathy Ciprian of Cisco Systems; Thom Clark and Melinda Thiel of Johnson & Johnson; Dave Moeller and Jen Sandhage of Graybar; and the wonderful Amy Linsenmayer and Amanda Bjerkan Hennessy of Disney. I count myself so fortunate that these are friends more than clients.

To the amazing Oratium team who never settles for anything other than the best: Mark Bourgeois, Jenn Callaway, Eli Murphy, JD, Michael Hubble, Sebastian Mathews, Rachael Hille, Kristin Jacobs, Alyssa Melder, and Sean Thom. No team ever cared more for each other than this one. Thanks for your constant support, and the same goes to the newly minted Oratium Europe, Marieke and Joost.

Huge thanks to my friends Park, Pastor Vern, Mark W, Michael M, Stevie G, Steve V, Mark and Sarah, Jen and Brock, Ted and

Dawn, Deri, Crull, and Jesus for keeping me sane. And of course, the most amazing family a person could ever dream of: my undeserved wife Ruth, and my incredible kids, Grace, Angus, Fergus, and Rosie.

And a special shout-out to my big brother Chris. Blood truly is thicker than water.

Soli Deo Gloria

INDEX

acoustics, 77, 79, 83–84, 87, 113, 114
ad-libbing, 63
Africa scam, 227–29
air conditioners, 79
Ali, Muhammad, 265
Allen, Woody, 121
alliteration, 264, 283–84, 298
ambiance, 78
anadiplosis, 247, 274–77, 298
anaphora, 267–71, 272, 273, 297
anecdotes, 56, 208, 308
antimetabole, 248, 257–60, 297
antithesis, 213, 253–57, 258, 265, 297
Apollo, 13, 90, 102
Aristotle, 182, 195, 246
Armstrong, Neil, 254
arrogant/arrogance, 38, 52, 107, 202,
    234, 278
A.R.T., 172
Art of War, The, 105
audience
    authority given by, 212
    collective brain of, 4
    comfort of, 87
    comprehension, 63, 71
    connection with, 87, 104, 167, 184,
        204, 209, 300, 301, 304
    desire of, 196, 197, 199
    diversity of, 27
    dynamic, 32, 150, 165, 166, 196
    firehosing of, 1
    impact of language on, 222–27,
        233–35, 240
    intellectual connection to, 37
    language of, 45–48, 51, 52, 113, 292
    lighting for, 80, 86
    makeup of, 166
    mental and physical state of,
        40–43, 55, 109, 124, 137–38, 291
    message anchored in, 4
    mock/test, 68, 243
    persuasion of, 182

audience (*continued*)
    Pre-Wiring Your, 170
    problem of, 20, 58, 105, 106, 108,
        132, 139, 140, 293
    rejection of speaker, 201–02
    retention, 63
    signals from, 59, 168
audience-centric, 25, 37, 108
Auschwitz, 19, 26, 181, 214
authenticity, 186, 188, 191, 193, 195,
    204, 206, 207
    of delivery, 15

ballroom, 1, 31, 79, 84, 165, 171
Battle of Britain, The, 60, 224, 246, 262
Bible, The, 10
bifold document, 20
Boardman, George Dana, 275
body language, 3, 11, 12, 33,
    150–51, 152, 159, 190, 192, 294
Botton, Alain de, 237
brain
    activity in audience, 133, 138, 139
    bandwidth of, 4, 73
    freezing up of, 7–8, 63, 98
    heightened focus of, 157
    left, 5, 241, 255
    limitations of, 111, 153, 200, 261
    image storage of, 3
    Riding the Rhythms of, 140–41
    right, 5, 241, 255, 258
    what it loves, 251, 258, 261, 262, 265,
        271, 274, 277, 283
    wiring of, 157
brain-aligned design, 4, 5, 19
brain-space, 20
breaks, 167, 168, 177, 199, 293, 295
breathing, 68, 103, 306
brevity, 76, 262
Bryan, William Jennings, 165
bullets, 5, 74, 299, 301, 308
Bush, George W., 162

ABOUT THE AUTHOR

Tim Pollard is the founder and CEO of Oratium, a leading messaging consulting firm. He is a sought-after speaker and author of the acclaimed book *The Compelling Communicator: Mastering the Art and Science of Exceptional Presentation Design.* Pollard draws insight from a long career in sales, marketing, and communications for companies such as Unilever, Barclays Bank, and the Corporate Executive Board.

CPSIA information can be obtained
at www.ICGtesting.com
Printed in the USA
LVHW031200081019
633523LV00004B/986/P